MALCOLM LEE PEEL

THE EPISTLE TO
RHEGINOS

A VALENTINIAN LETTER ON
THE RESURRECTION

Introduction, translation, analysis
and exposition

THE WESTMINSTER PRESS

PHILADELPHIA

STANDARD BOOK NO. 664–20877–0
LIBRARY OF CONGRESS CATALOG. NO. 70–89686
© MALCOLM LEE PEEL 1969 JUL 12 74

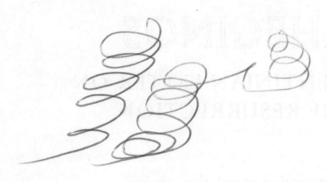

PUBLISHED BY THE WESTMINSTER PRESS®
PHILADELPHIA 7, PENNSYLVANIA
PRINTED IN GREAT BRITAIN

CONTENTS

INTRODUCTION

THE LAST TWO decades have witnessed a renaissance in the study of Gnosticism, that syncretistic religious movement first identified by the Christian heresiologists of the second century and characterized by pessimism and a dualistic conception of theology, cosmology, anthropology, and soteriology. This renewed interest has been stimulated through an astonishing discovery made by some Egyptian fellahin apparently in or near the ancient cemetery of Hamra-Doum, close by the present-day village of Nag Hammadi in Upper Egypt in 1945 or 1946.[1] Here were found thirteen papyrus codices written in Coptic and containing at least fifty-one separate tractates,[2] most of which are believed to emanate from a 'Sethian-Gnostic circle' probably existing in this area of Egypt in the third and early fourth centuries.[3] Although only partially published at present, the 'Library' of Nag Hammadi gives promise of providing important new information on such matters as the distinctive nature of Gnostic teachings, the fidelity of the heresiologists' reports on their Gnostic opponents, and the origins of this syncretistic religious movement.[4]

This book contains a fresh translation and exposition of one of the few writings thus far published from the Nag Hammadi Library, The

[1] Jean Doresse, upon whose initial reports most subsequent information on the discovery is based, offers the alternate date himself: *The Secret Books of the Egyptian Gnostics*, tr. Philip Mairet (London and New York, 1958/1961), p. xii; but, cf. p. 128 ' . . . about 1945'. Henri-Charles Puech, 'Découverte d'une bibliothèque gnostique en Haute Égypte', *Encyclopédie Française*, ed. Gaston Berger, Tome XIX (1957), 19.42–5, gives '. . . vers 1945, . . .' as the date of discovery.

[2] These figures are drawn from one of the most complete inventories of the Library, viz. that of Martin Krause, 'Der koptische Handschriftenfund bei Nag Hammadi. Umfang und Inhalt', *Mitteilungen des Deutschen Archäologischen Instituts*, Abteilung Kairo, Band 18 (1962), pp. 131–2.

[3] So Doresse, *The Secret Books*, p. 251. See, also, Henri-Charles Puech, 'Les nouveaux Ecrits gnostiques découverte en Haute-Égypte: Premier inventaire et essai d'identification', *Coptic Studies in Honor of Walter Ewing Crum: Bulletin of the Byzantine Institute*, Vol. 2 (1950), pp. 142, 145–8; Puech, *Encyclopédie Française*, p. 19.42–11.

[4] Some good impressions of the interest created by the Nag Hammadi find may be derived from Soren Giversen, 'Nag Hammadi Bibliography 1948–1963', *Studia Theologica*, Vol. 17, Fasc. 2 (1963), pp. 139–87: as well as from P. Nober, S.J., in the 'Elenchus bibliographicus biblicus' in the periodical *Biblica*.

Epistle to Rheginos concerning the Resurrection. Though less than eight full pages in length, the Epistle is of singular importance among the Nag Hammadi writings in that it provides us with the first Gnostic document devoted exclusively to the subject of individual eschatology.[5] According to the first editors of the Epistle, it presents a Valentinian conception of 'realized eschatology' which is similar to that heretical view combated in II Tim. 2.18 that the 'resurrection has already occurred'.[6] Such teaching is elaborated with the help of 'Pauline mysticism'—a rather rare occurrence of this segment of the Apostle's thought in a second century document.[7] Further, the Epistle's significance is enhanced by the possibility—which the editors claim as a probability—that it was penned originally by one of the greatest Gnostic teachers of the second century, Valentinus himself.[8]

Not all scholars familiar with the published official edition of the Epistle, De Resurrectione (Zürich-Stuttgart, 1963), are in accord with its editors' conclusions, however, and it is within this framework that the present volume finds its place. To acquaint the reader with the Epistle and the critical issues associated with its interpretation, Chapter I surveys the writing's place within the Nag Hammadi Library, the nature of its translation language, the literary form of its content, the historical context of its composition, and the use made of the New Testament by its author. There follows in Chapter II a new translation of the Epistle together with an analysis of its argument. In Chapter III appear exegetical and philological notes to the

---

[5] By 'individual eschatology' we mean religious or philosophical teachings about the 'last things' of a person's life, e.g. death, survival of death, etc. Dale Goldsmith also points to the unique contribution of the Epistle on this matter. See his Review of De Resurrectione, Journal of Religion, Vol. 45 (1965), p. 256.

[6] So Henri-Charles Puech and Gilles Quispel in Michel Malinine, Puech, Quispel, Walter Till, R. McL. Wilson, and Jan Zandee (trs. and eds.), De Resurrectione (Epistula ad Rheginum) (Zürich und Stuttgart, 1963), pp. x–xi, xxiii. Cf. further on this point: Gilles Quispel, 'Note on an Unknown Gnostic Codex', Vigiliae Christianae, Vol. VII (1953), p. 193; Henri-Charles Puech and Gilles Quispel, 'Les Écrits gnostiques du Codex Jung', VC, Vol. VIII (1954), p. 40.

[7] Such is the view of Puech and Quispel, De Resurrectione, p. XIII; and, the same authors in VC, Vol. VIII (1954), pp. 43–44. Cf. also Gilles Quispel, 'The Jung Codex and its Significance', in Quispel, Henri-Charles Puech, and Willem C. van Unnik, The Jung Codex, tr. F. L. Cross (London, 1955), pp. 55–56; Gilles Quispel, 'Neue Funde zur Valentinianischen Gnosis: Der Codex Jung', Zeitschrift für Religions- und Geistesgeschichte, Heft 4, Vol. VI (1954), pp. 299–300.

[8] See De Resurrectione, p. xxxiii; Puech and Quispel, VC, Vol. VIII (1954), p. 50. Cf. the cautious comments of Henri-Charles Puech on this matter in his Review of De Resurrectione, Académie des Inscriptions et Belles-Lettres: Comptes Rendus des Séances de l'Année (Juillet–Decembre, 1963), p. 319.

translation, together with Gnostic and New Testament parallels to the text. Chapter IV presents a new exposition of the Epistle's teaching, an exposition which challenges the prevailing interpretation of its eschatology. Chapter V concludes the study by submitting to critical re-examination the hypothesis that Valentinus composed the Epistle.

At the outset it is important that the presuppositions, as well as the objectives of this study be clearly understood. Throughout the whole, the reader will find the author in dialogue with the editors of the critical edition of *De Resurrectione*. Such procedure is made necessary by the fact that their pioneering efforts remain basic to any further serious study of the Epistle, and there is no sound reason for reproducing material they have already provided. In addition, the editors' hypothesis is presupposed, that the Epistle does originate from the Valentinian Gnostic sphere.[9] In our opinion, this hypothesis has been solidly established. Consequently, the reader is referred to the volume, *De Resurrectione*, for Valentinian parallels to the Epistle and for the editors' extensive argumentation concerning the probable milieu of composition.

The primary objective of this investigation is to provide a descriptive exposition of the eschatology of the Epistle without projecting on the meaning of the text what is known elsewhere about Valentinian teaching.[10] Only by such means, it would seem, can there be both an adequate test of the editors' hypothesis of authorship and an avoidance of undue prejudice in the interpretation of the Epistle's eschatology.[11] The latter consideration is of particular importance at this stage in the general study of Gnosticism since the Nag Hammadi

[9] More detail on this matter is offered below, pp. 13–17.

[10] Lucien Cerfaux has demonstrated the value of such an approach in his study of the use of the Pauline writings in the *Evangelium Veritatis* from the Jung Codex. See his article, 'De Saint Paul à l'Evangile de la Vérité', *New Testament Studies*, Vol. V (1958), pp. 103–12. Moreover, the approach becomes inevitable in view of Hans-Martin Schenke's recently-expressed doubts concerning the Valentinian nature of the Letter. See his Review of *De Resurrectione*, *Orientalische Literaturzeitung*, 60, Nr. 9/10 (1965), col. 473.

[11] The need for confirmation or repudiation of the editors' hypothesis of authorship is reflected in the comment of a recent reporter of work on the Jung Codex. He says:

'The editors themselves finally resolve to attribute this letter also to Valentinus, not to one of his pupils. Not all readers will follow this pleasant interpretation. Why really must all writings in this volume (the Jung Codex) be reckoned as originating from the head of the school? In the long run, is not the wish the father of thought here?'

texts are providing significant new data on the variety of thought within the total movement. Consequently, Gnostic studies may be said to exist at present in an 'interim time' when primary tasks are the study of individual documents and the particular theologoumena within those documents.[12] Both of these tasks are necessarily preliminary to any new syntheses on the distinctive nature and world view of Gnosticism, such as the classical one of Hans Jonas.[13] This volume seeks to make its own small contribution to such 'interim study'.

The author would extend a brief word of appreciation to some among the many who have given stimulus and encouragement. In particular, he would mention the late Dr Erwin R. Goodenough of Yale, under whom his initial study of Gnosticism was begun; Doctors Gilles Quispel and Willem C. van Unnik of the University of Utrecht, The Netherlands, whose counsel was most valuable in crystallizing the subject of the Yale dissertation which forms the basis of this volume, and who both read and constructively criticized the completed dissertation; Dr Jan Zandee of Utrecht, to whom the author owes his knowledge of Subakhmimic, and Dr Carsten Colpe of the University of Göttingen, whose seminar in Gnosticism at Yale in 1963–4 was most profitable. Dr Paul Schubert of Yale was very helpful as Advisor during preparation of the dissertation, and Dr Raymond Morris and Miss Jane E. McFarland of the Yale Divinity School Library Staff have assisted in countless ways. Special gratitude must be offered to Dr Robert M. Grant of the University of Chicago who read and encouraged publication of the dissertation, and to Professor Henri-Charles Puech of Paris, who graciously permitted the author to cite relevant passages from the published edition of De Resurrectione. Finally, adequate thanks cannot be accorded the author's wife, Ruth Ann Nash Peel, without whose constant support, long-suffering, and skilled typing this work might not have come to pass.

So Ernst Haenchen, 'Literatur zum Codex Jung', Theologische Rundschau (Juni 1964), p. 57. Cf. the interest expressed in this hypothesis in A. Orbe's Review of De Resurrectione, Gregorianum, Vol. 46, 1 (1965), p. 173.

[12] That these tasks are primary is affirmed by such writers as Carsten Colpe, Die religionsgeschichtliche Schule: Darstellung und Kritik ihres Bildes vom gnostischen Erlösermythus (Neue Folge, 60. Heft; Forschungen zur Religion und Literatur des Alten und Neuen Testaments, ed. Rudolf Bultmann, 78. Heft; Göttingen: Vandenhoeck & Ruprecht, 1961), pp. 5, 60, 68, and 201; Willem C. van Unnik, Newly Discovered Gnostic Writings (Studies in Biblical Theology 30; London, 1960), p. 92.

[13] Gnosis und Spätantiker Geist: Teil I: Die mythologische Gnosis. 3. Auflage (FRLANT, Neue Folge, 33. Heft; Göttingen: Vandenhoeck & Ruprecht, 1965).

ABBREVIATIONS

ACM	*Acta Congressus Madvigiani,* Copenhagen.
Acts of Th.	*The Acts of Thomas: Introduction, Text, and Commentary,* by A. F. J. Klijn (1962).
Ang. Rōs. I, II, etc.	*The Angad Rōsnan* from *The Manichaean Hymn-Cycles in Parthian,* translated by Mary Boyce (1954).
Apoc. Jac., II	*Die (Zweite) Apokalypse des Jakobus* in *Koptisch-Gnostische Apokalypsen aus Codex V von Nag Hammadi,* herausgegeben von Alexander Böhlig und Pahor Labib (1963).
Apoc. Joh.	*Die Drei Versionen des Apokryphon des Johannes,* herausgegeben von Martin Krause und Pahor Labib (1962).
Arndt-Gingrich, *Lexicon*	Arndt, William F. and F. Wilbur Gingrich, *A Greek-English Lexicon of the New Testament and Other Early Christian Literature* (1957).
Asclep.	*The Asclepius* from *Hermès Trismégistes: Corpus Hermeticum,* by A. D. Nock and A. J. Festugière, Tome II (1960).
BCLSMP	*Academie royale de Belgique: Bulletin de la Classe des Lettres et des Science Morales et Politiques,* Brussels.
BJRL	*Bulletin of the John Rylands Library,* Manchester.
Blass-Debrunner-Funk	Blass, Friedrich Wilhelm, and A. Debrunner, *A Greek Grammar of the New Testament and of Other Early Christian Literature.* Edited and translated by Robert Walter Funk (1961).
BO	*Bibliotheca Orientalis,* Leiden.
CGT	*A Coptic Gnostic Treatise Contained in Codex Brucianus.* Edited and translated by Charlotte A. Baynes (1933).
C.H. Excerpt I, II, etc.	Excerpts from the Hermetica collected in Walter Scott, *Hermetica,* Vol. I (1924).
C.H.	*The Corpus Hermeticum*—References are to the text established and translated by A. D. Nock and A. J. Festugière, *Hermès Trismégiste: Corpus Hermeticum,* Tomes I–IV (1954–60).

CRAIBL	Comptes Rendus de l'Académie des Inscriptions et Belles-Lettres, Paris.
Crum	Crum, Walter Ewing, A Coptic Dictionary (1962).
CSCO	Corpus scriptorum christianorum orientalium, Louvain.
D.R.	De Resurrectione, Ediderunt Michel Malinine, Henri-Charles Puech, Gilles Quispel, et Walter Till (1963).
E.V.	Evangelium Veritatis, Ediderunt Michael Malinine, Henri-Charles Puech, et Gilles Quispel (1956); and, Supplementum (1961).
Ev. Phil.	Das Evangelium nach Philippos, herausgegeben und übersetzt von Walter C. Till (1963).
EvTh	Evangelische Theologie, Munich.
Exc. Theod.	Clément d'Alexandrie: Extraits de Théodote. Texte grec, introduction, traduction et notes de F. Sagnard (1948).
FRLANT	Forschungen zur Religion und Literatur des Alten und Neuen Testaments, Göttingen.
FUG	Fragments of an Unknown Gospel and Other Early Christian Papyri, edited by H. I. Bell and T. C. Skeat (1935).
GCS	Die griechischen christlichen Schriftsteller der ersten drei Jahrhunderte, Berlin.
GLW	Alexander Böhlig, Griechische Lehnwörter im sahidischen und bohairischen Neuen Testament. Zweite Auflage (1958).
Goodspeed	Goodspeed, Edgar J., Index Patristicus: sive Clavis Patrum Apostolicorum Operum Ex Editione Minore Gebhardt Harnack Zahn, lectionibus editionum Minorum Funk et Lightfoot admissis (1907).
Gos. Heb.	The Gospel according to the Hebrews as it is found in Clemens Alexandrinus, Band II, Stromata (GCS), herausgegeben von Otto Stählin (1906).
Gos. Th.	The Gospel According to Thomas, text established and translated by A. Guillaumont, H.-Ch. Puech, G. Quispel, W. Till and Yassah 'abd al Masih (1959).
Grant, 2nd Cent. Christ.	Second-Century Christianity: A Collection of Fragments, by Robert M. Grant (1957).
Grant, Gnos.	Indicates the pages of texts collected and translated

	in *Gnosticism*, edited by Robert M. Grant (1961).
Greg.	*Gregorianum*, Rome.
Hatch-Redpath	Hatch, Erwin and Henry A. Redpath, Editors, *A Concordance of the Septuagint and the Other Greek Versions of the Old Testament* (1897–1906).
Heracleon, *Frag.*	*The Fragments of Heracleon*, edited by A. E. Brooke (1891).
HTR	*The Harvard Theological Review*, Cambridge, Massachusetts.
Huw I, II, etc.	Huwidagman, Canto I, II, etc. in *The Manichaean Hymn-Cycles in Parthian*, translated by Mary Boyce (1954).
IDB	*Interpreter's Dictionary of the Bible*, edited by George A. Buttrick, 4 vols. (1962).
Iren., *Adv. Haer.*	*Sancti Irenaei. Libros Quinque Adversus Haereses*, edidit W. Wigan Harvey, 2 vols. (1857).
James	Indicates the pages of texts collected and translated in *The Apocryphal New Testament*, by Montague Rhodes James (1953).
JBL	*Journal of Biblical Literature*, Philadelphia.
JEH	*The Journal of Ecclesiastical History*, Edinburgh.
Jeu I	*Das erste Buch des Jeu* from *Koptische-Gnostische Schriften, Erster Band*, herausgegeben von Carl Schmidt (3. Auflage, 1962).
JR	*The Journal of Religion*, Chicago.
JTS	*The Journal of Theological Studies*, Oxford.
Kümmel, *Einleitung*	Paul Feine und Johannes Behm, *Einleitung in das Neue Testament*, völlig neu bearbeitet von Werner Georg Kümmel (13. Auflage, 1964).
Lampe	*A Patristic Greek Lexicon*, edited by G. W. H. Lampe, 4 Fascicles (1961–5).
Liddell-Scott, *Lexicon*	Liddell, Henry G. and Robert Scott, *A Greek-English Lexicon*. A New Edition Revised and Augmented by Henry Stuart Jones and Roderick McKenzie (1940).
LNC	*La Nouvelle Clio*, Paris.
Mand. PB.	*The Canonical Prayerbook of the Mandaeans*, translated by E. S. Drower (1959). Occasionally the particular page in Drower's translation on which a parallel is found is referred to by 'Dr., p.———.'

Mand. Lit.	*Mandäische Liturgien,* übersetzt und erklärt von Mark Lidzbarski (1920).
Manich. Hom.	*Manichäische Homilien* (Band I, *Manichäische Handschriften der Sammlung A. Chester Beatty*) herausgegeben von Hans Jakob Polotsky (1934).
Manich. PsB.	*A Manichaean Psalm-Book,* edited by C. R. Allberry (Vol. II, *Manichaean Manuscripts in the Chester Beatty Collection,* 1938). References are to page numbers and lines of text.
MDAIK	*Mitteilungen des Deutschen Archäologischen Instituts,* Abteilung, Kairo.
NRT	*Nouvelle Revue Theologique,* Paris.
NTS	*New Testament Studies,* London.
NTT	*Nederlands Theologisch Tijdschrift,* Wageningen.
Odes of Sol.	*The Odes and Psalms of Solomon,* re-edited by Rendel Harris and Alphonse Mingana (1920).
OrL	*Orientalistische-Literaturzeitung,* Wiesbaden.
Orpheus	*Orpheus: Rivista di Umanità Classica e Cristiana,* Genoa.
Philo, *Abr.,* etc.	Abbreviations of the works of Philo correspond to those of Goodenough in his *By Light, Light* (1935), pp. XIIIf.
Pist. Soph.	*The Pistis Sophia* from *Koptisch-Gnostische Schriften: Erster Band,* herausgegeben von Walter C. Till (3. Auflage, 1962). References are to pages and lines of this text.
Plumley, par.	Plumley, J. Martin, *An Introductory Coptic Grammar* (*Sahidic Dialect*) (1948).
RGG[3]	*Die Religion in Geschichte und Gegenwart,* 3. Auflage (1957ff.).
RUB	*Revue de l'Université de Bruxelles,* Brussels.
Sophocles	Sophocles, E. A., *Greek Lexicon of the Roman and Byzantine Periods (from 146 BC to AD 1100)* 2 vols. (1887).
SOT	*Die Koptisch-Gnostische Schrift ohne Titel aus Codex II von Nag Hammadi,* herausgegeben von Alexander Böhlig und Pahor Labib (1962).
ST	*Studia Theologica,* Aarhus.
Steindorff	Steindorff, Georg, *Lehrbuch der Koptischen Grammatik* (1951).

Stu. Gen.	*Studium Generale*, Berlin.
ThR	*Theologische Rundschau*, Tübingen.
Till, *Dial.*	Till, Walter C., *Koptische Dialektgrammatik* (1961).
Till, *Sah.*	Till, Walter C., *Koptische Grammatik (Saïdischer Dialekt)* (1961).
TL	*Theologische Literaturzeitung*, Berlin.
TWNT	*Theologisches Wörterbuch zum Neuen Testament*, begründet von G. Kittel, herausgegeben von G. Friedrich (1933ff.).
UAW	*Unbekanntes altgnostisches Werk* from *Koptisch-Gnostische Schriften*, *Erster Band*, herausgegeben von Walter C. Till (3. Auflage, 1962).
VC	*Vigiliae Christianae*, Amsterdam.
Völker	Völker, Walther, *Quellen zur Geschichte der Christlichen Gnosis* (1932).
ZNW	*Zeitschrift für die Neutestamentliche Wissenschaft und die Kunde der älteren Kirche*, Berlin.
ZRGG	*Zeitschrift für Religions- und Geistesgeschichte*, Marburg.
ZTK	*Zeitschrift für Theologie und Kirche*, Tübingen.

For abbreviations of Patristic Writings utilized consult the Table of Abbreviations in G. W. H. Lampe (ed.), *A Patristic Greek Lexicon*, Fascicle 1 (1961).

Note to the Reader

For the convenience of the English reader, most quotations originally found in German, French, Dutch, Greek or Coptic have been translated into English by the author.

For typographical reasons, superlinear strokes in Coptic words have been made to conform to the conventional system, and do not attempt to reproduce the scribal usage in the original manuscript of 'Rheginos'.

I

THE NATURE OF THE DOCUMENT

A S IN SO MANY instances of a newly-discovered writing, the
recent history of the Epistle to Rheginos is known much better
than its ancient history. Thus, it is evident from the affinities
of its content, the overall size of its pages, and the Coptic dialect of its
translator that the eight papyrus sheets containing the text of 'Rheginos' constitute the third of five distinct writings found in Codex I[1] of
the Nag Hammadi Library.[2] The recent history of our text, therefore, is bound up with that of the thirteen Coptic-Gnostic codices
found in 1945/6 approximately thirty miles north of Luxor in Upper
Egypt.[3] However, the histories of 'Rheginos' and the Nag Hammadi
Codices are not synonymous, for soon after the discovery the bulk of
Codex I became separated from the other codices.[4] From that time

[1] The classification number given to the Codex is that provided in the inventory
of the Nag Hammadi Library by Martin Krause and Pahor Labib, *Die Drei
Versionen des Apokryphon des Johannes im Koptischen Museum zu Alt-Kairo (Abhandlungen
des Deutschen Archäologischen Instituts Kairo*, Band 1; Wiesbaden 1962), p. 7; by
Krause in *MDAIK*, 18 (1962), p. 124.

[2] Kendrick Grobel, *The Gospel of Truth: A Valentinian Meditation on the Gospel*
(New York, 1960), p. 8, prefers the designation 'Library of Chenoboskion' since
the actual place of discovery appears to have been on the eastern bank of the Nile,
whereas Nag Hammadi lies on the western bank about five miles to the south.
Nevertheless, the appellation 'Nag Hammadi Library' has remained dominant in
current usage.

[3] The existence of Codex I (XI in Doresse's classification) is mentioned in the
earliest reports of the Nag Hammadi find. See M. L. Th. Lefort, 'Note: Séance du
1er mars 1948', *Académie royale de Belgique: Bulletin de la Classe des Lettres et des
Science Morales et Politiques*, 5e Série, Tome XXXIV (1948), pp. 101–2; Henri-
Charles Puech and Jean Doresse, 'Nouveaux Écrits Gnostiques découverts en
Égypte', *CRAIBL*, Séance au 20 Fevr. (1948), p. 89; Togo Mina, 'Le Papyrus
Gnostique du Musée Copte', *VC*, II (1948), pp. 129–30.

[4] 'Rheginos' is first identified by name in Jean Doresse, 'Nouveaux Documents
Gnostiques coptes découverts en Haute-Égypte', *CRAIBL* (1949), pp. 177–9. Simi-
lar information is provided by Doresse in 'Douze volumes dans une jarre', *Les
Nouvelles Littéraires* (30. juin 1949), p. 1, cols. 1–3, p. 2, cols. 4–5; Jean Doresse and
Togo Mina, 'Nouveaux textes gnostiques coptes découverts en Haute-Égypte:

on, neither all eight pages of 'Rheginos' nor all 136 of Codex I were to be found in one place.[5] Rather, the first six papyrus sheets of 'Rheginos', Folios XXII–XXIV, were located in a lot of 100 sheets from Codex I found now in Zürich, Switzerland. Largely through the efforts of Prof. Gilles Quispel of Utrecht, this lot was purchased as a gift to the Jung Institute of Zürich on May 10, 1952, and named in honour of its founder 'The Jung Codex'.[6] The last two pages of 'Rheginos', Folio XXV, together with the remainder of Codex I were acquired by the Coptic Museum in Old Cairo, Egypt.[7] Fortunately, an agreement made between the Editorial Committee of the Jung Codex and the Egyptian Government permitted the Committee access to the pages in Cairo if they would agree to return the remainder of the Jung Codex to the Coptic Museum.[8] The Codex is gradually being returned following the publication of each writing in it. This agreement afforded publication of all eight pages of 'Rheginos' simultaneously.

The critical edition of our document, *De Resurrectione* (Zürich-Stuttgart, 1963), was published eight years after the acquisition of its text (1952). Reasons for the delay were legion but seem to have centred on an expansion of the original Editorial Committee working on the Jung Codex. The circle of investigators was extended to include two other Coptic experts, Walter Till of Austria and Jan Zandee of Utrecht, and an English-speaking consultant, Robert McL. Wilson of the University of St Andrews. The resulting need to co-ordinate contributions of this enlarged Committee, the desire to

---

La bibliotheque de Chenoboskion', *VC*, III (1949), pp. 129, 137; and by Doresse, 'Une bibliothèque gnostique copte découverte en Haute-Égypte', *BCLSMP*, 5e Série, XXXV (1949), 435, 444.

[5] On the divided state of the text of 'Rheginos', see Henri-Charles Puech and Gilles Quispel, 'Le quatrième Écrit gnostique du Codex Jung', *VC*, IX (1955), 'Note additionnelle', p. 102; *De Resurrectione*, p. viii. And, on the division of Codex I, see now Krause, *MDAIK*, 18 (1962), p. 131.

[6] For more detail on the acquisition and nature of the Jung Codex, see Quispel, Puech, and van Unnik, *The Jung Codex* (1955); Puech and Quispel, *VC*, VIII (1954), pp. 1–51.

[7] These last two pages of 'Rheginos' were actually published some time ago in Plates 1 and 2 of Pahor Labib's *Coptic Gnostic Papyri in the Coptic Museum at Old Cairo*, Vol. I (Cairo, Egypt: Government Press, 1956).

[8] In a personal conversation with Dr Quispel in February, 1965, it was learned that both he and Puech had travelled to Cairo to see the missing pages of the Jung Codex, but on separate occasions. The first mention in print of the agreement to return the Jung Codex to Cairo occurs in Puech's inventory in *Encyclopédie Française*, Tome XIX (1957), p. 19.42–5f.

supply editions of the writings from the Codex with introductions and full sets of Patristic and Gnostic parallels, and the meticulous editorial activity of Henri-Charles Puech all combined to retard publication.

A. THE LANGUAGE AND TRANSLATION OF THE DOCUMENT

Preliminary reports on the language of 'Rheginos' were somewhat confused. The dialect of all the writings in the Jung Codex was initially identified as Subakhmimic, with some grammatical peculiarities.[9] Later, however, both the papyrus sheets separated from the Codex[10] and those remaining with the bulk of the Codex[11] were described as having been redacted in a new Coptic dialect or subdialect hitherto unknown. Closer study of the Jung Codex in Zürich confirmed the original contention that all its writings were in Subakhmimic.[12] Even so, Walter Till detected in 'Rheginos' departures from classical Subakhmimic, departures which probably account for the earlier confusion.[13]

Its Subakhmimic dialect distinguishes the Jung Codex from the remainder of the Nag Hammadi Library, for all the other codices—with the possible exception of the first treatise in Codex XI—are written in pure Sahidic or in a Sahidic showing slight strains of Akhmimic and/or Subakhmimic.[14] Subakhmimic, a dialect

---

[9] Lefort, *BCLSMP*, 5e Série, Tome XXXIV (1948), p. 102; Puech and Doresse, *CRAIBL* (1948), p. 89; Mina, *VC*, II (1948), p. 130.

[10] Doresse, *CRAIBL* (1949), p. 178.

[11] Doresse and Mina, *VC*, III (1949), pp. 129, 132, 137; Doresse, *BCLSMP*, 5e Série, Tome XXXV (1949), pp. 438–9, 444; Doresse, 'Une bibliothèque gnostique copte', *La Nouvelle Clio*, Nr. 1 (1949), p. 61; and, Puech, *Studies in Honor of Crum* (1950), pp. 96 n.1, 104, and n.1.

[12] Puech and Quispel, *VC*, VIII (1954), pp. 2–3; Puech, *Encyclopédie Française*, Tome XIX (1957), p. 19.42–6; Doresse, *The Secret Books*, p. 239. This conclusion is repeated in the anonymous review in *Bibliotheca Orientalis*, Jahrgang XXI, No. 3|4 (Mei–Juli 1964), p. 250, and by Ernst Haenchen in his Review of *De Resurrectione*, *Gnomon*, 36 (1964), p. 359. Other Coptic scholars have confirmed the conclusion: J. W. B. Barns, Review of *De Resurrectione*, *The Journal of Theological Studies*, N.S., XV (1964), p. 163; Johannes Leipoldt, Review of *De Resurrectione*, *Theologische Literaturzeitung*, 90 (Juli, 1965), cols. 518–20; P. Lebeau, Review of *De Resurrectione*, *Nouvelle Revue Théologique*, Vol. 87 (1965), p. 319; Orbe, *Greg.*, 46 (1965), p. 173; Schenke, *OrL*, 60 (1965), col. 471.

[13] Till, *De Resurrectione*, pp. viii–ix.

[14] Krause and Labib indicate that Codices III, IV, and V are in pure Sahidic,

more closely related to the major southern Coptic dialect of Sahidic than to the northern dialects, seems to have arisen as a colloquial sub-dialect of Akhmimic in the middle of the third century AD, dying out again in the fifth century.[15] Since the domain of Subakhmimic was the vicinity around the ancient town of Assiût (or Asyût) which lay slightly more than 100 miles to the north of Nag Hammadi, the Jung Codex containing 'Rheginos' appears to have been transported a considerable distance south after it was translated or copied. This parallels the fate of another major group of Subakhmimic manuscripts in Egypt, viz. the seven collections of badly-defaced Manichaean texts which were discovered at Medinet Madi (the ancient Narmouthis) in the Fayyum, a region located quite a distance to the north of Assiût.[16] Thus it would seem that Assiût was something of a publication and distribution centre for Gnostic literature. Nevertheless, more orthodox Christian manuscripts in Subakhmimic have been found,[17] and during the period of AD 300 to 700 several Christian monastic communities were found in the area around Assiût.[18]

The first editors of 'Rheginos', noting such things as the slant to the right of the calligraphy and the less formally made uncial letters, attribute the script of the Epistle to a hand different from that found in the other four writings of the Jung Codex.[19] As to when this script

---

whereas II and VI show a Sahidic with light strains of Akhmimic and Subakhmimic. See *Die Drei Versionen*, pp. 10, 14, 19, 22, 23, and 25. For Codices VII–XIII we do not yet have their report and must be cautiously content with the information supplied by Doresse in *The Secret Books*, pp. 137–8.

[15] Walter C. Till, *Koptische Grammatik: Saïdischer Dialekt* (2., verbesserte Auflage; Leipzig, 1961), pp. 37–38. See also on the origins and development of Subakhmimic: Walter C. Till, 'Coptic and Its Value', *Bulletin of the John Rylands Library*, Vol. 40 (1957–58), pp. 231–2.

[16] See Carl Schmidt und Hans J. Polotsky, *Ein Mani-fund in Ägypten: Originalschriften des Mani und seiner Schüler (Sonderausgabe aus den Sitzungsberichten der preussischen Akademie der Wissenschaften. Phil.-hist. klasse*; Berlin, 1933).

[17] The only other major Subakhmimic manuscript known is that published by Herbert Thompson, ed., *The Gospel of St John According to the Earliest Coptic Manuscript* (London, 1924). It should be noted that the dimensions of the papyrus sheets of this manuscript are nearly identical to those of the 'Epistle to Rheginos': 14 × 29 cm in height and 9.5 × 24 cm in breadth of the written area in 'Rheginos'; 13 × 26 cm in height and 8.5 × 21 cm in breadth of written area in Thompson's 'John'. The tall, narrow format of both writings might be explained by a common source of supply for papyrus in the vicinity of Assiût and/or their provenance in a common scriptorium.

[18] See F. van der Meer and Christine Mohrmann, *Atlas of the Early Christian World* (Eng. trs., London and Edinburgh, 1958), Maps 18 and 34.

[19] Cf. Puech and Quispel, *VC*, VIII (1954), p. 2; and, the same authors with

should be dated, however, the editors have suggested both the end[20] and the middle of the fourth century.[21] Since we possess no dated Coptic texts from this century which could serve as a basis of comparison, it is probably not possible at present to date the script more precisely than the fourth century in general.[22]

The Subakhmimic is, in the opinion of the editors, only a vehicle of communication. That is, this dialect really represents an almost literal translation of a Greek original of 'Rheginos',[23] a translation presumably made for non-Greek speaking peoples of the area of Assiût. A re-translation into Greek, therefore, is utilized by Quispel to facilitate our understanding of certain passages, yield the meaning of some 'hapax legomena', and throw into prominence the style and language of the original writer.[24] One of the major arguments advanced to prove Valentinus was the author of 'Rheginos' is based upon such a re-translation, while the Coptic translator must bear the onus for passages difficult to understand.[25] We shall consider this hypothesis further when dealing with the question of the Epistle's authorship.

B. THE LITERARY FORM OF THE DOCUMENT

At present there is little agreement among scholars concerning the

---

Till in *De Resurrectione*, p. viii. This information is repeated with slight variation by Barns, *JTS*, N.S., XV (1964); Leipoldt, *TL*, 7, 90 (Juli 1965), col. 518; Haenchen, *Gnomon*, 36 (1964), p. 359. Schenke, *OrL*, 60 (1965), col. 471, adds independent confirmation of this view.

[20] *VC*, VIII (1954), pp. 5–6. Puech had earlier upbraided Doresse for his varying views on the date of the script, e.g. in *Coptic Studies in Honor of Crum* (1950), p. 103 and n.1.

[21] *De Resurrectione*, p. vii, n.1. Cf. Puech, *CRAIBL* (1964), p. 319.

[22] See the Epilogue by Walter C. Till, 'Die Edition der koptisch-gnostischen Schriften', in Willem C. van Unnik, *Evangelien aus dem Nilsand* (Frankfurt am Main, 1960), pp. 156–7.

[23] The presupposition of a translation Coptic has long been axiomatic for Quispel. See Gilles Quispel, *Gnosis als Weltreligion* (Zürich, 1951), pp. 2–3; also, his review of Walter Till's revision of Carl Schmidt, *Koptisch-gnostische Schriften* (*2. Auflage*), *TL*, Nr. 11 (1956), col. 686.

[24] See Puech and Quispel, *VC*, VIII (1954), p. 3. Cf. also Quispel, *VC*, VII (1953), p. 193; and his comments in *ZRGG*, Vol. VI, Heft 4 (1954), p. 290. Others would seem to disagree as to how 'literal' a translation the Coptic represents. See, e.g., Barns' comments in *JTS*, N.S., XV (1964), p. 163; Leipoldt's in *TL*, 7, 90 (Juli 1965), col. 520; and Haenchen's, *Gnomon*, 36 (1964), 362.

[25] Puech and Quispel, *De Resurrectione*, p. xxvi, cp. p. ix; Quispel in *The Jung Codex*, pp. 56f.

literary genre to which 'Rheginos' belongs. It has been called a treatise, a doctrinal letter, a letter, an epistle, a discourse, a tract, a pamphlet, and a book.[26] Except for the last-mentioned, all these terms have been used interchangeably by the first editors.[27] And, while more than one of these designations may be correct, others— such as 'book'—fail to describe the document with any accuracy. This ambiguity appears to stem from two problems: first, the meaning of the document's title; and, second, the identification of the addressee.

Like several other texts in the Nag Hammadi Library,[28] the Epistle to Rheginos has a subscript title at its end: ⲡⲗⲟⲅⲟⲥ ⲉⲧⲃⲉ ⲧⲁⲛⲁⲥⲧⲁⲥⲓⲥ. This, the editors maintain, is immediately re-translatable into λόγος περὶ τῆς ἀναστάσεως.[29] Of key significance is the meaning of the term λόγος in this title. In early Christian literature λόγος was used to denote a 'statement, word, report, proclamation, teaching, message, subject, matter, and revelation'.[30] In Patristic literature of the first few centuries, λόγος occasionally had the meaning of 'written words', or 'treatise', or the separate books of a larger work.[31] Conceivably the term could have been expanded to mean 'letter' or 'epistle', but the more normal Greek for these was γραφή, γράμμα, or especially ἐπιστολή.

Of related interest is the fact that while 'Rheginos' is most prob-

---

[26] These various designations appear in the following: Anonymous, *BO*, XXI, 3/4 (Mei–Juli, 1964), p. 250; Soren Giversen, A Review of *De Resurrectione, Journal of Ecclesiastical History*, XVI, No. 1 (April, 1965), p. 82; Goldsmith, *JR*, 45 (1965), pp. 256f.; Haenchen, *Gnomon*, 36 (1964), pp. 360 and 362–3; Haenchen, *ThR*, 30, Heft 1 (1964), pp. 43–44, 55, and 57; Lebeau, *NRT*, 87 (1965), p. 319; Leipoldt, *TL*, 90 (Juli 1965), cols. 518–19; Puech, *CRAIBL* (1964), pp. 317ff.; Puech, *Encyclopédie Française*, Tome XIX (1957), p. 19.42–8; Puech and Quispel, *The Jung Codex*, pp. 19, 24, 54, 56; Puech and Quispel, *VC*, VIII (1954), pp. 3–4, 50; Quispel, *VC*, VII (1953), p. 193; Quispel, *ZRGG*, VI, Heft 4 (1954), p. 290; Schenke, *OrL*, 60 (1965), pp. 471ff.; Willem C. van Unnik, 'The Newly Discovered Gnostic "Epistle to Rheginos" on the Resurrection: I & II', *JEH*, XV, No. 2 (1964), pp. 141, 143–7, 151–3, 159, and 165. The designation 'book' is only given by van Unnik, *JEH*, XV, No. 2 (Oct. 1964), pp. 144 and 147; Barns, *JTS*, N.S., XV (1964), p. 163.

[27] See Puech and Quispel, *De Resurrectione*, pp. vii–x, xiii, xvii, xx–xxi, xxiv–xxvii, xxix, and xxx–xxxiii.

[28] Cf. Krause, *MDAIK*, 18 (1962), p. 132.

[29] *De Resurrectione*, p. x.

[30] So, William F. Arndt and F. Wilbur Gingrich, *A Greek-English Lexicon of the New Testament and Other Early Christian Literature* (Fourth Revised and Augmented Edition; Chicago and Cambridge, 1957), pp. 478–80.

[31] See G. W. H. Lampe, *A Patristic Greek Lexicon*, Fascicle 3 (Oxford, 1964), p. 807. λόγος is cited with the meaning of 'treatise' only in Photius, *cod.*, 172–4.

ably translated from a Greek original, the Coptic translator has retained the Greek loan word ⲗⲟⲅⲟⲥ in the title. Such usage was not unusual, for we find this loan word in the Sahidic Coptic New Testament, as well as in the works of such indigenous Coptic writers as Schenute and Pachomius.[32] Nevertheless, when translated, λόγος was normally rendered by the substantive ϣⲁϫⲉ, meaning 'saying, word, affair, debate, or retort', but apparently never 'letter' or 'epistle'.[33] On the other hand, the usual Greek for 'letter' or 'epistle', viz. γράμμα or γραφή, was translated exclusively by the Coptic substantive ⲥϩⲁⲓ;[34] or, the Greek γραφή and ἐπιστολή were retained as loan words, e.g. ⲅⲣⲁⲫⲏ, ⲉⲡⲓⲥⲧⲟⲗⲏ.[35] In no instance known to the writer, however, is λόγος translated by ⲥϩⲁⲓ.[36] While not conclusive, then, the retention of ⲗⲟⲅⲟⲥ by the translator in the title affixed to 'Rheginos' seems to imply that 'letter' or 'epistle' was not the intended meaning of the word. If this were the case, we would expect the use of ⲥϩⲁⲓ, or the more usual ⲅⲣⲁⲫⲏ, ⲅⲣⲁⲙⲙⲁ, or ⲉⲡⲓⲥⲧⲟⲗⲏ instead of ⲗⲟⲅⲟⲥ. Therefore, ⲗⲟⲅⲟⲥ in the title probably denotes something other than formal description. To this point we shall return.

The second problem associated with attempts to define the literary form of our document is that of identifying the addressee. That is to say, is the writing directed to an individual, or is it intended for circulation among a larger audience? The editors of the document acknowledge that it has the '. . . form of an epistle, . . . written by a Gnostic master to one of his disciples named Rheginos . . . in response to some questions which that one had posed on the subject of the resurrection (p. 44.4–5)'.[37] But they continue:

Nevertheless, it is not destined for this person alone, but, at the same time, to his 'brothers', his fellow-disciples, to the spiritual 'sons' of the

---

[32] So, Alexander Böhlig, *Die griechischen Lehnwörter im sahidischen und bohairischen Neuen Testament* (*Studien zur Erforschung des christlichen Ägypten*, herausgegeben von Alexander Böhlig, Heft 2; Zweite Auflage; München, 1958), pp. 64–65 in the 'Register und Vergleichstabellen'.

[33] So, Walter Ewing Crum, *A Coptic Dictionary* (Oxford, 1939), p. 613b.

[34] *Ibid.*, 'Letter'—p. 861; ⲥϩⲁⲓ—p. 383a; γράμμα, γραφή,—p. 890 (Greek Index). Cf., also, René Draguet, *Index Copte et Grec-Copte de La Concordance du Nouveau Testament Sahidique* (*Corpus Scriptorum Christianorum Orientalium*, Vol. 196, Subsidia, Tome 16; Louvain, 1960), p. 159.

[35] Cf. Draguet, *Index Copte*, pp. 72 and 94; Böhlig, *Die griechischen Lehnwörter*, pp. 26–27, 42–43 (in the 'Register').

[36] Cf. Crum, *Coptic Dictionary*, pp. 613ff.; Draguet, *Index Copte*, p. 119.

[37] *De Resurrectione*, p. ix.

Master (p. 50.2–3), to whom, in the epilogue, the author asks that it be communicated, exhorting all to peace and saluting all in common.[38]

Being addressed to a larger audience, the editors continue, the letter contains only a few personal touches but much of convention.[39] For example, it complies with the epistolary genre of literature current in the Greco-Roman world and falls into the customary divisions of such literature:

A General Introduction	43.25–44.3
Statement of Theme	44.3–12
Argument	44.12–47.1
Brief Resume	47.1–4
A Refutation	47.4–49.9
Paraenetic Conclusion	49.9–36
Epilogue	49.37–50.16.[40]

Certain features of the Coptic text, however, make the determination of the addressee more complex than the editors seem to allow. For example, all references to the reader up to the 'Epilogue' (i.e. 49.37–50.17) are solely in the second person singular or a direct form of address:

(a) The reader as subject:

44.4	ⲉⲕϣⲓⲛⲉ	47.19	ⲟⲩⲛⲧⲉⲕ
44.18–19	ⲉⲧⲕ̅ⲟ̅ⲙⲁⲥⲧ̄	47.21	ⲛ̄ⲕⲛⲁϯ
45.15	ⲛ̄ⲕⲏⲡ	47.22	ⲉⲕϣⲁⲛⲃⲱⲕ
47.4	ⲛⲉⲕϣⲟⲟⲡ	48.6–7	ⲁⲕⲣ̄ⲡⲙⲉⲩⲉ
47.5	ⲁⲕⲝⲓ	49.11–12	ⲙ̄ⲡⲣ̄ⲣ̄ⲡⲟⲗⲓⲧⲉⲩⲉⲥⲑⲁⲓ (implied subject of the negative impv.)
47.5–6	ⲛ̄ⲧⲁⲣⲉⲕⲉⲓ		
47.7	ⲛ̄ⲕⲛⲁⲝⲓ	49.15	ⲟⲩⲛⲧⲉⲕ
47.7–8	ⲉⲕϣⲁⲛⲃⲱⲕ	49.22	ⲛ̄ⲕⲛⲉⲩ
47.14	ⲉⲕⲛ̄ⲛⲓⲙⲁ	49.23	ⲉⲁⲕⲧⲱⲟⲩⲛ
47.14–15	ⲉⲧⲕ̄ϣⲁⲁⲧ	49.25	ⲟⲩⲛⲧⲉⲕ
47.15–16	ⲛ̄ⲧⲁⲕⲣ̄ⲥⲡⲟⲩⲇⲁⲍⲉ		
		49.26	ⲕϭⲉⲉⲧ
47.18–19	ⲕϣⲟⲟⲡ	49.27	ⲉⲕⲛⲁⲙⲟⲩ

(b) The reader as object:

44.7	ⲛⲉⲕ	48.20–21	ⲙ̄ⲙⲁⲕ

---

[38] *Ibid.*   [39] *Ibid.*   [40] *Ibid.*

47.11	ⲉⲧⲃ̄ⲏⲧⲕ̄	49.24	ⲙ̄ⲙⲁⲕ
47.13	ⲛ̄ⲙⲙⲉ[ⲕ]		

(c) The reader as possessive pronoun or possessive article:

47.12	ⲡⲱⲕ....ⲡⲱⲕ	49.29–30	ⲧⲉⲕⲙ̄ⲛ̄ⲧⲁⲧⲣ̄ⲥⲟⲩⲙ̄ⲛⲁⲍⲉ

(d) The reader as direct address:

43.25–26	ⲣⲏⲅⲓⲛⲟⲥ	47.3	ⲣⲏⲅⲓⲛⲉ
44.22	ⲣⲏⲅⲓⲛⲉ	49.10–11	ⲣⲏⲅⲓⲛⲉ
46.6	ⲡⲁϣⲏⲣⲉ		

However, in the concluding section of 49.37–50.16 there appears a mixture of this second singular masculine form with plural forms of address:

(a) The readers as subject:

	Plural		Singular
50.7–8	ⲉⲣⲉⲧⲛ̄ϣⲓⲛⲉ	50.8–9	ⲙ̄ⲡⲣ̄ⲣ̄ⲫⲟⲟⲛⲉⲓ (implied subject of the negative imperative)

(b) The readers as object:

	Plural		Singular
50.4	ⲧⲏⲩⲧⲛ̄	50.1–2	ⲁⲓⲧⲥⲉⲃⲁⲕ
50.7	ⲁⲣⲱⲧⲛ̄	50.2	ⲛⲉⲕⲥⲛ[ⲏⲩ]
50.14	ⲛ̄ϧⲏⲧⲟⲩ	50.9–10	ⲁⲣⲁⲕ
50.15	ⲛⲉⲧⲙⲁⲉⲓⲉ	50.13	ⲛⲉⲕ
50.16	ⲙ̄ⲙⲱⲧⲛ̄	50.15	ⲁⲣⲁⲕ
		50.16	ⲙ̄ⲙⲱⲧⲛ̄

(c) The reader in direct address (?):

	Plural
50.2–3	ⲛⲁϣⲏⲣⲉ

If we follow the English translation of Robert McL. Wilson, the last-mentioned instance of a plural form is especially problematic. For up to 50.2–3 no one except Rheginos, the pupil, has been addressed. Then, suddenly and inexplicably there appears the following:

I have taught thee (Rheginos) and thy brethren concerning them, my sons (ⲛⲁϣⲏⲣⲉ), . . .[41]

---

[41] *Ibid.*, p. 67. The German translation of Walter Till (p. 57) corresponds to that of Wilson, and the French of Malinine and Puech (p. 17) differs only slightly.

Where have these other readers come from? Why are they not mentioned until this point? The difficulties here and those found elsewhere in the 'Epilogue' (49.37–50.16) stem in part, we maintain, from a defective translation. To help resolve some of these problems, we have offered a fresh translation below.[42]

From our new translation and the foregoing considerations, we believe we may draw some important conclusions. First, the eight pages of our text were originally addressed to an individual, Rheginos, and not to a larger audience. True, in 50.11–14 it is stated that others may desire to 'look into' what the author has written; however, the addressee has not been so broadened as to make the document a general epistle. Rather, it is a didactic and apologetic letter written by a teacher to one of his pupils in response to specific questions raised by the pupil. This means that we may look for more 'personal touches' in the letter than the first editors indicate are there. Second, the term λοϲοϲ in the subscript title of the text is more descriptive of the content than the literary form of the letter. That is, λοϲοϲ does not mean 'discourse', 'general epistle', or 'treatise' (the editors' preferred translations); it refers instead to the 'word of instruction' given to a pupil by his teacher on the subject of the resurrection. This conclusion is further confirmed by the fact that in the second or third century a personal letter would have had no such title affixed to it.[43] Consequently, the subscript title was not part of the original text of 'Rheginos' but was added either by the Coptic translator or by the editor-collector of the documents with which the Letter was originally grouped! Such a title would have served as a handy index to a particular writing contained in a codex. And, since the title is a late addition, its form cannot be utilized—as by the first editors—to argue for a Greek original of the Letter.[44]

An objection might be raised at this point: if 'Rheginos' is a personal letter, why is there no 'praescriptio' such as we commonly find in this type of literature? One suggestion offered is that the writing never had a 'praescriptio'. It should be identified with that ancient Middle Eastern epistolary form which lacks such a beginning,

---

[42] See *infra*, pp. 33f. Consult, also, the relevant notes to this passage, *infra*, pp. 99–104.

[43] On this, see Otto Roller, *Das Formular der Paulinischen Briefe: Ein Beitrag zur Lehre vom antiken Briefe* (Beiträge zur Wissenschaft vom Alten und Neuen Testament; Vierte Folge, Heft 6; Stuttgart, 1933), pp. 68–78, 85. Schenke, *OrL*, 60 (1965), col. 471, also considers this title to be clearly secondary.

[44] *De Resurrectione*, pp. ixf.

such as the Epistle to the Hebrews.[45] However, there are distinct differences between 'Rheginos' and a literary type like Hebrews: (1) the addressee is personal, not general; (2) there is no noticeable Semitic character; (3) while the content is didactic and apologetic, 'Rheginos' is still addressed to specific needs and questions. An alternate suggestion is that the translator, or an editor-collector, has intentionally removed the original 'praescriptio' to give the Letter a more general address. Or, if the author was Valentinus, as the first editors claim, the removal of an offensive heretical name from the 'praescriptio' would have made the letter much more serviceable for use as propaganda among 'orthodox' Christian contemporaries. Or, it may be that in copying the text, a scribe interested in including as many writings as possible in the codex he was compiling may have removed the 'praescriptio', indicating the separation of 'Rheginos' from the preceding text by means of the diamond and dot pattern found on page one of the letter.[46] But whatever the manner, the Letter to Rheginos does appear to have lost its initial address.

Because of the frequent echoing of Pauline motifs throughout and the clear citation of a passage from the 'Apostle',[47] one might expect the author of 'Rheginos' to have imitated the Pauline letter style. Certainly, numerous Christian writers of the second century were influenced by Paul's format.[48] However, there are more differences than similarities, such as the absence in 'Rheginos' of anything comparable to the Pauline 'praescriptio' with its well-known division into two sentences of greeting (in which sender and receiver are named) and of blessing. Also, the Letter contains no thanksgiving, which usually forms a transition to the body of the letter in Paul's authentic writings. Moreover, despite the similarity of the valediction in 'Rheginos' 50.14 (ⲁϯⲣⲏⲛⲏ ⲛ̅ϧⲏⲧⲟⲩ ⲙ̅ⲛ̅ ⲧⲉⲭⲁⲣⲓⲥ) to the Pauline formula of χάρις καὶ εἰρήνη, the formula in 'Rheginos' occurs

45 See Alfred Wikenhauser, *New Testament Introduction*, tr. Joseph Cunningham (New York and London, 1958/1967), pp. 349f.; Roller, *Das Formular der Paulinischen Briefe*, pp. 57–68, 78–84. Dr van Unnik seems to identify 'Rheginos' with the literary type represented by Hebrews, *JEH*, XV, No. 2 (Oct. 1964), p. 146; whereas Orbe, *Greg.*, 46 (1965), p. 173, considers the document to be more a 'homily' or 'sermon of the brotherhood' than a personal letter.

46 See the Plate of f. XXIIʳ in *De Resurrectione* for this pattern. Schenke, also, seems to think that the praescriptio 'is missing', *OrL*, 60 (1965), col. 471.

47 The Letter's use of Paul is discussed below, pp. 18f., 21, 23–26, 70ff.

48 On the extensive influence of Paul's epistolary style, see Roller, *Das Formular der Paulinischen Briefe*, pp. 136ff.; Paul Wendland, *Die Urchristlichen Literaturformen* (Handbuch zum Neuen Testament, herausgegeben von Hans Lietzmann; Band I, Teil 3; Tübingen, 1912), pp. 277ff.

at the end of the Letter, not in the salutation as in the Pauline and deutero-Pauline literature. Also, whereas Paul, the deutero-Pauline writings, the Petrine Epistles, and Revelation (1.4) never vary the order of χάρις καὶ εἰρήνη, in 'Rheginos' this order is reversed.[49] Thus, the author of our Letter does not seem to have consciously imitated the Pauline letter style.

We would conclude with respect to the literary form of 'Rheginos' that however one assesses our conjecture that its 'praescriptio' may have been intentionally removed, three other observations must stand until disproven: (1) that the subscript title has been added to the Letter by a later translator or editor, not by the original author; (2) that 'Rheginos' is a didactic letter to an individual, although its author implies that it might be shared with others; (3) that no consciously consistent attempt was made by the writer to imitate the Pauline letter style.

C. THE HISTORICAL CONTEXT OF THE LETTER

The Letter to Rheginos is one of 55-odd writings from a 'religious library' probably used by a fourth-century Gnostic community of Sethian disposition which was settled in or near the ancient town of Chenoboskion (Χενοβόσκιον—'Goose-pasture').[50] Since this 'library' is largely Sethian in nature, the Valentinian character of 'Rheginos' and its companion writings in the Jung Codex makes it appear rather unique. Its presence in the 'library' is probably best explained by the theory of Henri-Charles Puech that the Sethian community which made the collection was eclectic in its tastes and found the thought of certain Hermetic and Valentinian writings congenial to its own views.[51] The group which preserved the writings of the Jung Codex prior to their acquisition for the Sethian library may have been some Valentinians who, as Epiphanius (Pan., XXXI.7, 1) notes, were still found in the Thebaeid region in the fourth century.

---

[49] Contrast the editors' views in their 'Notes Critiques' to 50.14 and 50.15: De Resurrectione, p. 47.

[50] The community's founders are probably to be identified with a second-century group combated by Irenaeus (Adv. Haer. I.29, 30) whom subsequent heresiologists identify as 'Gnostics', 'Barbelognostics', 'Archontics', or 'Sethians'. On this, see Puech and Doresse, CRAIBL (1948), p. 91; Doresse, BCLSMP, Tome XXXV (1949), p. 435; Puech, Coptic Studies in Honor of Crum, pp. 142–9.

[51] Encyclopédie Française, Tome XIX (1957), p. 19.42–11.

The Greek autograph of 'Rheginos' was most likely composed sometime prior to the fourth century, the date assigned to the script of its Coptic text.[52] On the other hand, the utilization of Pauline and Marcan material in the Letter, plus the 'echoing' of other New Testament passages, presupposes the author's possession of an authoritative collection of Scripture which probably did not exist earlier than the first quarter of the second century. The problem of establishing a date for the text sometime between the first quarter of the second century and the fourth century is complicated, however, by the fact that no known text from this period mentions or quotes the Letter to Rheginos.[53]

In spite of our inability to date the Letter more precisely, some narrowing of the probable period of its composition has been achieved through two major investigations. Both of these take as their starting point a fundamental theme of the writing, viz. that the resurrection has already occurred.[54] One of them, the investigation of Puech and Quispel, has sought to find the setting for this teaching among the heretical views of the period. The Letter's fundamental Gnostic character is emphasized, together with its heterodox origin and features.[55] The other attempt, van Unnik's, has undertaken to place 'Rheginos' among the controversies over the resurrection which took place within the Great Church. In contrast to the views of Puech and Quispel, the content of 'Rheginos' is held to be surprisingly close to more orthodox Christian views of the time. For van

---

[52] On the Coptic text of 'Rheginos' as a translation Coptic as well as concerning the dating of the script, see *supra*, pp. 4–5.

[53] So Puech and Quispel, *VC*, VIII (1954), p. 40; van Unnik, *JEH*, XV, No. 2 (Oct. 1964), p. 144.

[54] All students of 'Rheginos' are agreed that this theme is central to the Letter's teaching. See, for example: Anonymous, *BO*, XXI 3/4 (Mei–Juli, 1964), p. 250; Barns, *JTS*, XV (1964), p. 163; Jean Daniélou, A Review of *De Resurrectione*, *VC*, XVIII, No. 3 (1964), p. 187; Giversen, *JEH*, XVI, 1 (April, 1965), p. 82; Haenchen, *ThR*, 30, Heft 1 (Juni 1964), p. 55; Lebeau, *NRT*, 87 (1965), p. 319; Leipoldt, *TL*, 7, 90 (Juli 1965), col. 519; Orbe, *Greg.*, 46 (1965), p. 173; Puech, *The Jung Codex*, p. 19; Puech and Quispel, *VC*, VIII (1954), pp. 40, 46; Quispel, *ZRGG*, VI, Heft 4 (1954), p. 299; Schenke, *OrL*, 60 (1965), col. 472; van Unnik, *JEH*, XV, No. 2 (Oct. 1964), p. 143; Jan Zandee, 'De Opstanding in de brief aan Rheginos en in het Evangelie van Philippus', *Nederlands Theologisch Tijdschrift*, 16 (1962), p. 361.

[55] See, for example, Quispel, *ZRGG*, VI, Heft 4 (1954), pp. 299–301; Puech and Quispel, *VC*, VIII (1954), pp. 40–50; Puech, *Encyclopédie Française*, Tome XIX (1957), p. 19.42–8; Puech and Quispel, *De Resurrectione*, *passim*; Puech, *CRAIBL*, (1964), pp. 317f. A similar point of view is taken by Leipoldt, *TL*, 7, 90 (Juli 1965), cols. 519–20; Zandee, *NTT*, 16 (1962), pp. 361–77.

Unnik, it remains an enigma why an author who is otherwise so 'orthodox' should continue to subscribe to the Gnostic cosmology so evident in the text.[56] Thus, as is the case with respect to the Apocryphon of James from the Jung Codex,[57] two angles of vision are represented in the approaches to the Letter to Rheginos. Nevertheless, these separate attempts concur in locating the historical setting of the Letter in the same period. It will be useful to see how they do this.

Christianity, state Puech and Quispel, has been in conflict from its inception with advocates of the view that the 'resurrection has already occurred' (II Tim. 2.18: λέγοντες ἀνάστασιν ἤδη γεγονέναι). Although several groups and individuals combated by the early Christian Apologists propounded this view, none did so more vigorously than the opponents of Tertullian in his treatise, *De Resurrectione Mortuorum*. These opponents appear to be Valentinians, and their teaching bears similarity to that of the Letter to Rheginos.[58] Closer study of other Valentinian texts has revealed some decisive parallels to our Letter. The Valentinians are said to have held the view of a 'pneumatic resurrection' obtainable during life.[59] Moreover, there are striking similarities in terminology, as evidenced by such expressions in 'Rheginos' as πλήρωμα, σύστασις, σπέρμα, ἀποκατάστασις, σαρκικός, ψυχικός, πνευματικός; as well as in the use of opposing concepts like κόσμος and αἰών, μερισμός and ἕνωσις. Further, a variant reading of Col. 1.16 in 'Rheginos' 44.34–39 is held to be paralleled only in Valentinian sources cited by Irenaeus (*Adv. Haer.*, I.4.5) and Clement (*Excerpta ex Theodoto*, 43.3).[60] Finally, the Valentinian nature of the Letter is said to be clearly confirmed by the numerous affinities it shares with the Gospel of Truth from the Jung Codex.

---

[56] See *JEH*, XV, No. 2 (Oct. 1964), pp. 151–2, 165. Cf., also, the appreciative comments of Haenchen on van Unnik's view in *Gnomon*, 36 (1964), p. 363; also the views of Barns, *JTS*, XV (1964), p. 163.

[57] Jan Zandee maintains that the 'Apocryphon' is clearly Valentinian. See his 'Gnostische trekken in een apocryphe brief van Jacobus', *NTT*, 17 (1962–63), pp. 401–22. The opposite view, viz. that the text is basically Christian with only slight heterodox traces, is supported by van Unnik. See the latter's comments in *Evangelien aus dem Nilsand*, pp. 100f.

[58] Puech and Quispel, *De Resurrectione*, pp. x–xii; [Quispel, *VC*, VII (1953), p. 193; Quispel, *ZRGG*, VI, Heft 4 (1954), p. 299; Puech and Quispel, *VC*, VIII (1954), p. 40; Quispel, *The Jung Codex*, pp. 54–55; Haenchen, *ThR*, N.F. 30, Heft 1 (1964), p. 56; Daniélou, *VC*, XVIII, No. 3 (Sept. 1964), p. 187.

[59] Puech and Quispel, *De Resurrectione*, pp. xvf.; cf. pp. xxiv and xxix.

[60] *Ibid.*, p. xx.

The editors cite as proof of this E.V. 24.32–25.2 compared to Rheg. 48.38–49.6.[61]

Since classical Valentinianism was divided into Oriental and Occidental Schools, however, the first editors are concerned to identify 'Rheginos' resurrection teaching with that of one or the other. Some similarities with the Occidental School are detected, such as the identical stress by Heracleon on the value of 'faith' and the disparagement of 'persuasion' (πείθειν; cf. Rheg. 46.3–13). Much more significant, though, are the similarities between our Letter and the Oriental School. Like Valentinus himself, members of the Oriental School apparently taught that the resurrection involved only the 'pneumatic element' or 'spirit' of a believer, not the 'psychic element' or 'soul'. So also, the Letter to Rheginos propounds the view that neither soul nor flesh participates in the resurrection, but only the spirit (46.21–24).[62] At death the 'pneumatics' (those possessing the spirit) are re-absorbed by their divine, consubstantial counterpart, God (cf. Rheg. 45.39–46.2).[63] By contrast, Occidental Valentinians taught that both 'psychic' and 'pneumatic' elements of believers were susceptible of salvation. Another parallel cited is in the area of Christology. The Oriental School taught that Christ had only a pneumatic body, no 'psychic' elements being present in him. In Rheg. 44.30–36, say the editors, Christ's nature is shown to be purely spiritual. The Occidental School, however, taught that the Saviour possessed both a spiritual 'seed' and a psychic body.[64] Such parallels lead the editors to conclude that the Letter to Rheginos must emanate from the Oriental branch of Valentinianism.

In the first of two lectures delivered at King's College, London, in 1963, Prof. Willem van Unnik of Utrecht argues that the Letter to Rheginos probably dates from the second century. This is because

[61] *Ibid.*, pp. xx–xxv. Cf., from some of the Valentinian parallels to 'Rheginos', the following: Quispel, *ZRGG*, VI, Heft 4 (1954), p. 299; Puech and Quispel, *VC*, VIII (1954), pp. 41ff., 45; *The Jung Codex*, Puech: p. 19; Quispel: pp. 55ff.; Haenchen, *ThR*, N.F. 30, Heft 1 (1964), pp. 56f.; Barns, *JTS*, XV (1964), pp. 163–4; Leipoldt, *TL*, 7, 90 (Juli 1965), col. 520; Giversen, *JEH*, XVI, 1 (April 1965), pp. 82–83.

[62] The interpretation is that of Puech and Quispel, *De Resurrectione*, pp. xi and xxiii; cf. the same authors in *VC*, VIII (1954), p. 49.

[63] So, Puech and Quispel, *De Resurrectione*, p. xiv; Puech, *CRAIBL* (1964), p. 318; Zandee, *NTT*, 16 (1962), p. 372; Daniélou, *VC*, XVIII, No. 3 (Sept. 1964), p. 188. Cf. the contrasting interpretation of Rheg. 45.14–46.2 in Haenchen, *Gnomon*, 36 (1964), p. 361.

[64] See the reference in note 62 just above.

the Letter's content reflects a time of serious debate over the resurrection, a time such as the second century when the resurrection doctrine was almost an *articulus stantis aut cadentis ecclesiae*.[65] Then, in his second lecture, van Unnik gathers evidence from Tertullian, Minucius Felix, the Acts of Paul and Thecla, Pseudo-Justin, and Athenagoras to demonstrate that the subject of the resurrection was indeed the 'storm centre' of debate in the second century. By contrast, minor differences about the resurrection, such as those between Jesus and the Sadducees (Mark 12.18ff. and parallels), between Paul and his opponents at Corinth (I Cor. 15), and Paul and the philosophers at Athens (Acts 17.30ff.) are taken to show that '. . . on the whole, this belief does not seem to have been a storm-centre of attack and defence in the first century'. After the second century, on the other hand, the front of battle turned to other matters.[66]

The remainder of this lecture is concerned with the important points of second-century dispute, including: the attack of pagans, such as Celsus, on the idea of corporeal resurrection as opposed to immortality of the soul; the contradictory views of eschatology held among poorly-educated Christians; the confused identification of Gnostic teaching on the resurrection with that of the Great Church; and the view that the resurrection has already occurred. Finally, van Unnik shows his agreement with Puech and Quispel in his conclusion that the Gnostic ideas of resurrection found in 'Rheginos' have many affinities with the Valentinian teachings on the subject which were combated by Irenaeus, Tertullian, and Justin.[67]

Thus, both the line of demonstration pursued by Puech and Quispel and that followed by van Unnik converge in their conclusions that the Letter to Rheginos finds its proper historical context in the second century. While van Unnik goes only so far as to show that the distinctive resurrection teaching in 'Rheginos' points toward a second-century Valentinian milieu for the Letter, the first editors push on to try to set it into the framework of Oriental Valentinianism. The latter effort involves a comparison of the teaching of 'Rheginos' with that of the Gospel of Truth (*Evangelium Veritatis*). Both documents are found to be quite similar in content and in the degree of development of Valentinian teaching. This, together with arguments yet to be reviewed, leads Puech and Quispel to the conclusion that the Letter to Rheginos must have been penned by Valentinus him-

---

[65] *JEH*, XV, No. 2 (Oct. 1964), pp. 142–4, 146.
[66] *Ibid.*, pp. 155–6.   [67] *Ibid.*, pp. 156–62, 164–5.

self sometime after AD 150, probably in Italy.[68] The soundness of these arguments and comparisons will be discussed more fully in Chapter V. For the present it may suffice to say that the degree of validity found in the authors' argumentation is in direct proportion to the extent of one's agreement with (a) their interpretation of the teaching of 'Rheginos'; (b) their reconstruction of Oriental and Occidental Valentinianism's resurrection teachings; and (c) the results of their comparison of 'Rheginos' with the Gospel of Truth. And, with respect to van Unnik's study, it satisfies in so far as one agrees that a text like 'Rheginos' can only emerge out of a 'storm-centre of debate' over the resurrection.

D. THE USE OF THE NEW TESTAMENT IN THE LETTER

In his argumentation on behalf of the resurrection, the author of the Letter to Rheginos treats the New Testament as his final court of appeal. Such matters as the guarantee of the resurrection for believers, the proof that men are raised in spiritual flesh, and the demonstration that one should consider himself already raised are all rooted ultimately in the author's 'exposition' ($\dot{a}\pi a\gamma\gamma\epsilon\lambda\dot{\iota}a$) of this written 'Word of Truth' (Rheg. 43.34; 45.4). Moreover, many have found the Letter's content to be permeated with Pauline thought and vocabulary, as in its stress on faith; its emphasis on life and resurrection in Christ, by him, and with him; its theme of the absorption of the visible into the invisible; and its use of the phrase 'putting on' or 'wearing' Christ.[69] The first editors think that Rheg. 45.24–40 is an important witness to the conservation and cultivation of a 'Pauline mysticism' during a period when such mystical motifs of the Apostle are largely absent from orthodox writings.[70] Thus, the author of our Letter gives ample

[68] Puech and Quispel, *De Resurrectione*, pp. xxxi–xxxiii. The editors do not actually specify Italy as the place of origin. Such an inference may probably be drawn, however, from their close association of 'Rheginos' with the Gospel of Truth.

[69] *Ibid.*, p. xiv. Cf., also, Quispel, *VC*, VII (1953), p. 193; Quispel, *ZRGG*, VI, Heft 4 (1954), p. 300; Puech and Quispel, *VC*, VIII (1954), p. 44; Zandee, *NTT*, 16 (1962), p. 377; Daniélou, *VC*, XVIII, No. 3 (Sept., 1964), p. 187; Gilles Quispel, 'Il Cristianesimo primitivo alla luce delle recenti scoperte', *Orpheus: Revista di Umanità Classica e Cristiana*, X, No. 1 (1963), p. 12; van Unnik, *JEH*, XV, No. 2 (Oct., 1964), p. 150; Haenchen, *Gnomon*, 36 (1964), pp. 361–2; Barns, *JTS*, XV (1964), p. 163; Giversen, *JEH*, XVI, No. 1 (April, 1965), p. 82.

[70] Puech and Quispel, *De Resurrectione*, pp. xiii and xxxi. It is notable that

evidence of his desire to base his teaching upon the authoritative written source of Christianity.

1. *New Testament Citations and Echoes*

Two methods are employed by the author in his use of the New Testament. The first of these is the citation or quotation of certain passages. The second involves the echoing of or allusion to characteristic terminology and ideas. For clarification we shall deal with each separately.

The introductory formulae of two passages in 'Rheginos' plainly indicate that both are intended as citations.[71] The first of these passages is Rheg. 45.24–28:

> Then, indeed, as the Apostle
> said, 'We suffered
> with him, and we arose
> with him, and we went to heaven
> with him'.[72]

The technical term 'Apostle' *(ἀπόστολος)* certainly refers to Paul here, as the content of the passage makes clear.[73] At the same time, the citation can by no means be called literal, since it is actually a composite one, made up of portions of at least two Pauline passages,[74] viz. a partial but nearly literal quotation of Rom. 8.17 and a para-

---

Haenchen, while agreeing on Pauline influence in this passage, does not mention the presence of any 'Pauline mysticism' and clearly distinguishes the Pauline view on the relations of believers to Christ from that of 'Rheginos': *ThR*, N.F. 30, Heft 1 (1964), p. 56. Also, van Unnik says that while Rom. 6 may lie behind Rheg. 45.24ff., there is no explicit mention of baptism in the Gnostic text, as the editors are inclined to believe. See *JEH*, XV, No. 2 (1964), p. 151.

[71] The editors attempt to identify a third citation, that of Col. 1.16, in Rheg. 44.34–39. See *De Resurrectione*, pp. xx, 24–25. Because of the omission of anything like a citation formula and because of the very fragmented nature of 44.34–39, however, we believe it is more properly treated as an 'echo' or 'allusion' than a citation. See *infra*, p. 63.

[72] The translation here, as in all other passages cited from 'Rheginos' except where indicated otherwise, is the author's. Similarities to the translation supplied by Wilson in *De Resurrectione* are due mainly to the use by both translators of Crum's *Coptic Dictionary*.

[73] However, the Valentinian exegetes used this term with reference to other Apostles, too: Luke: ὥς φησιν ὁ ἀπόστολος (Clement, *Exc. Theod.* 74); John: λέγει ὁ ἀπόστολος (Ptolemaeus, *ad Fl.* I 6); Peter: καὶ κατὰ τὸν ἀπόστολον (*Exc. Theod.* 12).

[74] This fact has been correctly noted by the editors in *De Resurrectione*, p. xxxi, cf. p. 27.

phrase of the ideas found in Eph. 2.5–6.[75] The non-literal and composite nature of the citation may stem from the author's attempt to recall relevant passages from a faulty memory, or its form may be due to the admixture of the author's own views with selected New Testament 'proof texts'. It is clear, however, that by this appeal to Paul the author seeks to clinch his arguments: (1) that the Saviour has destroyed death and opened the way of immortality; and (2) that this event has had decisive consequences in which the believer is a participant.

A second citation in the Letter is Rheg. 48.6–11:

> For if you
> recall reading in the
> Gospel that Elijah ap-
> peared and Moses
> with him, do not think the
> resurrection is an illusory thing.

The editors of our Letter have shown that this passage contains a clear allusion to the 'Transfiguration' pericope found in Matt. 17.1–8; Mark 9.2–8; Luke 9.28–36.[76] But the partial nature of the allusion and the simple reference to 'the Gospel' ($\epsilon\vec{v}\alpha\gamma\gamma\acute{\epsilon}\lambda\iota o\nu$) make complex the question of which Gospel is being cited. Nevertheless, from a detailed comparison of these passages in both Coptic and Greek,[77] we have been able to draw some important conclusions: (1) Although the key Coptic phrase in Rheg. 48.8–9 for 'appeared' (ⲟⲩⲱⲛⲏ ⲁⲃⲁⲗ—$\check{\omega}\phi\theta\eta$) most closely parallels the same phrase in the Sahidic Coptic Version of Luke 9.31a (ⲟⲩⲱⲛⲏ ⲉⲃⲟⲗ—οἱ ὀφθέντες), the order of appearance of Elijah and Moses corresponds to Mark's account instead of to Luke's or Matthew's. The latter conclusion seems decisive.[78] (2) The author of our Letter makes a number of important omissions from the Marcan text in citing this

---

[75] The Greek and Coptic parallels supporting this conclusion are offered in our critical notes, *infra*, pp. 70–72. We disagree with Ernst Haenchen, *Gnomon*, 36 (1964), p. 361, who contends that Col. 2.12–13 is the real source of this passage. Other texts suggested as background for 45.26–28 are I Cor. 15.20, 23; Rom. 8.29; Col. 1.18; Rev. 1.5—as allusions to the Christian view that Christ's resurrection guarantees that of his followers (van Unnik); also, Rom. 6.1–14; Phil. 3.10–11 (Zandee); II Cor. 4.10–13 and II Tim. 2.11–12 (Puech and Quispel).

[76] See *De Resurrectione*, p. xxx, and their 'Note Critique' to 48.1–12 on p. 38.

[77] These comparisons are offered in Chapter III, *infra*, pp. 89–90.

[78] Thus we concur with the editors' views in *De Resurrectione*, p. xxx; also with Haenchen, *Gnomon*, 36 (1964), p. 362.

pericope, for he excludes any mention of Jesus and his disciples; the conversation between Elijah, Moses, and Jesus; the 'Sitz' of this event; and the significance of the 'Transfiguration' within the life of Jesus as viewed by the Synoptic writers. Indeed, the figures of Elijah and Moses are introduced as proof of the non-illusory character of the resurrection, and they thus indirectly bear testimony to the author's view of a 'spiritual resurrection body' which retains personally identifiable traits.[79] Notable, however, is the omission of any mention of Jesus' transfiguration, as well as the fact that the names of Elijah and Moses are both given—two features which rather decisively tell against viewing this passage as a proof text for the theory that this story was originally a resurrection appearance transposed back into Jesus' ministry by Mark.[80] (3) The point of crucial significance in the passage as used in our Letter is that Elijah and Moses, who have presumably died centuries ago, have appeared on earth in a resurrected state. Jesus, on the other hand, is understood to have undergone a temporary transformation while still alive! Thus, he is not mentioned as a proof for the resurrection, while Elijah and Moses are.

The other method utilized by the author of our Letter in his employment of the New Testament is, as we have indicated, an 'echoing' of its terminology and ideas. Certainly it was not uncommon in the early centuries of the Roman Empire for the literary style of cultured men to reflect a distinct preference for language reminiscent and suggestive of well-known authors, as opposed to express citation.[81] Such usage was also prevalent among writers within the Great Church, for '. . . the Fathers were so steeped in Scripture that their

[79] This portion of the Letter's eschatological thought is discussed more fully *infra*, pp. 146-9.

[80] That such backdating was done by Mark to give a 'heavenly ratification of Peter's Confession and . . . a prophecy of the Resurrection in pictorial form' is the theory of Rudolf Bultmann. He contends that in the original form of the tradition of this resurrection appearance the two figures who appear with Jesus were 'originally two unidentified heavenly beings (angels or saints), providing the accessories to the Lord who had ascended into the heavenly places'. *The History of the Synoptic Tradition*, tr. John Marsh (Oxford and New York, 1963), p. 260. Some salient criticisms of Bultmann's theory are offered by C. H. Dodd, 'The Appearances of the Risen Christ: An Essay in Form-Criticism of the Gospels', *Studies in the Gospels: Essays in Memory of R. H. Lightfoot*, edited by Dennis Eric Nineham (Oxford, 1955), p. 25.

[81] On this matter see Walter Kroll, *Studien zum Verständnis der römischen Literatur* (Stuttgart, 1924), pp. 139ff. We are indebted to Dr van Unnik for this valuable reference.

Biblical echoes are even more extensive than their direct quotations.'[82] This style was designed to call to the reader's mind what was already familiar to him without the need for verbatim citation, or it was indicative of the saturation of a writer's vocabulary with the language of the literature he knew so well. For example, the expression 'to stand within the Word of Truth' in Rheg. 43.32–34 is strongly reminiscent of I Cor. 15.1: Γνωρίζω δὲ ὑμῖν, ἀδελφοί, τὸ εὐαγγέλιον ὃ εὐηγγελισάμην ὑμῖν, ὃ καὶ παρελάβετε, ἐν ᾧ καὶ ἐστήκατε. Or, the statement in Rheg. 45.36–37 that 'We are drawn to heaven by Him . . .' is a clear echo of such expressions as those found in John 12.32: κἀγὼ ἐὰν ὑψωθῶ ἐκ τῆς γῆς, πάντας ἑλκύσω πρὸς ἐμαυτόν (cf. John 6.44a).[83] Thus, as in the Gospel of Truth from the Jung Codex,[84] we find the practice of 'echoing' or 'alluding to' the New Testament. But, whereas this is the only style found in the Gospel of Truth, it is mixed with the citation-method in the Letter to Rheginos.

2. *The Author's New Testament Text*

Triple problems confront the investigator of the text type underlying the New Testament citations and echoes in 'Rheginos'. First, there is the problem involved in re-translation from the Coptic text of 'Rheginos' into its Greek 'Vorlage'. On this problem we shall say more later.[85] Second, it is extremely difficult to check possible 'echoes' and 'allusions' in the Coptic text of 'Rheginos' against the text of the Subakhmimic Coptic Version of the New Testament, that version probably most familiar to the translator of 'Rheginos'. This is so because there are almost no extant remains of the Subakhmimic Version. Thus, whenever Johannine parallels have been sought, we have had to have recourse to Sir Herbert Thompson's edition of a fourth-century Subakhmimic codex of the Fourth Gospel—the only extensive manuscript of the Subakhmimic New Testament preserved.[86] Beyond the Fourth Gospel, we have had to utilize the Sahidic Version for the remainder of the New Testament in Coptic, a version which may be both younger than and textually related to

[82] So H. E. W. Turner, *The Pattern of Christian Truth: A Study in the Relations between Orthodoxy and Heresy in the Early Church* (London, 1954), p. 273.

[83] These 'echoes' and others are presented in our critical notes in Chapter III.

[84] On the 'echoes' of the New Testament contained in the Gospel of Truth, see van Unnik, *The Jung Codex*, pp. 107ff.

[85] See *infra*, pp. 160–1.

[86] Thompson, *The Gospel of St. John According to the Earliest Coptic Manuscript* (1924).

the Subakhmimic, although the exact relationship is disputed.[87] For Acts and the Pauline Epistles we have used the superior text edited from the Chester Beatty Manuscripts by Thompson.[88] For the Synoptics, Catholic Epistles, and Revelation we have employed the text established by George Horner[89]—fully conscious of its deficiencies.[90] About all we can conclude concerning the text type represented by this mixture is that the Sahidic Version, like the Subakhmimic codex of John mentioned above, is most closely related to the Alexandrian text, although the Sahidic displays some influences from the Western text.[91] This combination of Subakhmimic and Sahidic texts—in spite of its inadequacy—has had to provide the Coptic New Testament text compared with 'Rheginos'.

The third problem encountered in working through the citations and echoes in 'Rheginos' is that they are neither literal nor clear enough to afford definitive identification of their underlying text type. It has become evident from comparisons made, however, that instead of translating the New Testament passages cited or echoed directly from the Greek New Testament, the translator has probably

---

[87] *Ibid.*, p. xxi. He believes that the Akhmimic Version and that of its sub-dialect are older than the Sahidic. There is some controversy among textual critics, however, over whether the Sahidic, the Akhmimic, and the Subakhmimic Versions have arisen independently of one another, or whether they are basically the same version. On this, see Arthur Vööbus, *Early Versions of the New Testament: Papers of the Estonian Theological Society in Exile* (Stockholm, 1954), pp. 238–9.

[88] Sir Herbert Thompson, *The Coptic Version of the Acts of the Apostles and the Pauline Epistles in the Sahidic Dialect* (Cambridge, 1932).

[89] George Horner, ed., *The Coptic Version of the New Testament in the Southern Dialect Otherwise called Sahidic and Thebaic* (Oxford, dates as follows): Vol. I— *The Gospels of S. Matthew and S. Mark* (1911); Vol. II—*The Gospel of Luke* (1911); Vol. VII—*The Catholic Epistles and the Apocalypse* (1924). Occasional use has been made of Vol. III—*The Gospel of S. John, Register of Fragments, Etc., Facsimiles* (1911), to supplement the text of John where Thompson's edition of that Gospel has lacunae.

[90] Vööbus, *Early Versions*, p. 217, writes:
'It must be borne in mind that Horner's Sahidic text is a mosaic with portions from all centuries—a fact which has not always been taken into account by students of textual history.'
Nevertheless, a critic such as Heinrich Vogels acknowledges that the authoritative edition of the Sahidic Gospels remains that of Horner. See *Handbuch der Textkritik des Neuen Testaments* (2. Auflage; Bonn, 1955), p. 129.

[91] On the text of Thompson's Subakhmimic Version of John, consult Bruce M. Metzger, *The Text of the New Testament: Its Transmission, Corruption, and Restoration* (New York and London, 1964), p. 81. On the basic text represented by the Sahidic Version, see the following: Vööbus, *Early Versions*, pp. 227–9; Vogels, *Handbuch*, pp. 128–9; Alexander Souter, *The Text and Canon of the New Testament* (Revised by C. S. C. Williams; London, 1954), pp. 61–62.

substituted familiar passages and expressions from his Coptic Version.[92] If so, this would indicate that at least the Coptic text of these citations and echoes in 'Rheginos' bears affinity to the Alexandrian text type.[93]

3. The Author's New Testament Canon

From the New Testament citations and reasonably distinct echoes identified in our Letter, it appears that the author knew and used the Gospels of Mark, John and probably Matthew, and the following Pauline Epistles: Romans, I–II Corinthians, Ephesians, Philippians, and Colossians.[94] Thus, when he alludes to the 'Gospel' (48.7–8), the author mentions only one of at least two Gospels which he knew. His reference to 'the Apostle' (45.24–25), on the other hand, conceals somewhat his knowledge of at least six Pauline letters. In brief, he does not cite particular writings by name, but his 'canon'—somewhat like Marcion's—is divided into a 'Gospel' and an 'Apostle'.[95] Moreover, if we add to this basic list other New Testament writings which may be vaguely alluded to in 'Rheginos', we could include Luke, Acts, I–II Thessalonians, II Timothy, Titus, Hebrews, I–II Peter, I John and III John.[96] We cannot so expand the list with much confidence, however, because of the fragmentary nature of the echoes mentioned earlier. Our investigation will demonstrate that Paul was the New Testament writer predominantly utilized by the author.

[92] Substantiation for this conclusion is provided by the Coptic New Testament parallels to the text of 'Rheginos' cited in the following relevant sections in Chapter III: 2; 6; (10;) 13 (?); 20; 23; 25 (idea of 'swallowing up'); 26; 27 (?); 29; 30; 31; 36; 45; 49; 53 (1); 55; 60; 61; 62; 65; 78 (?); and 79. Cf. also our note to 50.15. If this was the procedure of the translator of 'Rheginos', it is just the opposite of the practice of the translator of the Coptic-Gnostic 'Gospel of Mary'. Cf. Robert McL. Wilson, 'The Study of N.T. Allusions in the Gospel according to Mary', *NTS*, III (1957), pp. 236–9.

[93] We have previously commented on the text type of the Sahidic Version. See *supra*, p. 22.

[94] Support for this statement is provided in Chapter III in the sections of New Testament parallels numbered: 2; 3; 6; 13; 15; 20; 23; 25; 26; 27; 29; 31; 42; 45; 49; 53 (1); 55; 61; 62; 65.

[95] On Marcion's Bible, see Adolf von Harnack, *Marcion: Das Evangelium vom Fremden Gott, Neue Studien zu Marcion* (Zweite Auflage; Berlin, 1960 Reprint), pp. 35–73; Turner, *The Pattern*, pp. 252–3.

[96] Such allusions would encompass those found in Chapter III in the sections of New Testament parallels which are numbered: 1; 4; 5; 8; 10; 18; 21; 22; 24; 36; 41; 56; 60; 64; 67; 70; 76; 78; 79. In the remaining sections of New Testament parallels, the only additional writings to which allusion might be made are Galatians and James.

4. *The Author's Exegetical Method*

Unlike other Valentinian exegetes, our author does not approach the New Testament as an esoteric book whose literal sense conceals deep mysteries of true 'knowledge'.[97] For example, Elijah and Moses are not treated as transparent symbols of a higher reality in our Letter,[98] but they are simply mentioned as proofs of the fact that men do survive death (48.6–11). It is certainly true that Valentinian exegesis did occasionally engage in a more literal interpretation of Scripture,[99] but ingenious or fantastic allegory—the characteristic feature of the exegesis of Ptolemy, Heracleon, and other Valentinians[100] —is absent from our Letter. In fact, the 'symbols' and 'images' used are not provided by scriptural events, but by the concepts of the Valentinian myth itself (e.g. Rheg. 48.34–49.7—light flowing down on darkness, the Pleroma perfecting the Deficiency)! On the other hand, the author of 'Rheginos' may have made use of a typological allegory, but merely does not do so in our Letter. For example, although it is never made explicit, some relationship appears presupposed between the event of Christ's resurrection and the great metaphysical process of 'Restoration' *(ἀποκατάστασις).*[101]

Among other exegetical methods made use of in our Letter is the combination of several New Testament passages on the basis of a catchword. This is the case in Rheg. 45.24–28 where Rom. 8.17 and Eph. 2.6 appear to be combined on the basis of the phrase ⲛ̄ⲧⲙ̄ⲙⲉϥ

---

[97] Carola Barth has shown this to be the Valentinian approach to Scripture in her important study, *Die Interpretation des Neuen Testaments in der Valentinianischen Gnosis* (3. Reihe, 7 Band, Heft 3, Texte und Untersuchungen zur Geschichte der altchristlichen Literatur, herausgegeben von Adolf von Harnack und Carl Schmidt; Der ganzen Reihe XXXVII Band; Leipzig, 1911), pp. 44f., 116f.

[98] Barth, *ibid.*, pp. 76–84, has demonstrated that in Valentinian exegesis there is a great deal of fluidity between symbol and reality in the treatment of New Testament personalities. An example is provided by Heracleon's treatment of the Samaritan woman whom Jesus meets in John 4.4–42. She is not flesh and blood, but rather a symbol of the Spirit created by Sophia which dwells on earth, greatly in need of salvation (Frags. 18–19).

[99] See *ibid.*, pp. 102–8.

[100] See the examples given in *ibid.*, pp. 46–92.

[101] Barth helps to illuminate this matter:
'For (Valentinian) belief, which sees in earthly occurrence a likeness of heavenly event, the life of the Saviour on earth is only a visible representation of a great, metaphysical process.'
Die Interpretation des Neuen Testaments in der Valentinianischen Gnosis (Inaugural-Dissertation zur Erlangung der Licentiatenwürde der Theologischen Fakultät der Universität Jena; Leipzig, 1908), p. 3; cf. p. 9.

(σὺν . . . αὐτῷ). Such a practice was also known and used in Valentinian exegesis.[102] In addition, the author sometimes interprets the details of a passage to the neglect of their context. For instance, in his citation of the Transfiguration pericope (Rheg. 48.6–11), his focus on the appearances of Elijah and Moses draws attention to a feature of the story not emphasized in its original Marcan setting.[103] This approach is similar to that allegorical Valentinian interpretation which fastened on single aspects of the parables of or stories about Jesus.[104]

We also find in 'Rheginos' a tendentious type of interpretation which bends the scriptural text into conformity with the particular views of the author. For example, in 45.24–26 the present tense of συνπάσχομεν from Rom. 8.17 is changed to a past tense, apparently to support better the author's 'realized' eschatology.[105] Also, if 44.37–38 is really an allusion to Col. 1.16 (which we elsewhere dispute[106]), then the passage is severed from its context and given a new meaning by placing the creation of 'dominions' and 'deities' in antithesis to rather than within the creative work of Christ. In 45.39–46.2 the Pauline concepts of ψυχική, πνευματική, and σαρκική are drawn together from different scriptural contexts—possibly under the influence of the Valentinian tripartite division of mankind—and are used to describe the mode of the resurrection rather than the resurrection body as in I Cor. 15.[107] Further examples could be cited to confirm the fact that like other Valentinian exegetes,[108] our author's employment of certain New Testament passages reflects his intent to use them to promote a particular point of view.

Having said these things, however, it is important to reiterate that

[102] Cf., for example, the combination of echoes of Matt. 19.17 and 5.8 in the fragment of a letter of Valentinus preserved in Clement, Strom. ii, 36.2–4. Dr van Unnik has detected a similar practice in the Evangelium Veritatis. See The Jung Codex, pp. 114f.

[103] See our treatment of this pericope, supra, pp. 19–20.

[104] See Barth, Die Interpretation (1908), pp. 15, 21, 27, 30. An example of this kind of interpretation is provided by Irenaeus, Adv. Haer. I, 8.4, who reports that in Ptolemy's interpretation of Anna's meeting with the Christ child in Luke 2.36ff., the Valentinian seizes on the phrase 'she gave thanks'. Anna is then interpreted as a type of Achamoth who had been a widow for seven years. She 'gives thanks' at her husband's, the Saviour's, return. The Letter to Rheginos contains nothing quite so fanciful.

[105] Consult our critical note to this passage, infra, pp. 7of. The same tendency manifests itself in the whole combination of texts in this passage.

[106] Infra, p. 63.

[107] Cf. our comments, infra, pp. 74f., 148f.

[108] See Barth, Die Interpretation (1911), p. 42.

on the whole the author of 'Rheginos' uses a remarkably sober exegesis for a Gnostic. Thus, there are a number of relatively literal uses of the New Testament, e.g. in the use of the Johannine idea of the Saviour 'drawing men' to heaven in 45.36–37, and in the retention of the basic meaning of Paul's expression 'to swallow up' in 45.14, 19; 46.1; 49.4. But of greater significance in evaluating the sobriety of the author's exegesis are several passages where it is difficult to see how a Gnostic exegete could have bypassed the opportunity for allegorical interpretation. For example, the author leaves completely unaltered the New Testament expression that the Son of Man '. . . rose again from the dead' (46.16–17). Yet, how could any Gnostic professing a docetic Christology make that statement?[109] The more likely course would have been to find some allegorical interpretation explaining that the Saviour never really died. Moreover, several passages in 'Rheginos' give vent to the author's view that the Elect are subject to physical death![110] Other instances could be found in the failure to extend the list of demonic beings alluded to 44.37–38, or in the omission of any qualification of the inference to be drawn from 45.25–26 that the Saviour really 'suffered'.[111] In sum, it is rather remarkable to see either how apparently inconsistent the author was in trying to hold his Gnostic views together with his use of the New Testament, or how little his Gnosticism has affected his exegesis.

[109] Barth, *Die Interpretation* (1908), p. 12, gives an example of a docetically-motivated softening or alteration of this New Testament affirmation.

[110] For the relevant texts and interpretation, see *infra*, pp. 117–22.

[111] As background for the immediately preceding discussion here one should consult Barth, *Die Interpretation* (1908), pp. 11–16, where she offers five reasons why Valentinians employed allegorical interpretation.

II

THE LETTER AND ITS STRUCTURE

IN THE PRECEDING chapter an effort was made to introduce the reader to the nature of the Letter to Rheginos and to those critical matters fundamental to its interpretation. With this groundwork laid, we turn now to the Letter itself. First, we offer a fresh translation from the original text. Then, second, we undertake an analysis of the movement of thought in the Letter. Finally, we summarize important insights gained from the analysis.

A. THE LETTER TO RHEGINOS: A NEW TRANSLATION

To cite a truism, every translation is itself an interpretation. In order to circumvent the possibility of erroneous interpretation at the level of translation, therefore, we have worked directly with the Coptic text of 'Rheginos'. Generally, the English translation by Robert McL. Wilson of St Andrews,[1] which is given in the first critical edition of the Letter, *De Resurrectione* (pp. 60–67), has been found to be quite faithful to the Coptic. His translation has been conformed to the German of Walter Till and shares in the understanding of the language which that master of Coptic possessed. Nevertheless, there are points wherein this writer finds himself at variance with Dr Wilson:

1. There is some inconsistency in his use of critical marks, e.g. parenthesis marks, square brackets, and arrows are all used to indicate conjectural reconstructions of lacunae in the Coptic text.

[1] Dr Wilson (private letter of April 13, 1968) writes that in the actual division of the labour it was agreed that Dr Wilson should have the last word in matters of English style and idiom, since that was his native tongue. Dr Zandee, as the Coptic specialist, claimed the right of final decision in matters of Coptic idiom. Differences of opinion were discussed by correspondence and agreement reached, so that both share responsibility for the English version.

2. The desire to match a line of English translation exactly with a line of Coptic, while commendable, occasionally produces an awkward translation.

3. Some renderings of the Coptic are too much paraphrase, others too literal.

4. In general, Wilson is consistent in translating key expressions into English. There are a few exceptions, however, which may mislead those unable to use the Coptic text.

5. The sporadic excursions into 'King James English' are prompted by Wilson's desire to indicate the difference between the singular and plural forms of the pronoun 'you'. He accordingly adopts the same style for the immediate contexts involved, e.g. in 47.4–8. However, his effort is not consistent (cf. 45.15—'you'); and, as we have already shown,[2] the plural form of 'you' does not appear until the final page of the text. For this reason, we think the use of modern English throughout with the addition of an asterisk after the few plural forms is preferable to the highly formal and anti-quated 'King James' vernacular.

6. At several points we believe prior interpretation of the meaning of the text has resulted in erroneous translation, e.g. 45.11–13.

Having reached these conclusions, a new translation seemed justi-fied, especially if it was to serve as the basis for the interpretation of the Letter. This translation we present here, reserving discussion of the philological and grammatical matters which support it until Chapter III. We would note at the outset that where Wilson's trans-lation is a clear rendering of the Coptic we have refrained from substi-tuting synonyms simply for the sake of novelty.

Key to Signs in the Translation

1. *(δέ)* Greek words in parentheses appear as loan words in the Coptic text.

2. ((. . .)) denotes an addition by the translator to convey the sense of the passage. These words do not appear in the Coptic text.

3. (. . .) indicates a parenthetical remark by the author of the Letter.

4. [. . .] indicates a conjectural emendation for a lacuna in the papyrus text.

5. * will follow the second person plural pronoun, 'you', wherever it occurs.

---

[2] *Supra*, pp. 8–10.

6. *Capitalization*. Used at the beginning of sentences, for proper names, and for certain 'technical expressions'.

The Translation

Page 43

25 Some there are, my son Rheginos,
who desire to learn much.
They have this aim *(σκόπος)*
when they are occupied with questions *(ζήτημα)*
which lack their answer; and
30 if they succeed with these, they customarily
think very highly of
themselves. But *(δέ)* I do not think
they have stood within
the Word *(λόγος)* of Truth. Rather,
35 they seek their own Rest, which
we have received through our
Saviour *(σωτήρ)*, our Lord Christ *(χρηστός)*.

Page 44

1 We received it ((i.e. 'Rest')) after we
had known the Truth and rested
ourselves upon it. But *(ἀλλά)*
because *(ἐπειδή)* you ask us
5 pleasantly what is proper
concerning the resurrection *(ἀνάστασις)*, I am writing
you ((to say)) that it is necessary *(ἀναγκαῖον)*.
To be sure *(μέν)* many are
lacking faith *(ἄπιστος)* in it, but *(δέ)*
10 there are a few who find it.
So then, let us discuss *(λόγος)*
the matter.
How did the Lord make
use *(χρῆσθαι)* of things while existing
15 in flesh *(σάρξ)* and after
He had revealed himself as Son
of God? He lived
in this place *(τόπος)* where you
remain, speaking

20 about the Law (νόμος) of Nature (φύσις). (But (δέ) I
call it 'Death.') Now (δέ) the
Son of God, Rheginos,
was Son of Man.
He embraced both of them,
25 possessing the
humanity and the divinity,
so that on the one hand (μέν) he might conquer
death through his being
Son of God,
30 and that on the other (δέ) through the Son of
Man the restoration (ἀποκατάστασις)
to the Pleroma (πλήρωμα)
might occur because (ἐπειδή)
originally He was from above,
35 a seed (σπέρμα) of Truth before
this structure (σύστασις) had come into being.
In this ((i.e., 'structure')) many dominions and
deities came into existence.
I know I am giving

Page 45
1 the solution in difficult (δύσκολον)
things, but (ἀλλά) there is nothing
difficult (δύσκολον) in the Word (λόγος)
of Truth. But (ἀλλά) since (ἐπειδή)
5 the solution appeared
so as not to leave anything hidden,
but (ἀλλά) to reveal all
things openly (ἁπλῶς) concerning
existence—the destruction of evil on the one hand (μέν),
10 but (δέ) the revelation
of the Elect on the other—this is
the emanation (προβολή) of Truth and
Spirit (πνεῦμα). Grace (χάρις) is of Truth.
The Saviour (σωτήρ) swallowed up
15 death. (You are not reckoned as being ignorant.)
For (γάρ) He put aside the
world (κόσμος) which is perishing. He transformed
[himself] into an imperishable Aeon (αἰών)

and raised himself up, having
20 swallowed the visible
by the invisible,
and He gave us
the way of our immortality.
Then (τότε), indeed, as the Apostle (ἀπόστολος)
25 said, 'We suffered
with him, and we arose
with him, and we went to heaven
with him.' Now (δέ) if we
are revealed in
30 this world (κόσμος) wearing (φορεῖν)
him, we are that one's beams (ἀκτίς),
and we are
enclosed by
him until our setting, that is to say,
35 our death in this life (βίος).
We are drawn to heaven
by him like the beams (ἀκτίς)
by the sun, not being restrained
by anything. This is
40 the spiritual (πνευματική) resurrection (ἀνάστασις)

Page 46
1 which swallows up the psychic (ψυχική)
alike (ὁμοίως) with the other fleshly (σαρκική).
But (δέ) if there is one who
does not believe (πιστεύειν), he does not have
5 ((the capacity for)) persuasion (πείθειν). For (γάρ)
it is the place (τόπος) of faith (πίστις),
my son, and not
of persuasion (πείθειν). He who is dead shall
arise. There is one who believes (πιστεύειν)
among the philosophers (φιλόσοφος) who are in this world.
10 At least (ἀλλά) he will arise. And let not the philosopher (φιλόσοφος)
who is in this world be caused
to believe (πιστεύειν) that he is a man who returns
himself (and ((that)) because of our faith (πίστις)).
For (γάρ) we have known the Son of

15 Man, and we have believed (πιστεύειν)
   that He arose from among the
   dead. This is He of whom we say,
   'He became the destruction
   of death', as (ὡς) He is a great One
20 who is believed in (πιστεύειν). Among
   the im[mortal] are those who believe (πιστεύειν). The
   thought of those who are saved shall
   not perish. The mind (νοῦς) of
   those who have known him shall not perish.
25 Therefore, we are elected to
   salvation and redemption,
   since we are predestined from the beginning
   not to fall into the
   foolishness of those who are without knowledge,
30 but (ἀλλά) we shall enter into the
   wisdom of those who have known the
   Truth. Indeed, the Truth which they keep
   cannot be abandoned,
   nor (οὔτε) has it been.
35   'Strong is the system (σύστημα) of the
      Pleroma (πλήρωμα); small is that which
      broke loose ((and)) became ((the))
      world (κόσμος). But (δέ) the All is
      what is encompassed. ((Before))

Page 47
 I   it came into being, it was existing.'
      Therefore (ὥστε),
      never doubt (διστάζειν) concerning
      the resurrection (ἀνάστασις), my son Rheginos.
      For (γάρ) if you did not exist
 5   in flesh (σάρξ), you received flesh (σάρξ) when
      you entered this world (κόσμος). Why ((then))
      will you not receive flesh (σάρξ) when you
      ascend into the Aeon (αἰών)?
      What is better than the flesh (σάρξ) is
10   for it ((the)) cause (αἴτιος) of life.
      Is not (μή) that which comes into being on your account
      yours? Does not (μή) that which is yours

exist with you?
Yet (ἀλλά), while you are in this world, what is it
15 that you lack? This is what you
have been making every effort (σπουδάζειν) to learn.
The afterbirth (χόριον) of the body (σῶμα) is
old age, and you
exist in corruption. You have
20 absence (ἀπουσία) as a gain.
For (γάρ) you will not give up what is
better if you should depart. That which is worse
has diminution,
but (ἀλλά) there is grace for it. Nothing,
25 therefore, redeems us from
this world. But (ἀλλά) the All which
we are—we are saved. We have received
salvation from ((one)) end of it
to the other. Let us think in this way.
30 Let us comprehend in this way. But (ἀλλά)
there are some ((who)) wish to
understand in the enquiry about
those things they are looking into, whether
he who is saved, if he leaves behind
35 his body (σῶμα), will
be saved immediately? Let
no one be given cause to doubt (διστάζειν) concerning
this,
. . . indeed, the visible members (μέλος)
39 which are dead shall

Page 48
1 not be saved,
((only)) the living [members—μέλος] which exist within
them would arise. Then, what
is the resurrection (ἀνάστασις)? It is always the
5 disclosure of
those who have arisen. For (γάρ) if you
remember reading in the
Gospel (εὐαγγέλιον) that Elijah appeared and Moses
10 with him, do not think the

resurrection *(ἀνάστασις)* is an illusion *(φαντασία)*.
It is no illusion *(φαντασία)*, but *(ἀλλά)*
it is truth. It is more
suitable to say, then *(δέ)*, that
15 the world *(κόσμος)* is an illusion *(φαντασία)*,
rather than the resurrection *(ἀνάστασις)* which
came into being through
our Lord the Saviour *(σωτήρ)*,
Jesus Christ.
20 But *(δέ)* what am I telling
you now? Those who are
living shall die. How *(πῶς)*
do they live in an illusion *(φαντασία)*?
The rich have become poor
25 and the kings have been overthrown, everything is wont to
change. The world *(κόσμος)*
is an illusion *(φαντασία)* (so that I
should not rail at *(καταλαλεῖν)*
30 things exceedingly). But *(ἀλλά)*
the resurrection *(ἀνάστασις)* does not have
this aforesaid character; for
it is the Truth, that which stands firm.
And it is the revelation of
35 that which exists, and the transformation
of things, and a
transition *(μεταβολή)* into
38 newness. For *(γάρ)* imperishability

Page 49
1 de[scends] upon the
perishable; and the light flows
down upon the darkness,
swallowing it up; and the Pleroma *(πλήρωμα)*
5 fills up the deficiency.
These are the symbols *(σύμβολον)* and
the images of the resurrection *(ἀνάστασις)*.
He it is who makes the
good. Therefore *(ὥστε)*, do not

10 think *(νοεῖν)* in part *(μερικῶς)*, O Rheginos,
neither *(οὔτε)* live *(πολιτεύεσθαι)*
in conformity with *(κατά)* this flesh *(σάρξ)* for the
    sake of
unanimity, but *(ἀλλά)* flee
from the divisions *(μερισμός)* and the
15 fetters, and already *(ἤδη)* you have
the resurrection *(ἀνάστασις)*. For *(γάρ)* if
he who will die knows
himself that he
will die (even if *(κἄν)* he spends many
20 years in this life *(βίος)* he is
brought to this),
why not consider yourself
as risen and ((already))
brought to this?
25 If you have the
resurrection but *(ἀλλά)* continue as if *(ὡς)*
you will die (and yet *(καίτοι γε)* that one
knows that he has died), why then
do I ignore your
30 lack of exercise *(-γυμνάζεσθαι)*? It is right for
each one to practise *(ἀσκεῖν)*
in a number of ways, and
he shall be released from this Element *(στοιχεῖον)*,
so that he may not be misled *(πλανᾶν)* but *(ἀλλά)*
35 shall himself receive again
what at first was.
    These things I have received
38 from the trust *(-φθονεῖν)* of my

Page 50
1 Lord Jesus Christ. [I have] taught
you and your broth[ers], my sons, concerning them,
while I have not at all omitted any of
the things suitable for strengthening you.*
5 But *(δέ)* if there is one thing written
which is obscure in my exposition *(ἀπαγγελία)* of
the Word *(λόγος)*, I shall interpret it for you*

when you* ask. But *(δέ)* now,
do not be jealous *(φθονεῖν)* toward anyone who is in
   your number
10 when it is possible for him to
help *(ὠφελεῖν)*. Many may look at
this which I have written
to you. To these I say,
'Peace *(εἰρήνη)* ((be)) among them and grace *(χάρις)*.'
15 I greet you and those who love
you* in fraternal love.

> The Word *(λόγος)* concerning the
> Resurrection *(ἀνάστασις)*

B. AN ANALYSIS OF THE LETTER

As previously demonstrated,[3] the text of 'Rheginos' has the form of a
didactic letter addressed primarily to one individual, with the pro-
vision that it might be shared with his immediate co-disciples. This
conclusion, based as it is on a literary-critical study, is confirmed, we
believe, by a thorough analysis of the internal movement of the letter's
argument. Such an analysis uncovers a rather personal 'Sitz im
Leben' for the letter,[4] the progression of the authors' argument reflecting efforts to answer certain objections to the resurrection raised
by Rheginos, the pupil. It appears that in several of these Rheginos,
in turn, has echoed objections offered by those who are sceptical of
this neophyte's belief in the resurrection. And, despite the fact that
these sceptics and their objections are sometimes only vaguely recognizable, the general outlines of their positions are discernible. Thus,
the didactic portions of the letter are interwoven with apologetic.
These things only become apparent, however, from a form-critical
and analytical examination of the document. To this task we now
turn.[5]

---

[3] See the full discussion, *supra* pp. 5–12.

[4] Contrast the view of the first editors in *De Resurrectione*, p. ix: 'There are for
all that, however, few personal touches and much of convention (in the Letter)'.

[5] Of course, such an analysis presupposes certain interpretations of the Letter,
interpretations which are more fully supported by the critical notes given in
Chapter III and the interpretation offered in Chapter IV following.

I. *Rheg. 43.25–44.10. Introduction and Occasion of the Letter:*
'*False and True Seeking*'

A. *The False Seekers of 'Rest'* (*43.25–35*)

1. The author begins with a description—which could serve as a warning—of those who hold themselves to be self-sufficient in answering important questions. They easily become self-inflated by their successes (43.25–32).

2. Then the description of these false seekers is drawn more closely: (*a*) The real nature of their search is indicated (43.35), i.e. the questions which occupy them are soteriologically and eschatologically oriented. They are seeking their own 'Rest' (ἀνάπαυσις). Also, (*b*) the real objections to these false seekers are articulated (43.32–35), including the facts that they have not sought the answers to such questions in the sufficiency of the Scriptures (—'Word of Truth' 43.33–34) and that they have sought their 'Rest' by and of themselves (43.35—emphasis on 'seeking their *own*').

B. *The True Receivers of 'Rest'* (*43.35–44.3*)

1. The expressed objections to the false seekers lead the author to a statement of the two opposite marks of the true seekers. First, 'Rest' is that which must be 'received' from the Saviour, the Lord Christ. It cannot be obtained by one's own effort (43.35–37).

2. Second, knowledge of the Scriptures (—'Truth') and confidence in their proclamation represent the essential requirements for the attainment of 'Rest' (44.1–3).

C. *The True Seeker and Statement of his Problem* (*44.3–10*)

1. ἀλλά ('but') indicates a second contrast, this one between the manner of questioning practised by the false seekers (43.25–35) and that of the pupil Rheginos. The contrast is emphasized with the term ϩⲛ ⲟⲩⲣⲗⲁϭ ('sweetly' or 'pleasantly'—44.5). ἀλλά also introduces the occasion of the letter, viz. Rheginos' query about the correct views of the resurrection (44.3–6). The mention of 'resurrection' (ἀνάστασις) in 44.6 permits a more explicit definition of 'Rest' (ἀνάπαυσις—43.35; 44.1), for we shall see that 'resurrection' has both present and future dimensions and that 'Rest' has eschatological overtones.

2. The author then moves to give his initial response to Rheginos' question (44.7–10). The resurrection, he states, is indispensable to

the faith (44.6–7). And although he concedes that many have no faith in the resurrection, there are a few who do believe and share in it (44.7–10).

D. A Transitional Passage to the Body of the Letter (44.11–12)

II. Rheg. 44.13–46.2. The Main Discussion. 'The Resurrection: Its Christological Foundation'

A. The Lord's Activity in the Sphere of 'Flesh' (σάρξ) (44.13–21)

1. (44.13–17). A rhetorical question introduces the discussion. Its answer gives the author the opportunity to affirm the reality of the Lord's sojourn in the flesh, the period of his self-revelation as Son of God.

2. (44.17–20). In answering his own question, the author emphasizes two aspects of the Lord's earthly activity:

(a) his walking 'the walk of life' (περιπατεῖν) in this world (τόπος) where Rheginos now remains (44.17–19);

(b) his teaching (44.20).
The subject of the latter is: the 'Law of Nature' (ὁ νόμος τῆς φύσεως).

3. (44.20–21). The author parenthetically remarks that in his opinion, the 'Law' of which the Lord spoke is the 'Law of Death'.

B. The Lord's Nature and Saving Work (44.21–38)

1. (44.21–26). The particle δέ marks a transition in the author's thought. He affirms that the Son of God who appeared 'in flesh' was also Son of Man, the two titles recalling his participation in the spheres of humanity and divinity.

2. (44.27–37). By participation in those spheres, the Lord effects the work of salvation. As Son of God he conquers death (44.27–29); while as Son of Man, he will bring about the 'restoration' (ἀποκατά-στασις) of the 'Pleroma' (πλήρωμα—44.30–33). Mention of the work of 'restoration', however, prompts an explanation from the author introduced with the causal ἐπειδή (44.33). The Lord will accomplish such a work because of his pre-existent nature, which implies his reconstitution of that which was present in his pre-existence.

C. The Author's Digression: An Excuse and an Assurance (44.39–45.13)

1. (44.39–45.2). The author interrupts his presentation of the

Christological foundation of the resurrection to offer an excuse for the difficulty of the things he is presenting. The excuse has a twofold interest: (1) it is an interesting concession to Rheginos' imperfect knowledge of the Saviour (44.21–26), of the 'restoration of the Pleroma' (44.30–33), of the pre-existence of the Son of Man as a 'seed' *(σπέρμα)* from above (44.33–36); (2) it is also an implicit admission by the author of his own shortcoming in his effort to present such difficult matters clearly.

2. (45.2–3). The simplicity and clarity of the solution to the problem of the resurrection found in the 'Word of Truth' (Scriptures) stands in contrast to the difficulties posed by the author's presentation of that solution. There is no confession here of a fundamental disparity between the author's solution and that of the 'Word of Truth'. Rather, there is an acknowledgement that what he presents is an interpretation which makes use of images that may be difficult to one not fully versed in them. Indeed, in 49.6–7 we read that much of what this author has written about the resurrection in this letter has been given in 'symbols' and 'images'.

3. (45.4–9). The solution contained in Scripture centres in the teaching and work of the Saviour. Its, and thus the Saviour's, manifestation in the world cleared away the enigmas surrounding the problem of existence (45.4–9).

4. (45.9–11). The author interjects an explanatory gloss concerning what those enigmas were and how they were overcome: (1) the existence of evil and death—now destroyed in Christ; (2) the fate of believers—now revealed as those chosen for salvation.

5. (45.11–13). This solution, embodied in Christ, is really that which was 'put forth' or 'emanated' *(προβολή)* by the deities of the Pleroma, Truth and Spirit. 'Grace' *(χάρις)*, which we may probably identify as a blessing coming with the solution in Christ, is that which pertains to and comes from the deity Truth.

D. *The 'Spiritual Resurrection' provided through the Saviour (45.14–46.2)*

1. (45.14–15). Here is resumed the presentation of the Christological basis for the resurrection which was left at 44.39. The affirmation that the Saviour destroyed ('swallowed up') death both picks up an earlier theme (44.27–29) and simultaneously announces the theme of the ensuing section (45.16–28).

2. (45.15). Parenthetically the author acknowledges that Rheginos is no stranger to the truth he has just affirmed or will be affirming. In

brief, Rheginos is a Christian, a pupil who has received prior instruction from this author, and therefore one well-acquainted with these elementary facts of the Faith.

3. (45.16–23). Having acknowledged what his pupil already knows, the author proceeds with an explanation of how the Saviour destroyed death. (1) The Saviour cast off and thereby withdrew from association with the perishing sphere of the 'world' (κόσμος—45.16–17). (2) He transformed himself into an imperishable, invisible, divine Aeon, becoming just opposite in nature to the κόσμος (45.17–21). (3) He caused himself to ascend from this sphere (45.19). (4) He thereby opened up to believers the way by which they themselves could achieve immortality and imperishability (45.22–23).

4. (45.24–28). The affirmation of the Saviour's destruction of death and opening of the way of immortality are now given support by appeal to Scripture, viz. to the Apostle Paul. The citation reaffirms that there were three stages of the Saviour's work: (1) his 'suffering', and thus his putting aside the perishable 'world' (45.25–26; cf. 45.16–17); (2) his ascension (45.26–27; cf. 45.17–19, 20–21); (3) his entrance into heaven (45.27–28; cf. 45.22–23). The representative participation of the Elect in each of these stages of the Saviour's saving work is emphasized through the triple occurrence of the preposition ⲘⲚ̄ ('with' him).

5. (45.28–29). The particle δέ marks a simple transition in the author's thought to a further illustration of: (1) how the Saviour's destruction of death affects us; and, (2) how we at present participate in his saving work. Throughout the passage the author employs figurative language drawn from astronomy: (1) as the already transformed believers of the Saviour, we are like his 'beams'; (2) he keeps us enclosed in the number of his Elect until our death, i.e. our 'setting'; (3) like the 'beams' which appear to return to the sun as it sinks in the west, so are we believers drawn up to heaven at our death.

6. (45.39–46.2). The author concludes his demonstration of how the Saviour destroyed death and how the Elect share in the victory with the summation that this is what constitutes the 'spiritual resurrection' (πνευματικὴ ἀνάστασις). This type of resurrection destroys the possibility of a 'psychical' or 'fleshly' resurrection. Yet, as we shall see, there is a 'resurrection flesh' which is conferred upon the faithful.

III. *Rheg. 46.3–49.9. The Problems and Questions of Rheginos Answered*

A. *First Problem: The Resurrection is Undemonstrable and Unsure (46.3–47.10)*

1. First Answer: The Resurrection is a Matter of Faith, not of Demonstration (46.3–20)

(a) (46.3–8). From the passage we may infer that Rheginos has apparently been troubled by someone's denial of the verity of the resurrection and has discovered his inability to argue persuasively on behalf of it. The author responds to his pupil's frustration by stating that those who lack faith cannot be persuaded by argument, for the resurrection is fundamentally a matter of faith. The truth is, the author reaffirms, that he who has died will be raised.

(b) (46.8–20). But even among the philosophers, whose business it is to persuade by argument, there is one who has faith and who shall be resurrected because of it. This philosopher (as our critical note to this passage will show) stands in sharp contrast to those 'philosophers of this world' who falsely think they have the capacity to make themselves immortal. Such philosophers are deluded, for the resurrection—the author states parenthetically (46.13)—is a matter of our faith! (A re-emphasis on the theme of 46.3–8.) Then follows the author's statement of the content of that faith (46.14–19); it includes knowledge *(γνῶσις)* of the Son of Man and belief *(πίστις)* in his resurrection from the dead. Mention of this saving work prompts the author to conclude with a declaration of the 'greatness' of the Saviour. (Note that here, too, the theme of the Saviour's destruction of death is picked up again. Cf. 44.27–29; 45.9 (?); 45.14–15.)

2. Second Answer: The Real Basis for Assurance about Immortality and Resurrection is Election (46.21–47.1)

(a) (46.21–24). A second answer offered by the author to the problem posed by Rheginos is that the nature of the Elect is that they are immortal. This means especially that their facility for 'thought', their 'mind' *(νοῦς)*, which is also their receiver of 'knowledge' *(γνῶσις)*, shall not perish in death but is given its immortality through faith.

(b) (46.25–34). 'Therefore,' the argument continues, the immortality of our 'thought' and 'mind' shows that we are actually predestined to the resurrection, i.e. 'to salvation and redemption' (46.26). Such 'predestination' took place 'from the beginning' (possibly meaning before the 'world' existed), and it was double: some shall fall or have fallen into the 'foolishness' of those who lack γνῶσις, while others shall partake of that 'wisdom' which is the possession of those having 'knowledge' of the 'Truth'. This 'Truth', once received by the Elect, cannot be let go. Possession of it seems bound up with the state of salvation which the Elect enter.

(c) (46.35–47.1). Confirmation of the preceding affirmation is supplied by the author's citation of a stanza from a Valentinian hymn, a hymn which presupposes some extra-contextual understanding and which therefore was previously known to Rheginos. The stanza declares the strength and permanence of the 'Pleroma', of which the Elect are originally a part, over against the subsidiary and inferior nature of the 'world' wherein the Elect are presently found. The 'All', i.e. that whole body of the Elect which pre-existed in the 'Pleroma' prior to the world's creation, is at present encompassed by and is under the Saviour's protection (cf. our critical note to this passage).

3. A Concluding Assurance (47.1–10)

Having completed his arguments that the truth of the resurrection can only be apprehended by faith and that the guarantee of the resurrection is found in the election of believers, the author concludes by exhorting Rheginos never to doubt the truth of the resurrection. Doubt is to be dispelled, for even if Rheginos pre-existed in the 'All' as a fleshless being (46.39–47.1), he received flesh when he entered this world (47.4–6). And this flesh, which gives personal identity to Rheginos while on earth, is to be replaced by a new, transformed flesh upon his ascension to heaven at death (47.6–8). The real continuity between pre-existence in the 'All', existence in the 'flesh' (σάρξ) of this world, and existence in the new 'flesh' of the resurrection is provided by that which is better than and the cause of life for the 'flesh', viz. the 'spiritual, inner man' (cf. 45.17–21; 45.39–46.2; 46.21–24; 46.38–47.1; 47.34–48.3).

B. A Question: What is Deficient about the Present Bodily State that the Resurrection can supply? (47.11–30)

1. Statement of the Question (47.11–16)

Two rhetorical questions (47.11–13), both expecting positive answers, lead into the author's consideration of another problem perhaps posed by Rheginos. The two anticipated answers reflect Rheginos' contention that the 'flesh' (47.5–6) and 'body' (47.17) are his own, that they came into existence for his sake (cf. 47.4–6), and that they thus co-exist with him (47.12–13). If this be true, continues Rheginos' line of thought, what is it that is deficient about this bodily state in which I now live? That is, why does the resurrection not entail a simple retention of my present bodily state? (47.14–16).

2. The Author's Answer (47.17–26)

The response comes first through a statement of a fact of existence, viz. that old age, the period of decay and increasing uselessness, is the inevitable fate of this life's body (47.17–19). Thus, escape from such is certainly a gain (47.19–20). Moreover, this escape or ἀπουσία does not entail loss of the 'better', i.e. the spiritual part of man; but, rather, a decrease in that which is experiencing decay, viz. the 'body' (47.21–23). Nevertheless, there is blessing for the corruptible part of man, for its personally identifiable traits will appear in the new 'flesh' of the resurrection (see our critical note to 47.24).

3. An Admission and a Reassurance (47.24–29)

Just as old age was admitted by the author to be the inevitable fate of the Elect (47.17–19), so now he draws out the logical conclusion of that admission: nothing exempts the Elect from 'somatic' (bodily) existence in this world of corruption (47.24–26). Still such existence is more tolerable when it is remembered that the 'All', of which the Elect are the constituting members, has already been saved (47.26–29).

4. A Concluding Exhortation to Correct Thought and Belief (47.29–30).

C. The Second Problem: An Immediate, Bodiless Resurrection is a Paradox (47.30–48.3)

1. The Question (47.30–36)

Rather than being a general refutation, the author's allusion here to the questioning of some may be the reflection of another objection passed along to him by his pupil Rheginos. This objection seems to echo an orthodox Christian view. It is, how can an immediate resurrection at death—which is clearly the author's teaching, e.g. 45.36–39—take place without a body? For the resurrection of the righteous in Christian thought of the time—whether it be thought of as immediate or after an interim of 'sleep'—usually involved a raising of the body (so, following Paul, Irenaeus, Justin, Tertullian, etc.).

2. The Answer (47.37–48.3)

The author defends his teaching with an exhortation not to doubt concerning its truth, viz. that the visible members of the 'body' will not be resurrected (47.36–48.1). It is only the inward, spiritual members, the inner spiritual man, who is resurrected (48.2–3; cf. our analysis of 47.1–10 given above).

D. *The Third Problem: The Resurrection is Fantasy, not Reality (48.3–38)*

1. An Opening Rebuttal and Allusion to the Problem (48.3–13)

(*a*) (48.3–11). A rhetorical question (48.3–4) provides the author with an opportunity to answer still another objection to the resurrection (48.4–6). It appears that his pupil, Rheginos, has been assured by some (possibly by the false seekers of 43.25–32) that the resurrection is an 'illusion', a fantasy of deluded minds (48.10–11). So the author begins with the statement that the resurrection is always the disclosure of those who have arisen (48.4–6). The tangible proof of this is furnished in the Gospel, where the appearance of Moses and Elijah with Christ is undeniable testimony to the truth of the resurrection (48.6–10).

(*b*) (48.12–13). The proof thus given, the author reaffirms his position in the face of the objection: the resurrection is no illusion, but a reality.

2. The 'world' *(κόσμος)* is Illusion, not the Resurrection (48.13–30)

(*a*) (48.13–19). The author then reverses the objection levelled at the resurrection. It is actually the world, that sphere against which those sceptical of the resurrection measure its reality, that is illusory. The resurrection, on the contrary, is what the Saviour has brought into being.

(*b*) (48.20–21). At this point, however, the author pauses in his rebuttal. He acknowledges what he has just said may need some substantiation or elaboration.

(*c*) (48.21–27). He continues with a demonstration of how the Elect, who shall die as all men, may be said to be at present living in an illusory world (cf. our critical notes to 48.21–23). His two examples are drawn from the economic and political realms, both showing the unpredictability, the insecurity, and the transitoriness of earthly possessions and offices.

(*d*) (48.27–30). Having completed his demonstration of the instability of the cosmic sphere, the author reiterates as a fact to be accepted his earlier statement (48.14–15) that the 'world is an illusion'. Then, parenthetically, he explains the brevity of his demonstration: he does not want to tire Rheginos by ranting in excess about the world's illusory character (48.28–30; cf. our critical note to this passage). In brief, the author feels he has made his point!

3. A Concluding Summation: The Real Character of the Resurrection (48.30–49.9)

(a) (48.30–38). The ἀλλά introducing this sentence indicates a contrast with what has preceded. In distinction to the illusory nature of the world, the firm and secure nature of the resurrection is asserted. A threefold definition of the resurrection follows: it is (a) the disclosure of that which truly exists (48.34–35; cf. 48.4–6); (b) the transformation of things (48.35–36; cf. 45.16–19); (c) a transition into a new existence (48.36–38; cf. 45.19; 45.34–39). As we indicate by the passages for comparison, we feel that all three definitions run parallel to what has been said earlier about the process of the resurrection.

(b) (48.38–49.7). In addition to having the character just attributed to it, the resurrection is bound up in a whole movement of salvation—a movement now briefly summarized in the symbolic imagery of the Valentinian school. Involved is the descent of immortality upon that which is perishable, the coming down of light over darkness, and the filling up of that which is void in the 'Pleroma' itself. The section ends with an explanation that these are the symbols and images of the resurrection (49.6–7).

(c) (49.8–9). The preceding statement of what the resurrection is concluded with the declaration that it is the Saviour who brings about these 'good things' (see our critical note to 49.8–9).

IV. *Rheg. 49.9–36. A Final Warning, An Existential Proof, and an Exhortation*

A. *A Warning Against Erroneous Thought and Action (49.9–16)*

The ϩⲱⲥⲧⲉ (ὥστε) at the beginning of this section indicates that what is about to be said should follow logically from what has been said. There then follows the author's warning against those who have raised for Rheginos the problems and questions treated in the preceding portion of the Letter (48.30–49.9). Rheginos is told not to be misled by half-truths (49.9–10), nor to be accommodating to the views of those who represent this 'fleshly' sphere of corruption (49.11–13). Rather, he should withdraw from their divisive views and the snares which accompany them (49.13–15). Doing this, Rheginos will find that he already possesses the resurrection (49.15–16).

B. An Explanation of what it means already to have the Resurrection (49.16–24)

With the conjunction γάρ the author moves to an explanation of what he has just said concerning Rheginos' present possession of the resurrection. The explanation is offered in the form of a question, the answer to which is self-evident and is also demonstrative of the author's assertion. Simply expressed, the author asks: If one knows of the inevitability of death (despite whatever longevity he may have), should he not consider himself really as being already dead? And, if this be true, it follows from what the author has already said about the salvation of the Elect through Christ's resurrection that the believer should consider himself also as already raised!

C. An Exhortation to Live as One Already Resurrected (49.24–36) (cf. our critical notes to this Section)

Having shown Rheginos how he may consider himself as dead already, and raised already, the author progresses in this section to the imperative for which this new existence calls. Once again, the construction is that of a conditional sentence whose apodosis is a question. The condition is considered as fulfilled: 'you, Rheginos, already possess the resurrection, although you continue to act and think as if you were going to die' (49.25–27). A parenthesis intervenes between protasis and apodosis: but the logic of what I (the author) have just shown you (49.16–21) should make known to you (Rheginos) that you have already died (49.26–27). Then follows the apodosis in the form of a question which is also a rebuke: 'why do you (Rheginos) not act upon what you know to be true?' (49.28–30). We might paraphrase the whole: 'If you, Rheginos, are already resurrected, and if you know that you have already died, then why do you continue to act and think as one who is concerned about death?' The rebuke may well be due to the gullibility of Rheginos as demonstrated in his susceptibility to the seductiveness of the arguments of those who doubt the resurrection, arguments which the author appears to have been combating in the previous pages of this letter. Following the rebuke, however, the author proceeds to remind Rheginos of what probably was taught him at an earlier time, viz. that it is necessary to practise diligently in order to be freed from this cosmic 'Element' (στοιχεῖον—49.30–33). Only in this manner is it possible to avoid error and receive again that pre-existent state of bliss which the Elect formerly possessed (49.35–36; see the critical note to 49.36–37).

V. Rheg. 49.38–50.16. The Conclusion

A. *The Source and Scope of the Author's Instruction* (49.38–50.4)

At this point the author offers the basis and authority for that which he has communicated to Rheginos. The source, explicitly named, is the 'Lord Jesus Christ' himself (50.1). The assurance is then given that nothing of value for the confirmation in the faith of Rheginos and his brethren has been omitted from the author's instruction of them both in this letter and in his former instruction (50.3–4; see our critical notes to 50.1–4).

B. *Some Encouragements to Seek Further Help* (50.5–11)

1. (50.5–8). From the Teacher himself. Rheginos and his brethren are invited to raise any further questions they may have concerning the Teacher's 'exposition' of the 'Word of Truth'. This may be a reference to a written exposition of Scripture which Rheginos and his companions have in their circle (see our critical note to 50.6–7).

2. (50.8–11). From Rheginos' co-disciples. The author also encourages Rheginos not to be envious of the superior insight and 'knowledge' (γνῶσις) of some of his brethren, for they may be of real help to him with other difficult problems which may arise (see our critical note to 50.10–11).

C. *A Greeting to Others who may read the Letter* (50.11–14)

The author indicates to Rheginos that there may be many in his circle who might also read this letter with profit. This is probably intended as a request that Rheginos share the letter, although we must emphasize that this request is implicit rather than explicit. That is, the letter is addressed to Rheginos, not to a wide circle of readers. To such other possible readers, however, the author extends a greeting of 'peace' and 'grace' (50.14; see our critical note to 50.10–11).

D. *A Final Greeting to Rheginos and his Brethren* (50.15–16)

VI. Rheg. 50.17–18. A Title Descriptive of the Letter's Content

48 THE LETTER AND ITS STRUCTURE

C. SOME CONCLUDING OBSERVATIONS

The preceding analysis makes possible several remarks which are helpful for an understanding of the Letter's argument. In the first place, the analysis supports our view that the document is a personal, apologetic, didactic letter written by a teacher to one of his pupils. Doubts expressed by the pupil, Rheginos, have prompted the author's replies and have—to a degree—governed the outline of 46.3–49.9. Thus, we attach little significance to the theory that a Stoic-Cynic diatribe style has moulded some of the Letter's structure.[6] The author contends not with straw men nor generally held objections to the resurrection, but with specific issues and questions raised in earlier conversation or correspondence by Rheginos.

Secondly, the author's apologetic appears directed against two types of objector. On the one hand, behind some of the questions raised by Rheginos appear the sceptical views of those who deny the resurrection of any type of body, and who consequently accuse Christians of illusory and fanciful thinking (cf. 46.3–47.10; 48.3–38). Such opponents could be complete sceptics regarding the afterlife,[7] or they could be those who denied the resurrection of the flesh while affirming the immortality of the soul.[8] In either case, our author is

[6] This theory has been advanced by van Unnik in *JEH*, XV, 2 (1964), p. 146.

[7] Such scepticism may have been held by those who exterminated the Christians at Lyon and swept the ashes of their burned bodies into the Rhone River in order to destroy their resurrection hope: see Eusebius, *HE*, v, 1.62–63; cf. Minucius Felix, *Octavius* 11.4. Tertullian and Theophilus apparently knew of some who entertained this view: see the former's *De Res. Carnis*, i; Theophilus, *ad Autolycum*, 1.13. Franz Cumont, *After-Life in Roman Paganism* (New York, 1959, new edition), p. 39, remarks that pagan thought in the second century AD generally subscribed to belief in an afterlife, but there were still Stoics, like the Emperor Marcus Aurelius, '. . . for whom the future life was a mere hypothesis and sceptics like Lucian of Samosata, whose irony mocked all beliefs'. We might add to his list the Stoic Panaetius, whose words are recorded by Cicero, *Tusc.* i.79. See A. J. Festugière, *Epicurus and his Gods*, tr. C. W. Chilton (Oxford, 1955), pp. 18ff.

[8] Representatives of such an opinion may be found among Paul's opponents on the Areopagus (Acts 17.31–32). Celsus states that God cannot perform shameful acts—he would not raise corpses, flesh full of unspeakable things: '. . . corpses are more to be thrown away than dung' (Origen, *Con. Cels.* 5.14; cf. 2.55–70). A similar view is found in Porphyry, *Frags.* 34 and 92 (Harnack's Edition). See, also, Arthur Darby Nock, *Conversion* (Oxford, 1933), pp. 247–9; Pierre Champagne de Labriolle, *La réactione païenne: étude sur la polémique anti-chrétienne du Ier au VIe siècle* (Paris, 1934), p. 277.

defending the truth of the resurrection—albeit his own version of that doctrine—against those who deny it. This fact indicates that while our Letter does not emanate from an exclusively 'intra-Christian' debate over the resurrection, it does emerge from a deeply Christianized form of Gnosticism.

On the other hand, there have been objections raised by others who seem to be more orthodox Christians. These objectors have had difficulty with the idea of a *spiritual resurrection*[9] occurring *immediately at death*, with no interval of 'sleep' nor raising of the physical flesh involved (47.30–48.3). This more 'orthodox' objection may also have included a protest against the author's contention that if the resurrection were a surety for the Christian, it could be viewed in faith as having already taken place. But nowhere does the author contend with such an objection. His main argument for the view that the resurrection has already occurred seems designed to remove from Rheginos' mind any anxiety he may have concerning the inevitable event of death (49.9–36). In the face of this 'orthodox' objection the author re-emphasizes that a spiritual resurrection of the individual takes place immediately at death,[10] with no post-mortem interim. At the same time, by so strongly stressing the faith-view that the resurrection has already occurred, the author gives the impression of holding an 'over-realized eschatology'.[11]

Thirdly, from within the author's own framework of thought, the argument of the Letter displays considerable inner consistency—more, in places, than its first editors allow. Thus, after affirming the reality and necessity to faith of the resurrection (43.25–44.12), the author has proceeded to establish the Christological foundation for this teaching (44.13–46.2), and to meet certain objections raised against it (46.3–49.9). The remainder of the Letter contains a warning against erroneous thinking, a reminder of the imperatives of life with which present possession of the resurrection confronts the

[9] Evidence that the Great Church early felt the need to polemize against the view that the resurrection was only spiritual is provided by the insistence upon the resurrection of the flesh *(σαρκὸς ἀνάστασιν)* in the early Creeds. See, on this, H. B. Swete, 'The Resurrection of the Flesh', *JTS*, XVI (1917), pp. 135–41.

[10] Substantiation for this interpretation is provided below, pp. 143–6.

[11] The phrase is drawn from a suggestive article by William L. Lane, 'I Tim. IV. 1–3. An Early Instance of Over-Realized Eschatology?', *NTS*, XI, No. 2 (January 1965), pp. 164–7. Lane holds that a fundamental misunderstanding of Paul's teaching on the shift of the Aeons connected with the Christ Event has led those in I Tim. 4.1–3 and II Tim. 2.18 to the erroneous view that the Parousia has already occurred.

believer, and some concluding matters (49.9–50.14). Throughout, the author has consistently argued for the verity of the resurrection. There is a resurrection for the believer at death, its surety is rooted in Christ's victory over death, its guarantee is our election by Christ, its appropriation comes through faith, its actualization involves a retention of personally identifiable traits in a new spiritual flesh, and its expectation is a matter of such confidence that one should consider himself already raised from the dead! Nevertheless, a lack of clear logic manifests itself in the author's attempt to hold together such seemingly contradictory things as (1) the impending death and destruction of the visible, external body and flesh with the resurrection of the inward, spiritual members in a spiritual flesh; (2) the affirmation that the resurrection has already occurred with the expectation that its full realization awaits physical death in this sphere. These things are held side by side with one another, as we shall attempt to show in Chapter IV.

Fourthly, our analysis provides some substantiation for van Unnik's view that the specifically Gnostic features and terminology of our document are peripheral to the fundamentally Christian nature of its main argument.[12] That is, the scattered Valentinian terminology and imagery (e.g. 48.38–49.5) and the fragment of a Valentinian hymn (46.35–47.1) are not as integrally woven into the eschatology as we might otherwise expect in a Gnostic text. But of this we shall say more in Chapter V.

[12] For van Unnik's view, see *supra*, p. 14 and n.56 on that page.

CRITICAL NOTES TO THE TEXT

IN SUPPORT OF THE translation and analysis in the preceding chapter and as background for the exposition in Chapter IV, we offer in the succeeding pages three types of material. First, some technical notes on the Coptic grammar and syntax of our Letter are presented. Many of these notes make clear wherein and why our translation differs from that made by Jan Zandee and Robert McL. Wilson in the critical edition of the Letter.[1] Second, important parallels from other Gnostic texts are given, parallels not hitherto cited. And third, New Testament parallels, quotations, and 'echoes' are noted in order to demonstrate the influence of this literature upon the thought of the author of 'Rheginos'.[2] New Testament quotations and 'echoes' are numbered consecutively for easy reference.

43.25 'Some there are'. Our analysis (*supra*, pp. 36–37) has shown that a contrast is contained in this passage between those who self-centredly seek knowledge and the addressee, Rheginos (44.3–5). The contrast is made clearer by translating 'some' first, as the construction ογπ ϩⲁⲉⲓⲛⲉ fully permits (cf. Plumley, par. 184, p. 79).[3]

43.26 'who desire'. In the verbal form ⲉⲧογⲱϣⲉ, which this phrase translates, the Circumstantial converter ⲉ- has been combined with the third person plural of the I Present tense, ογ. In such con-

---

[1] See *De Resurrectione*, pp. 60–67, for the English translation.

[2] Because of limitations of space, the full Coptic and Greek texts of NT passages cited could not be given. These may be found, however, in the writer's original dissertation: 'The Epistle to Rheginos: A Study in Gnostic Eschatology and Its Use of the New Testament'. Unpublished doctoral dissertation, Yale University, 1966 (Copyright, University Microfilms, 1967). Nevertheless, an effort has been made to retain Coptic and Greek phrases where these are essential to the comparisons made.

[3] Because of the frequency of their citation in this chapter, the various grammars, lexicons, Gnostic and Patristic sources, and secondary works utilized have been referred to by means of abbreviations within the text (see list on pp. xi–xv).

struction the **є-** does service as a 'virtual relative pronoun', introducing a modifying relative clause following an undefined antecedent
(cf. Till, *Sah.* par. 475, p. 233).

43.27 'this aim (goal, objective)'. Study of the photograph of the
Coptic text (*De Resurrectione*, Plate 43, f. XXIIʳ) shows a correction of
ѕкопос to **скопос**, perhaps reflecting the influence of the Greek
script from which the translator works. **скопос**, which is a hapax
legomenon in the New Testament (Phil. 3.14), is retained in the Sahidic Version of Philippians (see Böhlig, *GLW*, Register, pp. 98–99).

43.28 'when they are occupied with questions'. The literal meaning of the intransitive verb **амаѕте** (**емаѕте** A²), which we translate
as 'occupied', is 'to be laid hold on' or 'to be restrained' (Crum 9a).
The meaning here, then, is that these 'questions' have a 'hold upon'
or are 'engaging the attention of' these seekers. Further, although
there might be some affinities in this mode of inquiry to the 'Questions and Answers' literature cited by the editors (*De Resurrectione*,
p. 19), in our Letter these questions are not general, but are defined by
the manner in which they are asked (43.32–34) and by their eschatological objective ('Rest'—43.34–35).

43.29 '; and . . .' We have altered the punctuation of this conjunction from that which is found in the Wilson-Zandee translation
so as to improve the English style and to help emphasize the following
'real prospective' conditional clause (cf. Plumley, par. 377, p. 182).
Such a conditional clause indicates that fulfilment of the supposition
contained in the protasis is reasonably likely (cf. Steindorff, par.
483, p. 234).

43.30–31 'they customarily think' (**ѱатмеѕе**). Although the
'Praesens Consuetudinis' tense may be translated as a simple infinitive (see Till, *Dial.*, par. 249, pp. 53–54), a rendering of it which
expresses its basic meaning of repeated, instantaneous past action
seems to accentuate best the prospective nature of the protasis here.

(1) The editors (*De Resurrectione*, p. 20) think that the clause, 'they
customarily think very highly of themselves' (43.30–32) recalls
similar expressions in I Cor. 8.1 and Rom. 12.3. If so, the mode of
influence would be that of an idea, as opposed to any literal 'echoing'
of Paul.

43.31–32 'very highly of themselves'. Literally the Coptic
means, 'some greatnesses within themselves'. We accept, however,
the arguments of Puech (*De Resurrectione*, pp. 19–20) for the translation offered. The meaning is that of self-inflating, vain thought.

43.33–34 'that they have stood within the Word of Truth (ⲙ̄ⲡⲗⲟⲅⲟⲥ ⲛ̄ⲧⲙⲏⲉ)'. The Coptic verb ⲁⲩⲁϩⲉ ('they have stood') indicates by its Qualitative form, that a state resulting from completed action is denoted (cf. Till, *Sah.*, par. 313, p. 159). To the expression 'Word of Truth', compare the following: E.V. 16.31 (ⲡⲉⲩⲁⲅⲅⲉⲗⲓⲟⲛ ⲛ̄ⲧⲙⲏⲉ); *Odes of Sol.* VIII.8; XII.1, 3; XIV.7; XXXII.2; *Manich. Hom.* I–7.2; *Pist. Soph.* 153.9, 20; *Mand. Lit.* 214.8, 9.

(2) The striking expression 'stood within the Word of Truth' (ⲁⲩⲁϩⲉ ⲁⲣⲉⲧⲟⲩ ⲙ̄ⲫⲟⲩⲛ ⲙ̄ⲡⲗⲟⲅⲟⲥ) echoes I Cor. 15.1b–c: '. . . I preached to you the gospel, which you received, in which you stand (ⲡⲁⲓ̈ ⲟⲛ ⲉⲧⲉⲧⲛ̄ⲁϩⲉⲣⲁⲧ ⲧⲏⲩⲧⲛ̄ ⲛ̄ϩⲏⲧϥ̄), . . .' Other instances of the phrase, 'standing within', but without 'Gospel' or 'Truth' as its object, are Rom. 5.2; I Cor. 16.13; Phil. 1.27; 4.1; Col. 4.12; I Thess. 3.8; II Thess. 2.15; I Peter 5.12. The echo seems clearly Pauline.

(3) The expression 'Word of Truth' (ⲡⲗⲟⲅⲟⲥ ⲛ̄ⲧⲙⲏⲉ) in 43.34 is certainly an echo of an identical phrase in the New Testament (cf. *De Resurrectione*, p. 20). Nevertheless, in our Letter it appears to refer to the 'written' Gospel as opposed to the 'oral.'. Further, the translations of this phrase in the Coptic New Testament are always different from that of our Letter, e.g. Col. 1.5 (ϩⲙ̄ⲡϣⲁϫⲉ ⲛ̄ⲧⲙⲉ); Eph.1.13 (ⲉⲡϣⲁϫⲉ ⲛ̄ⲧⲙⲏⲉ); II Cor. 6.7 (ϩⲛ̄ ⲟⲩϣⲁϫⲉ ⲛ̄ⲧⲉ ⲧⲙⲉ); II Tim. 2.15 (ⲙ̄ⲡϣⲁϫⲉ ⲛ̄ⲧⲙⲉ); James 1.18 (ⲡϣⲁϫⲉ ⲛ̄ⲧⲙⲉ). Thus, it appears that the translator of our Letter retained in his loanword, ⲡⲗⲟⲅⲟⲥ, the Greek of his original text, viz. ὁ λόγος τῆς ἀληθείας.[4]

43.34–35 'Rather, they seek their own Rest' (ⲉⲩϣⲓⲛⲉ ⲛ̄ϩⲟⲩⲟ ⲁⲡⲉⲩⲙ̄ⲧⲁⲛ). In contrast to McL. Wilson and Zandee (*De Resurrectione*, p. 60), we think that ⲉⲩϣⲓⲛⲉ is II Present instead of Circumstantial. This is because the stress of the verb is on the following adverb, ⲛ̄ϩⲟⲩⲟ, which emphasizes the contrary of what has just been intimated (cf. Crum 736a and b; Plumley, par. 192, p. 86). Further, we disagree with Henri-Charles Puech (*De Resurrectione*, p. 20) that ⲛ̄ϩⲟⲩⲟ translates ἐπὶ πλεῖον instead of μᾶλλον. He cites the Greek texts of II Tim. 2.16b and 3.9a in support of his contention, but unfortunately the Coptic version of neither passage exactly supports his view: II Tim. 2.16b: ἐπὶ πλεῖον (=ⲉⲡⲉϩⲟⲩⲟ, not ⲛ̄ϩⲟⲩⲟ); II Tim. 3.9a:

---

[4] On the meaning of 'Word of Truth' in the NT, see Heinrich Schlier, *Die Brief an die Epheser: ein Kommentar* (2. Auflage: Düsseldorf, 1958), p. 69; Martin Dibelius, *An die Kolosser, Epheser, und Philemon* (Handbuch zum Neuen Testament, herausgegeben von G. Bornkamm; Dritte Auflage. Neu Bearbeitet von D. Heinrich Greeven; Tübingen, 1953), p. 6.

ἐπὶ πλεῖον (=ЄΜΑΤЄ). Certainly, the II Present Tense of ЄⲦⲨⲒⲚЄ makes sufficiently clear that the passage refers to the *continuing* quest for 'Rest' by those mentioned. Finally, we must also reject J. W. Barns' reading of the Ⲁ- before ⲚЄⲦⲘ̄ⲦⲀⲚ as a comparative particle (*JTS*, N.S., XV (1964), p. 165) since this would hardly make sense in the context.

On the meaning of 'Rest' (Ⲙ̄ⲦⲀⲚ = ἀνάπαυσις), see *infra*, Chapter IV, pp. 140–3, and the following parallels: *Jeu I*—257.8; *UAW*— 336.17–20; 341.3–4; 350.28–30; and, 367.2–3; *Pist. Soph.* 134.16; *Apoc. Joh.* III, 35.1–2; II, 26.26–32; IV, 41.14–21; *Apoc. Jac.* II–56.2–3; *SOT*—173.7–11; *Odes of Sol.* III.5; XI.12; XX.8; XXVIII.3 ('. . . believed; therefore, I was at rest'); XXXV.1; XXXVII.4; XXXVIII.4; Iren., *Adv. Haer.* I, 2.6a; III, 15.2; *Exc. Theod.*, LXIII.2; LXV.2; Heracleon, *Fr.* 12.31; *E.V.* 22.9f.; 23.29; 40.32; 41.13, 29; 43.1; *Ev. Phil.* 119.13–15; 120.9–12; *Gos. Th.*— Log. 50, 51, 60; *Gos. Heb.* (*Strom.* V, 14.96); *Mand. Lit.* 25; 75.6; 80.4; 125.4; and, 129.4; *Manich. Hom.* I—15.17; 61.5; *Manich. PsB.* 136.9–12; 63.3–4; 26.24–26; 155.16–19.

43.35–37 'their own Rest, . . . received through our Saviour, our Lord Christ'. Although a definite article appears in the text prior to the name 'Christ' (ⲚЄⲬⲢⲎⲤⲦⲞⲤ), it is commonly left untranslated (see Till, *Sah.*, par. 96, p. 61).

(4) The title, 'our Saviour, our Lord Christ', finds no exact parallel in the NT, even though the separate designations it contains are found in a different combination: II Peter 1.11; 2.20; 3.18, all three—'our Lord and Saviour Jesus Christ'. Thus, the composite title appearing in 'Rheginos' gives evidence of considerable development, its closest counterpart being found in the second century writing of II Peter. (For the designation 'Lord Christ' by itself, cf. Rom. 16.18 and Col. 3.24.)

(5) The idea of receiving 'Rest' from the Saviour vaguely recalls the Synoptic saying of Jesus in Matt. 11.28f.—'Come to me, all who labour and are heavy laden, and I will give you rest. Take my yoke upon you, and learn from me; for I am gentle and lowly in heart, and you will find rest for your souls.' But cf. also Heb. 4.1–3a, where the last segment reads, 'For we who have believed enter that rest (Ⲙ̄ⲦⲀⲚ), . . .' (See *infra*, p. 142, n.126.)

44.1 'We received it ((i.e. "Rest")) after we had known' (Ⲛ̄ⲦⲀϨⲚ̄ⲭⲒⲦϤ̄ Ⲛ̄ⲦⲀⲢЄⲚⲤⲞⲦⲱⲚ). Instead of taking Ⲛ̄ⲦⲀϨⲚ̄ⲭⲒⲦϤ̄ as a Relative form of the I Perfect, as do Wilson and Zandee (*De Resurrec-*

tione, p. 61), we believe it to be II Perfect. This is because a certain stress seems present on the adverbial extension represented by the following Temporalis Tense prefix, ⲛ̄ⲧⲁⲣⲉⲛ-. Such is the basis for our translation. The giving of 'Rest' by the Lord in the present is also found in such Gnostic texts as *Acts of Th.* 19; 39; 50; 60; 139; 141; *Odes of Sol.* III, 5; XI, 12; *Manich. PsB.* 26.26, 31; 185.23–24; *Ev. Phil.* 119.13–15; *Gos. Th.*, Log. 51; Heracleon, *Frag.* 33.

44.2–3 'rested ourselves' (ⲁⲛ̄ⲙⲧⲁⲛ ⲙ̄ⲙⲁⲛ). The verb ⲙ̄ⲧⲁⲛ (AA²F form of ⲙ̄ⲧⲟⲛ Sah., Crum 193b) is transitive in meaning, as is shown by the following object pronoun. The construction is thus reflexive and should be so translated. Note the interesting variation in the form of the Perfect prefix here with what we find in 43.36 -ⲛ̄ⲧⲁⲣⲛ̄-.

44.4 'But because you ask us'. The conjunction used here is the Greek loanword ⲁⲗⲗⲁ, an adversative particle clearly indicating a contrast with what precedes. The object pronoun ⲙ̄ⲙⲁⲛ ('us') is used to designate the author himself, the usage being that of the 'literary plural' ('pluralis sociativus', cf. Blass-Debrunner-Funk, par. 280, pp. 146–7). Elsewhere in the Letter the author uses the first person singular, i.e. in 43.32; 44.6; 44.21; 44.39; 48.20; 48.28; 49.29; 49.37; 50.1 (?); 50.7; 50.12, 13, 15; or he makes use of a collective 'we' to denote what affects the author himself, Rheginos his pupil, and perhaps others: 43.36; 44.1; 44.11 (only the author and Rheginos); 45.22; 45.25–38; 45.31–32, 35–36; 46.14–15, 17; 46.25, 27–28, 30; 47.26.

44.5 'pleasantly what is proper'. We render the adverbial expression ϩⲛ̄ ⲟⲩϩⲗⲁϭ, which literally means 'in a sweetness' or 'sweetly' and normally translates the Greek γλυκύτης or γλυκασμός (Crum, 673a), with a metaphorical synonym, 'pleasantly'. The adverb refers to the manner in which Rheginos, the pupil, has asked the author of our Letter about the resurrection. Cf. the use of ϩⲗⲁϭ in *Manich. Hom.* I, 36.19; 37.16; 78.21; *Manich. PsB.* 8.9; 33.23; 45.20; 46.9; 55.31; 70.28; 167.17.

44.7–8 '((to say)) that it is necessary'. The verb of saying is supplied since it was often omitted in Coptic texts preceding the conjunction ⲝⲉ, as here (cf. Plumley, par. 337, p. 160). The copula, which is translated as 'it' (ⲧⲉ), indicates by its feminine gender that its antecedent is ⲁⲛⲁⲥⲧⲁⲥⲓⲥ ('resurrection') in 44.6. We agree with Quispel's reconstruction of the Greek underlying ⲁⲛⲁⲅⲕⲁⲓⲟⲛ ⲧⲉ, viz. ἀναγκαία ἐστι, rather than with Puech's, viz. ἀναγκαῖον ἐστι (*De*

Resurrectione, p. 21). The presence of the neuter form ⲁⲛⲁⲥⲕⲁⲓⲟⲛ cannot be taken as determinative of the gender of the underlying Greek adjective it translates since, as Böhlig has shown (*GLW*, p. 126), the feminine form of Greek loanwords in Coptic early disappeared and was replaced interchangeably by masculine or neuter forms.

44.8–10 'To be sure *(μέν)* many (ⲅⲁⲣ) are lacking faith (ⲁⲡⲓⲥⲧⲟⲥ) in it, but *(δέ)* there are a few (ⲅⲛ̄ⲕⲟⲩⲉⲓ) who find it'. As opposed to Wilson and Zandee (*De Resurrectione*, p. 61), we leave untranslated an initial ⲁⲩⲱ ('and') in line 8 since its retention detracts from the following correlative clause construction and is rather pleonastic in English style. Our translation also attempts to make clear a contrast indicated by the δέ of the second clause (cf. Arndt-Gingrich, pp. 503–4 for this usage). A similar contrast between the few who will be saved and the many who will not is to be found in the Gospel of Thomas, Log. 75; *C.H.* IX,4b; *Asclep.* I.10; III.22a; cf. Basilides' teaching as reported in Iren., *Adv. Haer.* I, 24.6.

ἄπιστος, which occurs in twenty-two passages in the Greek New Testament, is retained as a Greek loanword in all of these passages in the Sahidic Version (Böhlig, *GLW*, p. 415). This substantive is often used of the heathen (e.g. I Cor. 6.6; 10.27) and the condemned. Cf. the rebuke of Andrew by the Saviour for his 'faithlessness' in matters eschatological in *Pist. Soph.* 162.2.

(6) Similar opposition of the elect 'few' and the non-elect 'many' is found in Matt. 7.13–14 (cited in *De Resurrectione*, p. 21): 'Enter by the narrow gate; for the gate is wide and the way is easy, that leads to destruction, and those who enter by it are many (ⲅⲁⲣ). For the gate is narrow and the way is hard, that leads to life, and those who find it are few (ⲅⲉⲛⲕⲟⲩⲓ).' Cf. also Matt. 22.14:—'For many (ⲅⲁⲣ) are called, but few (ⲅⲉⲛⲕⲟⲩⲓ) are chosen.'

44.11–12 'let us discuss the matter'. Literally: 'let the word *(λόγος)* be to us concerning it, i.e. the Resurrection'.

44.13–14 'How did the Lord make use . . .' (ⲛ̄[ⲧ]ⲁⲟⲩⲁⲛⲝⲁⲉⲓⲥ ⲣ̄ⲭⲣⲱ ⲛ̄ⲉϣ ⲛ̄ϩⲉ). The editors' conjectural reconstruction of the nominal subject form of the II Perfect is certainly correct (*De Resurrectione*, p. 4), for II Tenses normally show stress on a following adverbial extension.[5] Here such extension is provided by the interrogative ⲛ̄ⲉϣ ⲛ̄ϩⲉ (cf. Till, *Dial.*, par. 327, p. 76). On the unusual form

---

[5] On the use of the Second Tense, see H. J. Polotsky, *Études de Syntaxe Copte* (Publications de la Société d'Archaeologie Copte; Le Caire, 1944), p. 30, par. 8.

of ⲭⲣⲱ, which appears closer to the substantive χρέω(ν) than to the second person singular, middle, imperative form which is normal for such Greek loanwords in Coptic, see Böhlig's comments (*GLW*, p. 135).

44.14–15 'while existing in flesh' (ⲉϥϣⲟⲟⲡ ϩⲛ̄ ⲥⲁⲣⲝ). The Circumstantial Tense (ⲉϥϣⲟⲟⲡ) is often used to translate a Greek participle (see Plumley, par. 197, p. 89). In spite of Wilson's studious avoidance of the translation 'exist' for the SA² Qualitative ϣⲟⲟⲡ, this is one of the fundamental meanings of that form (see Crum, 578a).

The assertion that the Saviour existed 'in flesh' is another bit of evidence which shows that the Gnostics were not uniformly docetic in their Christology. On the one hand, there were those who, like the 'orthodox' author of the Epistle of Barnabas (6.14), seem to affirm that Jesus existed on earth like other men of the flesh, e.g. Carpocrates (Iren., *Adv. Haer.* I, 25); Cerinthus (Iren., *Adv. Haer.* I, 26.1); *Gos. Th.*, Logia 28; *FUG* 3. On the other hand, the vast majority denied that Jesus existed 'in the flesh', e.g. Saturninus (Iren., *Adv. Haer.* I, 24.1); Cerdo (Ps.-Tert. 16, Grant, *2nd Cent. Christ.*, p. 136); Marcus and Colorbasus (Ps.-Tert. 15, Grant, p. 135); Valentinus himself (Ps.-Tert. 12, Grant, p. 133). Cf. the docetic qualification in E.V. 31.4f.: 'a similitude of flesh' (ⲛⲟⲩⲥⲁⲣⲝ ⲛ̄ⲥⲙⲁⲧ).

(7) The expression 'in flesh' is used to denote the earthly existence of Christ in a number of NT passages: Eph. 2.15; Heb. 2.14; 5.7; I Peter 3.18; 4.1; I John 4.2; II John 7; I Tim. 3.16. The Coptic translation of several of these passages is identical to the expression 'in flesh' in our Letter. Especially notable is the fact that in Heb. 2.14f. and John 1.14 the Saviour's pre-existence, descent, and temporary abode in the 'flesh' are implied. 'Flesh' also appears as a designation of the earthly Jesus in the Apostolic Fathers (I Clem. 32.2; Ign., *Smyrn.* 1.1; *Eph.* 20.2; *Magn.* 13.2), as well as a special term for his human side (II Clem. 8.2).[6]

44.15–16 'after he had revealed himself (ⲛ̄ⲧⲁⲣⲉϥⲟⲩⲁⲛϩϥ̄) as Son of God'. The Temporalis Tense is used reflexively here, as is indicated by the pronominal suffix ϥ. Note, also, that 'Son of God' appears here with the indefinite article, ⲉⲩϣⲏⲣⲉ, whereas in 44.21 it has the definite article, ⲡϣⲏⲣⲉ. The difference between them seems due to stylistic preferences of the translator, rather than to any

---

[6] See the comments of Schweizer in Eduard Schweizer, Friedrich Baumgärtel, and Rudolf Meyer, 'σάρξ, σαρκικός, σάρκινος', *Theologisches Wörterbuch zum Neuen Testament*, VII (1964), pp. 138–42, 145–6.

effort to make subtle distinctions in Christology. On the idea of the Saviour 'revealing himself', cf. *Ev. Phil.* 105.28–106.

(8) Only in two passages in the Fourth Gospel do we find expressions of Jesus' self-revelation: John 10.36: 'I am the Son of God'; John 21.1: '. . . after this Jesus revealed himself in this way'. Everywhere else in the New Testament Jesus is *revealed by* the Father instead of revealing himself, e.g. Luke 17.30; John 21.14; II Thess. 1.7; etc.

44.17 'He lived' (ⲁϥϩⲙⲁϩⲉ). The editors (*De Resurrectione*, p. 22) offer two conjectural emendations to make the text here intelligible. First, Walter Till wants to read ϩⲙⲁⲥⲧ (AA² of ϩⲙⲟⲟⲥ SF; Crum, 679a—'to sit, dwell, remain') for ϩⲙⲁϩⲉ. This emendation has in its favour the occurrence of the same word in the same sentence, i.e. -ⲉⲧⲣϩⲙⲁⲥⲧ in 44.18–19. Second, Jan Zandee makes a conjecture whose strength lies in the fact that it requires no internal change of the word as it stands in the text. He thinks that ϩⲙⲁϩⲉ is a form in which a prosthetic ϩ has been added to the SᵃA form of ⲙⲁϩⲉ (Crum, 203b—'walk, go'). We, however, would argue that metathesis has occurred between ϥ and ϩ. What would normally have been the I Perfect form ⲁϩϥⲙⲁϩⲉ has been changed to ⲁϥϩⲙⲁϩⲉ. Thus, ⲙⲁϩⲉ is probably a translation of περιπατεῖν (Crum, 203b), meaning, as in Paul, 'walk of life'. We translate metaphorically, 'live' (Arndt-Gingrich, p. 655). Cf. Rom. 6.4: '. . . we too might walk (ⲛ̄ⲧⲛ̄ⲙⲟⲟϣⲉ) in newness of life'; Rom. 8.4: '. . . who walk not (ⲉⲧⲉⲛ̄ⲥⲉⲙⲟⲟϣⲉ ⲁⲛ) according to the flesh . . .'; Rom. 13.13; 14.15; I Cor. 3.3; 7.17; II Cor. 4.2; 5.7; 10.2, 3; Gal. 5.16; Eph. 2.2; 4.1; Phil. 3.17, 18; Col. 1.10; 2.6; I Thess. 2.12; 4.1.

44.20 'The Law of Nature'. The editors (*De Resurrectione*, pp. 22–23) think it possible that certain NT texts used in other Valentinian writings to link the Jewish Law to death may have given rise to this statement, e.g. Rom. 7.10; 8.2; II Cor. 3.7. We, on the contrary, argue below (pp. 117–21) that there is no reference to the Jewish Law here at all. Rather, a philosophical teaching about the corruptible nature of man has been offered as Jesus' intended meaning.[7] Therefore, any hunt for a NT parallel or agrapha similar to this expression is futile.

---

[7] Cf. with our view that of Haenchen, *Gnomon*, 36 (1964), p. 362. Schenke, *OrL*, 60 (1965), col. 475, has recently offered a translation similar to ours in 44.20–21: '. . . mit seiner (the Son of Man's) Predigt gegen das Gesetz der Natur; ich nenne es aber "den Tod".' Contrast, however, the opinion of Zandee, *NTT*, 16 (1962), p. 374, who thinks that Rom. 7 may have informed the author's usage here.

It should be noted, however, that Clement of Alexandria calls Paul's reference to the Law a reference to the 'lex naturalis' (*Strom.* IV.83; *Frag.* 3). But note the different meanings given 'Law' by Ptolemy (*ad Floram*, 4.2–10) and Heracleon (*Frag.* 40).

44.21 'But I call it death' (ⲉⲉⲓϫⲟⲩ ⲛⲇⲉ ⲙ̄ⲙⲁϥ ϫⲉ ⲡⲙⲟⲩ). The conjecture that the author of our Letter attributes this statement to the Lord's earthly teaching (*De Resurrectione*, pp. 22–23) must be rejected for three reasons: (1) The Circumstantial converter ⲉ-, generally used to introduce a dependent clause amplifying the main sentence, scarcely permits ⲉⲉⲓϫⲟⲩ to be understood as introducing a direct quotation (cf. Plumley, par. 195, p. 89). (2) The absence of the conjunction ϫⲉ preceding what is supposed to be a direct quotation is contrary to the accepted rules of Coptic grammar (see Steindorff, par. 207, p. 100). (3) The presence of the adversative particle ⲛⲇⲉ (δέ) plus the first person singular (ⲉⲉⲓ-) indicates a slight contrast with what precedes. We are reminded, therefore, of a qualifying statement like Paul's in I Cor. 7.12a: 'To the rest I say, not the Lord, that if . . .'

The critical edition of the text gives the impression of a 'house divided against itself' in the interpretation of 44.20–21. In the 'Notes Critiques' (*De Resurrectione*, p. 22), Puech states:

. . . more probably, it is necessary to see in it (i.e. 44.20–21) a gloss, a personal remark of the author of the Treatise added by him to the passage and, so to speak, stated between parentheses.

But in the 'Introduction' of the same volume (*De Resurrectione*, p. XXVII), we read this remarkable statement:

He (Christ) has also come 'to vanquish death' (p. 44.27–29). Previously he had *declared himself against the law of Nature* (identical to that of the Demiurge) and had affirmed about it that it was death (p. 44.17–21).

In our translation, we treat 44.20–21 as a parenthetical remark by the Letter's author.

44.21–26 If, as the editors believe (*De Resurrectione*, p. xxviii), the title 'Son of God' refers to Christ's divine nature and 'Son of Man' to his human nature, then we have here the construction known as 'chiasmus', i.e. the literary pattern of *a b/b a* (see Blass-Debrunner-Funk, par. 477, p. 252). The reconstructed Greek text of this chiasmus, then, might be as follows:

(a) Ὁδὲ υἱὸς τοῦ θεοῦ, ὦ 'Ρηγῖνε, ἦν (b) υἱὸς ἀνθρώπου
καὶ περιεῖχε ταῦτα τὰ δύο
ἔχων (b) τὴν ἀνθρωπότητα καὶ (a) τὴν θεότητα

Christ, as 'Son of Man', also identifies himself as 'Son of God' in the *Odes of Sol.*, XXXVI.3.

In 44.22 the conjunction ⲡⲗⲉ *(δέ)* indicates a transition in the author's thought rather than a contrast.

The indefinite article preceding ϣⲏⲣⲉ ⲛ̄ⲣⲱⲙⲉ (lit.: 'a Son of Man') in 44.23 does not imply the existence of more than one 'Son of Man' in the author's thought. Cf., with this, the use of the same title with the definite article in 44.30–31. See also our note on 44.15–16 given earlier.

The conjunction ⲁⲩⲱ ('and') in 44.23 gives evidence of a paratactic style in the underlying Greek. Cf. our earlier note on 44.8–10. We leave the conjunction untranslated so as to improve the English style.

Before concluding our treatment of 44.21–26 we should also comment upon the phrase: 'the humanity (ⲛ̄ⲧⲙ̄ⲛ̄ⲧⲣⲱⲙⲉ) and the divinity (ⲧⲙ̄ⲛ̄ⲧⲛⲟⲩⲧⲉ)'. The first of these Coptic nouns probably translates the Greek ἀνθρωπότης ('abstract humanity', cf. Liddell and Scott, I, p. 142) since even though it is not found in the New Testament or the Apostolic Fathers, this term early became a *'terminus technicus'*, e.g. Iren., *Adv. Haer.* III, 18.3; Clem., *Paed.* I.5; Acts of Thomas A, 80; Origen, *Jo.* 1.18; Epiph., *Pan.* 65.7; Bas., *Eun.* 1.18; etc. On this, see Lampe, *Lexicon*, Fasc. 1, p. 144a. The second abstract noun, ⲧⲙ̄ⲛ̄ⲧⲛⲟⲩⲧⲉ, translates the Greek θειότης ('divine nature, divinity'—Rom. 1.20) or θεότης ('deity, divinity'—esp. Col. 2.9). Both terms are hapax legomena in the NT, and only the second appears in the Apostolic Fathers (viz., in Her. *Mand.* 10.1, 4; cf. 5f.; 11.5, 10, 14). Very early, however, θεότης as a designation of Christ's divine nature gained wide currency, e.g. Or., *Jo.* 1.18; Cyr., *Hom. Cat.* 10.3; referring to the relationship of Christ's two natures—Or., *Or.* 26.4; Meth., *Symp.* 3.4; especially of Christ's 'revealed' divinity —Epiph., *Pan.* 54.4; Or., *Con. Cels.* 2.33; etc.[8] In the view of the Early Church, Christ's 'humanity' refers to his weakness in human nature and humility in the assumption of flesh, whereas his divinity denotes his unity with God and participation in incorruptible nature. Cf. Melito of Sardis' discussion 'On the Incarnation of Christ', Book III (Grant, *2nd Cent. Christ.*, p. 73).

---

[8] For the texts of these citations, see Lampe, *Lexicon*, Fasc. 3, pp. 637–8.

(9) Two NT passages identify the Son of Man with the Son of God in a manner similar to 44.21–23: Matt. 16.13, 16: '... "Who do men say that the Son of Man is?" ... Peter replied, "You are the Christ, the Son of the living God." '; John 5.25, 27: '... the hour ... now is, when the dead will hear the voice of the Son of God, ... he is the Son of Man.'

(10) Although there are no exact NT parallels to the statement in 44.25–26 that the Saviour possessed 'humanity' (ἀνθρωπότης), behind the ascription of 'divinity' (ⲧⲙⲛ̅ⲧⲛⲟⲩⲧⲉ = θεότης) to him in the same passage may lie the thought of Col. 2.9: 'For in him the whole fullness of deity (ⲛ̅ⲧⲙⲛ̅ⲧⲛⲟⲩⲧⲉ) dwells bodily'.

44.27–28 'so that on the one hand he might conquer death'. The tense of the main verb in this final clause is II Future (ⲉϥⲛⲁϫⲡⲟ), which indicates that the action is regarded as instantaneous and so certain of achievement that it is viewed as if it were already completed (cf. Plumley, par. 208, p. 96).

44.27–33 The chiasmus noted in 44.21–26 is here reversed again, creating a sort of double chiasmus. Thus, the sequence in 44.26 of (a) 'humanity' of the Son of Man and (b) 'divinity' of the Son of God, is reversed in lines 27–33 where the Son of God's work (b) is mentioned preceding that of the Son of Man (a). On the concept of 'restoration' among the Gnostics, see Ev. Phil. 115, 16–18; Mand. PsB. 9; the view of the Sethian-Ophites in Iren., Adv. Haer. I, 30; Basilides in Hippolyt., Ref. VII.25.2; 27.5; Pist. Soph. 126.34–127.2.

(11) Nowhere in the NT is Jesus as 'Son of God' said to have conquered death. Nevertheless, this passage is reminiscent of several NT affirmations of Jesus' destruction of death, e.g. Heb. 2.14–15; II Tim. 1.10; and, more vaguely, Acts 2.24 and Rom. 1.4.

(12) The single usage of ἀποκατάστασις ('restoration') in the NT (Acts 3.21) in no way parallels what is said about it in Rheg. 44.30–33. Later, however, Origen interpreted the term allegorically and used it as a terminus technicus descriptive of the universal salvation of souls following their purification in heaven.[9] Behind the Saviour's 'restoration of the Pleroma', however, may stand such a thought as that expressed in Eph. 1.9–10:

> For he has made known to us in all wisdom and insight the mystery of his will, according to his purpose which he set forth in Christ as a

---

[9] See further on this, Albrecht Oepke, 'ἀποκαθίστημι, ἀποκατάστασις', TWNT, I (1933), pp. 391–2.

plan for the fullness of time, to unite all things in him, things in heaven and things on earth.

Cf. also Col. 1.19–20. It is of interest that in these passages, as in others, such as Eph. 4.13; 3.19; Col. 2.9, the Coptic NT never retains πλήρωμα as a Greek loanword but translates it with such expressions as ⲡϫⲱⲕ ⲉⲃⲱⲗ or ⲡϫⲱⲕ ⲧⲏⲣϥ̄.

44.33–35 'because originally He was from above, a seed of Truth'. We translate the Greek loanword (conjunction) ⲉⲡⲉⲓⲁⲏ in a casual sense since the ensuing passage serves as the author's explanation of how and why the Son of Man has brought about the 'restoration' of the Pleroma. The adverbial phrase ⲁⲃⲁⲗ ϩⲙ̄ ⲡⲥⲁ ⲛ̄ⲧⲡⲉ means literally, 'out of (from) the side of heaven', but often carries the idiomatic meaning of 'above, upward' (cf. Crum, 259b). The pre-existence of Christ is assumed by the phrase, as well as his transcendence.

(13) The idea of Christ being 'from above' is especially Johannine in character. Cf. John 3.31a: 'He who comes from above (ⲉⲃⲟⲗ ϩⲛ̄ ⲧⲡⲉ) . . .'; 6.38: 'For I have come down from heaven (ⲛ̄ⲧⲁⲉⲓ ⲉⲛ ⲁⲃⲁⲗ ϩⲛ̄ ⲧⲡⲉ), . . .'; 8.23: 'He said to them, . . . I am from above ([ⲟⲩ]ⲁⲃⲁⲗ', ϩⲛ̄ ⲧⲡⲉ); . . .;' and, less closely, John 3.13 and I Cor. 15.47f.

(14) Jesus is called a 'seed' in Gal. 3.16, but without allusion to his heavenly origin: 'Now the promises were made to Abraham and to his offspring (seed). It does not say, "And to offsprings (seed)"; but, referring to one, "and to your offspring (seed)", which is Christ.' 'Seed', σπέρμα, in the plural usually denotes 'descendants' in biblical literature. But see John 7.42.[10]

44.35–36 'before this structure (σύστασις) had come into being'. The tense of the verb here is that of 'Unfulfilled Action', i.e. action not yet effected but due to be so in the future (see Till, *Sah.*, p. 242; Plumley, par. 224, p. 104). For a similar use of 'structure', see *SOT*, 171.25–26.

44.37–38 'in this (i.e. structure) many dominions and deities came into existence' (ϩⲛ̄ ⲧⲉⲉⲓ ⲁϩⲛ̄ⲙⲛ̄ⲧϫⲁⲉⲓⲥ ⲙⲛ̄ ϩⲛ̄ⲙⲛ̄ⲧⲛⲟⲩⲧⲉ). Two abstract nouns used here represent some technical Greek expressions: ⲙⲛ̄ⲧϫⲁⲉⲓⲥ translates κυριότης (as in Eph. 1.21; see Crum, 787b) and ⲙⲛ̄ⲧⲛⲟⲩⲧⲉ (see our note above on 44.21–26). 'Lordships'

---

[10] Cf. the comments of Gottfried Quell and Siegfried Schulz, 'σπέρμα', *TWNT*, VII (1964), pp. 545–6.

or 'Dominions' seem to be special classes of angelic powers similar to those mentioned in Enoch 61.10; Col. 1.16; Eph. 1.21. But, compare also to 'dominions', *SOT* 149.29; *Apoc. Jac.* II, 49.7.

(15) The editors (*De Resurrectione*, p. xx) think that 44.37–38 is a citation of Col. 1.16 which contains a variant reading peculiar to the Valentinians (cf. Iren., *Adv. Haer.* I, 4.5 and *Exc. Theod.*, 43.3). We, on the contrary, think that while there may be an 'echo' of Col. 1.16 here, it is by no means a quotation. Our reasons for drawing this conclusion are as follows: (*a*) There is no citation-formula such as we have found in the two clear citations-passages elsewhere in the Letter (see *supra*, pp. 18–20). (*b*) In 'Rheginos' no mention is made of the other powers named by both Paul and the Valentinians who quote him. (*c*) In 'Rheginos' κυριότητες precedes θεότητες, whereas in Iren., *Adv. Haer.* I, 4.5, this order is reversed, and in *Exc. Theod.* βασιλεῖαι (a probable interpretative rendering of ἀρχαὶ or ἐξουσίαι from the Colossians passage) appears inserted between κυριότητες and θεότητες. (*d*) In Col. 1.15–16 these 'dominions' and 'deities' have been created 'in Christ', indicating their subservience to but also origin in Christ. In Rheg. 44.37–38, however, the creation of these 'powers' has taken place completely apart from Christ, and they are thoroughly inimical toward him.

Even if the preceding reasons are not considered decisive, we also find that the manner in which Col. 1.16 is supposedly cited in Rheg. 44.37–38 is at variance with Valentinian usage of the passage elsewhere. Thus, Carola Barth (*Die Interpretation* (1911), p. 41, note 'b') has shown that in the citation of Col. 1.16 by *Exc. Theod.* 43.3 there is evidenced a Gnostic tendency to extend the list of metaphysical spirit-beings named: πάντα γὰρ ἐν αὐτῷ ἐκτίσθη τὰ ὁρατὰ καὶ τὰ ἀόρατα θρόνοι κυριότητες βασιλεῖαι θεότητες λειτουργίαι. Even the citation given in Iren. I, 4.5 has the list of beings shortened by only one from that found in Col. 1.16. Clearly, if Rheg. 44.37–38 is a quotation of Col. 1.16, it shows a very un-Valentinian tendency to abbreviate radically the list of powers. It is in this light that we would raise the question of whether the passage in 'Rheginos' is not actually a random allusion to two orders of beings known in the Valentinian system or remembered vaguely from Paul's writings? Cf., for example, the Marcosian initiation formula in Iren., *Adv. Haer.* I, 21.3, where both θεότης and κυριότης appear independently of one another.[11]

[11] On the issue of whether the powers in Col. 2.9 were Gnostically conceived, see G. H. C. Macgregor, 'Principalities and Powers: The Cosmic Background of

45.1–2 'the solution in difficult things'. The 'solution' (ⲛⲃⲱⲗ =
ἡ λύσις, Crum, 32b) mentioned here is defined as (*a*) that which
false seekers seek with their soteriological questions (43.29); (*b*) that
which our author attempts to give in response to Rheginos' query
about the resurrection (45.1); and (*c*), that which, in conjunction with
Christ's advent, revealed evil's destruction and the elects' identity
(45.5–11). That is, our author is occupied with a 'solution' to the
problem of salvation, a 'solution' which he believes is provided
through Christ's life and work. (Cf. with this interpretation that of
Puech in *De Resurrectione*, p. 25.)

Of interest also in 45.1–2 is the author's concession concerning the
difficulty of the imagery with which he presents the 'solution'. He
appears to indicate thereby both his pupil's still-immature knowledge and his shortcoming as a teacher in failing to present the matter
with clarity.

45.5–8 'the solution appeared so as not to leave anything hidden,
but to reveal all things openly . . .' Although Wilson and Zandee
wish to translate 45.5–6 '. . . to leave nothing hidden' (*De Resurrectione*, p. 62), we think that the author has placed his emphasis on the
negation of the infinitive (ⲁⲧⲙ̅ⲕⲉ = 'not to leave hidden'). Another
construction is used in the Letter for the expression 'nothing', viz.
ⲙⲛ̅ ⲗⲁⲧⲉ in 45.2 and 47.24–25.

'Openly' in 45.8 translates the Coptic ϩⲁⲡⲗⲱⲥ, a form of the
Greek adverb-loanword ἁπλῶς. As in numerous other Coptic texts
(see Crum, 632a), the 'spiritus asper' of the original Greek has been
replaced by a prosthetic ϩ-. Further, to attempt to distinguish between 'simply' or 'openly' for the meaning of ἁπλῶς (as does Puech in
De Resurrectione, pp. 25–26) seems superfluous since the context implies
both shades of meaning are present. Actually, the adverb indicates a
contrast between what Christ's life and work have made clear, and
both the difficulty of the author's imagery (45.1–2) and the enigma of
the truth about things prior to Christ's coming (45.4–6). Cf. to the
idea of Christ's revelation of things formerly hidden the following:
I Clem. 18.6; *Gos. Th.*, Logia 5 and 6; Oxy. Pap. 654, iv (James,
p. 26).

(16) The editors suggest (*De Resurrectione*, p. 25) that we are to

---

St. Paul's Thought', *NTS*, I (1955), pp. 22–28; Clinton Morrison, *The Powers That
Be: Earthly Rulers and Demonic Powers in Romans 13:1–17* (Studies in Biblical
Theology, No. 29; London, 1960), pp. 25, 29, 34, and espec. p. 36.

compare, 'in a sense', the concept of 'solution' in 45.5–11 (which they identify as 'the solution personified in Christ') with Mark 4.34. We have difficulty, however, in seeing any direct connection or dependence here.

(17) The statement in 45.5–9 concerning the revelation of things formerly hidden vaguely recalls, according to the editors (*De Resurrectione*, p. 25), some Synoptic passages, such as Mark 4.22: 'For there is nothing hid, except to be made manifest; nor is anything secret, except to come to light'; Matt. 10.26. But compare also such Pauline expressions as are found in I Cor. 4.5 '. . . before the Lord comes, who will bring to light the things now hidden in darkness . . .'; Eph. 3.9; Col. 1.26; I Cor. 2.7. While none of these passages are truly 'echoed' in 45.5–9, the ideas they contain may have been a stimulus to our author.

45.8–9 'concerning existence' (ⲉⲧⲃⲉ ⲡⲓϣⲱⲡⲉ). The translation of ⲡⲓϣⲱⲡⲉ by Wilson and Zandee as 'the origin' (*De Resurrectione*, p. 62) we believe to be incorrect. They obviously infer from the *terminus technicus* προβολή ('Emanation') in 45.12 that ⲡⲓϣⲱⲡⲉ has some cosmogonic connotation. However, the Coptic verb ϣⲱⲡⲉ in its substantized form means basically 'being' or 'existence' (Crum, 580a). Indeed, Till himself (*De Resurrectione*, Index, p. 71) states that the term means 'être'. The ensuing parenthetical expansion in 45.9–11 defines ⲡⲓϣⲱⲡⲉ in terms of (1) the destruction of evil, and (2) the manifestation of the elect—both having more to do with 'existence' than with 'origin'.

45.10–11 'the revelation of the Elect'. Against Puech, Malinine, and Barns,[12] we agree with Quispel, Wilson and Zandee (*De Resurrectione*, pp. 26 and 62) that the Coptic ⲙ̄ⲡⲉⲧⲥⲁⲧ̄ⲡ̄ used in this passage means 'Elect' and not 'better'. While the context does show that ⲥⲁⲧ̄ⲡ̄ means 'better' (= κρεῖττον) in 47.9, 22, the term has the connotation of 'to be chosen' or 'elected' (ὁ ἐκλεκτός) in 46.25 (and Puech, Malinine, and Till all so translate it). But the usage of ⲙ̄ⲡⲉⲧⲥⲁⲧ̄ⲡ̄ vs. ⲡⲉⲑⲁⲩ in 47.21–22 on which Puech bases his argument for the meaning 'better' in 45.11 does not appear to mean the same as that of ⲙ̄ⲡⲡⲉⲑⲁⲩ and ⲙ̄ⲡⲉⲧⲥⲁⲧ̄ⲡ̄ in 45.10–11. In the former, 'worse' and 'better' refer to the perishable nature ('worse') of the Elect and to the

---

12 Till translates: '. . . das Erscheinen anderseits des Vorzüglichen', (*De Resurrectione*, p. 53); while Puech and Malinine offer: '. . . la manifestation du meilleur, . . .' (*ibid.*, p. 7). Barns agrees with them in his critical note to this passage (*JTS*, N.S., Vol. XV (1964), p. 165), as does now Schenke, *OrL*, 60 (1965), col. 475.

immortal nature ('better') retained in the after-life. The contrast in
45.10–11, however, defines what is revealed about existence through
the solution that Christ brings. 45.10–11 seems to recapitulate what
was said in preceding lines about Christ's work: (1) the Son of God
conquered death (44.27–29)//the destruction of evil (45.9–10);
(2) the Son of Man restored the Pleroma (44.30–33)//the revelation of
the Elect (45.10–11). The following chapter will show that there is a
clear election teaching in our 'Letter' which supports the translation
that we have given (cf., e.g. Rheg. 48.3–6, 34–35).

(18) The thought of 'revelation of the Elect' in 45.10–11 bears
some similarity to ideas expressed in Mark 4.22 and Luke 8.17. In
Paul, such revelation is linked to a future eschatological hope, not a
'realized' one as in 45.10–11. Cf. Rom. 8.19: 'For the creation waits
with eager longing for the revealing of the sons of God; . . .'

45.11–14 'this is the emanation of Truth and Spirit. Grace is of
Truth'. Although the Coptic forms of the words translated 'Truth',
'Spirit', and 'Grace' all have definite articles, we do not translate
them since these expressions are obviously the names of three divine
emanations in the Valentinian Pleroma.[13] On the omission in translation of definite articles preceding proper names, see Walter Till's
comments (*Sah.*, par. 96, p. 61).

The term 'emanation' *(προβολή)* is most certainly a *terminus technicus* drawn from the Valentinian sphere, for after the Classical
period (cf. Liddell-Scott, II, p. 1472), it appears neither in the
Septuagint (cf. Hatch-Redpath, p. 1205), nor in the New Testament
(cf. Arndt-Gingrich, p. 709), nor in the Apostolic Fathers (cf. Good-
speed, p. 205). Its first occurrence in the Christian era seems to be
among the Valentinians (cf. E. A. Sophocles, II, p. 923).

'Truth' is an emanation in the system of Ptolemaeus (Iren., *Adv.
Haer.* I, 1.1) and of the *Pistis Sophia* (77.3–6); 'Grace' appears as an
Aeon in *CGT* XXVIII, m.s.f. 110, c.s., p. 18; *Apoc. Joh.*, Cod. II,
p. 8.3–4. The hypostatization of both is found in Ptolemaeus (Iren.,
Adv. Haer. I, 1.1 and the *Pistis Sophia* (80.20–30). For Valentinian
parallels, see *De Resurrectione*, p. 26.

(19) The editors (*De Resurrectione*, p. 26) offer for comparison (without claiming that the passages are distinctly 'echoed' here), the
following: John 1.14: 'and the Word became flesh and dwelt among

---

[13] Puech and Malinine also support this view (*De Resurrectione*, pp. 7 and 26);
but, contrast the translation by Wilson and Zandee (*ibid.*, p. 62) where the capitalization of 'Spirit' only implies another interpretation of 'grace' and 'truth'.

us, full of grace and truth . . .'; John 1.17b: '. . . grace and truth came through Jesus Christ'.

45.14–15 'The Saviour swallowed up death. (You are not reckoned as being ignorant.)' The initial clause in the parenthetical remark, viz. 'you are not reckoned', is a translation of the negated form of нп (SA²BF Qualitative of ѡп, Crum 526a). In the Qualitative, a tense denoting the result of verbal action, нп means 'to count, esteem, reckon as'. Puech, Malinine, and Till all indicate the presence of this verb in their translations (*De Resurrectione*, pp. 7 and 62). Wilson and Zandee, however, pass over it: 'You are not to be ignorant' (p. 62). Indeed, if the latter translation were correct, it might parallel the Pauline expression: οὐ θέλω δὲ ὑμᾶς ἀγνοεῖν, ἀδελφοί, Rom. 1.13 (cf. Rom. 11.25; I Cor. 10.1; 12.1; II Cor. 1.8; I Thess. 4.13). However, the Qualitative indicates that the author is not proposing to illuminate Rheginos on a point of Christology; rather, he is reminding Rheginos parenthetically that he already possesses such knowledge.

(20) As the editors and Zandee have indicated,[14] the statement that the Saviour 'swallowed up death' (45.14–15: ациѡмпк ппмот) clearly echoes Paul's expressions in I Cor. 15.54c: ' "Death is swallowed up in victory" ' (атемк пмот); II Cor. 5.4d: '. . . what is mortal may be swallowed up by life' (етеѡмк пнешациот евоλ).

45.16–23 'For He put aside the world which is perishing. He transformed [himself] into an imperishable Aeon and raised himself up, having swallowed the visible by the invisible, and he gave us the way of our immortality.'

The clause, 'he transformed [himself]', in 45.17–18 translates the verb ациш︢т︦[ц], which is probably an SA² form of the verb шıве (Crum, 551a). This verb normally translates the Greek ἀλλοιόω (see Herm., *Mand.* 12.4.1) or ἀλλάσσω (cf. I Cor. 15.51f.). Against Puech (*De Resurrectione*, p. 27), who instead favours the Greek ἀπαλάσσεσθαι (i.e. 'he has departed for an Aeon or an eternity, imperishable') as the underlying text, we agree with Till, Wilson and Zandee that the meaning here is reflexive, i.e. 'He changed himself'. To translate as does Puech (1) would make 45.19 redundant; (2) it would break the contrast between the Saviour's 'putting aside the perishing (еациτεκο) world' (45.16–17) and 'transforming himself into an imperishable (пαττεκο) Aeon' (45.18); (3) it finds no more support in the Gnostic sources than the idea that the Saviour becomes fully divine again upon his ascent. Cf., for example, the identification of the

---

[14] See *ibid.*, pp. 26–27; Zandee, *NTT*, 16 (1962), p. 362.

Saviour with an imperishable Aeon in *Apoc. Joh.*, Cod. II, 1.27–28; and, in Ptolemaeus' system in Iren., *Adv. Haer.* I, 3.1. The Tenth Treatise of the C.H. speaks of the need for a soul's 'transformation' for it to become divine (X.6); while the Sethian-Ophites tell of the aspiration of the Son for an 'imperishable Aeon' (Iren., *Adv. Haer.* I.30). Finally, (4) in the phrase 'into an imperishable Aeon' (ⲁϩⲟⲩⲛ ⲁⲩⲁⲓⲱⲛ ⲛ̄ⲁⲧⲧⲉⲕⲟ), it should be noted that ⲛ̄ⲁⲧⲧⲉⲕⲟ is linked to ⲁⲓⲱⲛ with the attributive particle ⲛ- (cf. Till, *Sah.*, par. 114, pp. 67–68). Thus, ⲁⲧⲧⲉⲕⲟ is an attribute of ⲁⲓⲱⲛ (= 'imperishable Aeon'), not—as Puech would seem to have it—an adverb. Elsewhere in our Letter ⲧⲉⲕⲟ and ⲁⲧⲧⲉⲕⲟ both refer either to the imperishable nature of what is saved or the perishable nature of what is not (cf. Rheg. 45.17; 46.21, 23; 47.19; 48.38; 49.2).

(21) A Johannine theme may be suggested by the assertion that the Saviour disassociated himself from the world (45.16–17): John 13.1b: '. . . when Jesus knew that his hour had come to depart out of this world to the Father . . .' Cf. John 16.28b: '. . . again, I am leaving the world and going to the Father'.[15]

(22) To the passage in 45.16–17, 'the world which is perishing', compare I John 2.17a: 'And the world passes away, and the lust of it; . . .'; I. Cor. 7.31b: '. . . For the form of this world is passing away'.[16]

(23) The expression 'transformed [himself] into an imperishable Aeon' (45.17–18) is nowhere exactly paralleled in the NT, the personification of 'Aeon' *(αἰών)* actually being foreign to it, with the possible exception of Eph. 2.2. However, in the concept of the Saviour's 'transformation' (ⲁϥϣⲓϥ[ϥ] from ϣⲓⲃⲉ) we do seem to find an echo of I Cor. 15.51–52:

> Lo! I tell you a mystery. We shall not all sleep, but we shall all be changed (ⲁⲛⲟⲛ ⲇⲉ ⲧⲏⲣⲛ̄ ⲧ̄ⲛ̄ⲛⲁϣⲓⲃⲉ), in a moment, in the twinkling of an eye, at the last trumpet. For the trumpet will sound, and the dead will be raised imperishable, and we shall be changed (ⲁⲩⲱ ⲁⲛⲟⲛ ⲧ̄ⲛ̄ⲛⲁϣⲓⲃⲉ).

[15] As we shall see in the following chapter, *infra*, pp. 108–10, the 'world' has very negative overtones for our author. Such a view is comparable to that of the Fourth Gospel, where the world is at enmity with Christ (John 8.23; 12.31a), as well as with believers (John 12.25; cf. I Cor. 11.23). Christ does not belong to the world at all—John 17.14c, 16b; 14.27. See, further, Hermann Sasse, 'κόσμος', *TWNT*, III (1957), pp. 894–5.

[16] These parallels were discovered independently by the writer and by van Unnik, *JEH*, XV, No. 2 (1964), p. 166.

(24) The only NT reference to Jesus raising himself up from the dead is found in John's Gospel: John 2.19: 'Jesus answered them, "Destroy this temple, and in three days *I will raise it up*." ' Elsewhere in the NT Jesus is always raised by the Father. Yet, compare the remarkable parallel to this expression in Ign., *Smyrn.* 2.1: 'For he suffered all these things for us that we might attain salvation, and he truly suffered even as he also truly raised himself, . . .'

(25) There are three expressions in the passage 45.20–23 which may claim inspiration from the NT. First, van Unnik (*JEH*, XV, No. 2 (1964), p. 166) would have us think of II Cor. 4.18 in connection with the idea of the Saviour swallowing up 'the visible by the invisible'. It is doubtful, however, that this or any other NT expression really provides stimulus here, for in the NT the attribute 'invisible' is postulated only of God: Rom. 1.20; Col. 1.15; I Tim. 1.17; Heb. 11.26. Ignatius, however, does speak of the 'invisible' (τὸν ἀόρατον) Christ who became 'visible' (ὁρατόν) for the sake of men (*Poly.*, 3.2). Cf. *Exc. Theod.* 59.

Second, the Pauline expression to 'swallow up' is echoed in 45.20, as we have found it to be in 45.14.

Third, behind the phrase 'way of immortality' in 45.23 may lie the NT idea of Christ's opening of the 'way' to heavenly life for the believer, e.g. John 14.3–6:

> And when I go and prepare a place for you, I will come again and will take you to myself, that where I am there you may be also. And you know the way where I am going. Thomas said to him, 'Lord, we do not know where you are going; how can we know the way?' Jesus said to him, 'I am the way, and the truth, and the life; no one comes to the Father but by me.'

Cf. also Heb. 10.1–20.[17]

---

[17] Of course, Bultmann and Käsemann think that the imagery of Christ's 'opening of the way' is really provided for these NT authors by the Gnostic Redeemer Myth. See Rudolf Bultmann, γινώσκω', *Theological Dictionary of the New Testament*, ed. Gerhard Kittel; tr. Geoffrey W. Bromiley (Vol. I; Grand Rapids, Michigan, 1964), pp. 9–12; Ernst Käsemann, *Das wandernde Gottesvolk: Eine Untersuchung zum Hebräerbrief* (*FRLANT*, N.F. 55, Heft 37; Göttingen: Vandenhoeck & Ruprecht, 1952), pp. 82–90. Contrast, however, the opposite views of the following: Gilles Quispel, 'Het Johannesevangelie en de Gnosis', *NTT*, 11 (1956–57), pp. 175, 177, 203; Robert McL. Wilson, *The Gnostic Problem* (London, 1958), pp. 81–82, 88; Robert M. Grant, *Gnosticism and Early Christianity* (New York, 1959), pp. 171–5; E. M. Sidebottom, 'The Ascent and Descent of the Son of Man in the Gospel of St. John', *Anglican Theological Review*, 2, 2 (1957), pp. 115–22.

45.24–28 'Then, indeed, as the Apostle said, "We suffered with him, and we arose with him, and we went to heaven with him."' Note that the author in no way qualifies the suffering of the Saviour implied in the first of these lines. Ptolemaeus, by contrast, taught that only the 'psychic' but not the 'spiritual' Christ suffered (Iren., *Adv. Haer.* I, 7.2); while Basilides held that he really did not suffer (Hippolyt., *Ref.* VII, 27.11–12). Simon Magus, who is described as descending from a heavenly state in order to rescue his Helen, is said by Irenaeus (*Adv. Haer.* I, 23.3) to have '. . . appeared as a man, though he did not suffer'. Normally, proponents of a docetic Christology could support only the idea of an apparent but not real suffering of the Saviour (cf. the heretical views attacked by Ignatius in *Trall.* 10.1).

To the idea of believers having already 'gone to heaven' while in this life (Rheg. 45.27–28), compare *Mand. PB.* 29, 30, 58, 65, 71, 99; *Manich. PsB.* 63.2–4.

(26) We have stated earlier[18] that 45.25–28 contains a composite citation based on Rom. 8.17 and Eph. 2.5–6. Here we undertake to substantiate that conclusion by treating each component of the citation separately, offering first a re-translation of the Coptic text of 'Rheginos' into Greek and appropriate NT parallels, and then comparing the Coptic texts of both:

Rheg. 45.24–26	*New Testament*
Τότε οὖν, ὡς εἶπεν ὁ ἀπόστολος συνεπάθομεν αὐτῷ	The language of 'Rheginos' is most closely paralleled by Rom. 8.17— συγκληρονόμοι δὲ Χριστοῦ, εἴπερ συνπάσχομεν ἵνα καὶ συνδοξασθῶμεν.

ⲧⲟⲧⲉ ϭⲉ ⲛ̄ⲑⲉ ⲛ̄ⲧⲁ̅ⲣⲁⲡⲁⲡⲟⲥⲧⲟⲗⲟⲥ ϫⲟⲟϥ ϫⲉ ⲁⲛ̄ϣ̄ⲡ ϩ̄ⲓⲥⲉ ⲛ̄ⲙ̄ⲙⲉϥ ⲉϣϫⲉ ⲁⲛⲟⲛ ⲛ̄ϣⲏⲣⲉ ⲉⲓ̈ⲉ ⲁⲛⲟⲛ ⲛⲉⲕⲗⲏⲣⲟⲛⲟⲙⲟⲥ ⲙⲉⲛ ⲙ̄ⲡⲛⲟⲩⲧⲉ ⲛ̄ϣⲃⲣⲕⲗⲏⲣⲟⲛⲟⲙⲟⲥ ⲇⲉ ⲙ̄ⲡⲉⲭ̅ⲥ̅ ⲉϣϫⲉ ⲧⲛ̄ϣⲡ ϩ̄ⲓⲥⲉ ⲛ̄ⲙ̄ⲙⲁϥ ϫⲉ ⲉⲛⲉϫⲓⲉⲟⲟⲩ ⲟⲛ ⲛ̄ⲙ̄ⲙⲁϥ·

With the exception of a change in tense of the main verb (viz. from the I Present in Romans to the I Perfect in 'Rheginos') and a slight variation due to dialectical differences (ⲛ̄ⲙ̄ⲙⲁϥ is Sahidic, ⲛ̄ⲙ̄ⲙⲉϥ is Subakhmimic), the expression in our Letter of 'suffering

[18] See *supra*, pp. 18f.

with him' is identical to that of Rom. 8.17 in the Coptic New Testament. While this does not definitively prove the case for literal citation in 45.24–26, it does render it probable.[19]

Rheg. 45.26–27	New Testament
26 καὶ συνηγέρθημεν	Col. 2.12a & b: συνταφέντες αὐτῷ ἐν
27 αὐτῷ	τῷ βαπτίσματι, ἐν ᾧ καὶ συνηγέρθητε διὰ τῆς πίστεως . . .
	Col. 3.1: Εἰ οὖν συνηγέρθητε τῷ Χριστῷ, τὰ ἄνω ζητεῖτε, οὗ ὁ Χριστός ἐστιν ἐν δεξιᾷ τοῦ θεοῦ καθήμενος.
	Less literally parallel, but perhaps closer in thought is Eph. 2.6:
	καὶ συνήγειρεν καὶ συνεκάθισεν ἐν τοῖς ἐπουρανίοις ἐν Χριστῷ Ἰησοῦ, . . .

26–27 ⲁⲩⲱ ⲁⲛⲧⲱⲱⲛ ⲛⲙ̄ⲙⲉϥ	Col. 2.12b: . . . ⲡⲁⲓ ⲟⲛ ⲉⲛⲧⲁⲧⲉⲧⲛ̄ⲧⲱⲟⲧⲛ ⲛ̄ⲟⲏⲧϥ̄ ⲟⲛ̄ⲧⲡⲓⲥⲧⲓⲥ
	Col. 3.1a: ⲉϣϫⲉ ⲁⲧⲉⲧⲛ̄ⲧⲱⲟⲧⲛ ϭⲉ ⲙⲡⲛⲉⲭ̄ⲥ̄
	Eph. 2.6: ⲁⲩⲱ ⲁϥⲧⲟⲩⲛⲟⲥⲛ̄ ⲛⲙ̄ⲙⲁϥ. ⲁϥⲑⲙ̄ⲥⲟⲛ ⲛⲙ̄ⲙⲁϥ ⲟⲛ̄ⲙⲡⲏⲩⲉ ϩⲙⲡⲉⲭ̄ⲥ̄ ⲓ̄ⲥ̄.

It is difficult to determine the exact source of our author's citation in 45.26–27, although the use of ⲧⲱⲟⲛ plus ⲙⲛ̄ (a translation of συνεγείρω) in all three NT passages we cite seems to show our author's dependence on at least one of them. Due to the absence of any mention of baptismal practice in the Letter, Col. 3.1 seems a less likely source; while only differences in person and number keep the Coptic text of Eph. 2.6 from being virtually identical to Rheg. 45.26–27.

---

[19] Some other NT passages displaying parallel thought but not language are: II Cor. 1.5; Phil. 3.10–11. The latter reads:
. . . that I may know him and the power of his resurrection and may share his sufferings, becoming like him in his death, that if possible I may attain the resurrection from the dead.
Zandee (NTT, 16 (1962), p. 364) thinks that behind the author's thought here is the Pauline conception of 'dying with Christ' in baptism. However, as van Unnik states (JEH, XV, No. 2 (1964), p. 151), '. . . it is not clearly expressed; there are no references to baptism'. Cf. Ignatius, Letter to Polycarp, VI.1.

Rheg. 45.27–28
καὶ συνανέβημεν αὐτῷ
or
καὶ συνανέβημεν αὐτῷ εἰς τὸν
οὐρανόν, . . .

New Testament
Eph. 2.4–6: ὁ δὲ θεὸς πλούσιος ὢν ἐν
ἐλέει, διὰ τὴν πολλὴν ἀγάπην αὐτοῦ
ἣν ἠγάπησεν ἡμᾶς, καὶ ὄντας ἡμᾶς
νεκροὺς τοῖς παραπτώμασιν συνεζωο-
ποίησεν τῷ Χριστῷ,—χάριτί ἐστε
σεσωσμένοι,—καὶ συνηγείρεν καὶ
συνεκάθισεν ἐν τοῖς ἐπουρανίοις ἐν
Χριστῷ Ἰησοῦ, . . .
Col. 3.1–3: Εἰ οὖν συνηγέρθητε τῷ
Χριστῷ, τὰ ἄνω ζητεῖτε, οὗ ὁ
Χριστός ἐστιν ἐν δεξιᾷ τοῦ θεοῦ
καθήμενος· τὰ ἄνω φρονεῖτε, μὴ τὰ
ἐπὶ τῆς γῆς. ἀπεθάνετε γάρ, καὶ ἡ
ζωὴ ὑμῶν κέκρυπται σὺν τῷ Χριστῷ
ἐν τῷ θεῷ.[20]

ⲁⲧⲱ ⲁⲛⲃⲱⲕ ⲁⲧⲡⲉ ⲛ̄ⲙ̄ⲙⲉϥ,

Eph. 2.6: Given above (p. 71).
Col. 3.1–3: ⲉϣϫⲉ ⲁⲧⲉⲧⲛ̄ⲧⲱⲟⲧⲛ
ⲥⲉ ⲙ̄ⲡⲉⲭ̄ⲥ̄ ϣⲓⲛⲉ ⲛ̄ⲥⲁⲛⲁⲧⲡⲉ
ⲡⲙⲁ ⲉⲧⲉⲣⲉⲡⲉⲭ̄ⲥ̄ ⲛ̄ϧⲏⲧϥ̄
ⲉϥϩⲙⲟⲟⲥ ϧⲓⲧⲟⲛ̄ⲁⲙ
ⲙ̄ⲡⲛⲟⲩⲧⲉ. ⲙⲉⲉⲩⲉ ⲉⲛ ⲁⲧⲡⲉ·
ⲛⲉⲧϧⲓϫⲙ̄ⲡⲕⲁϩ ⲁⲛ.

Once again, the author does not literally cite but rather summarizes
his understanding of the Pauline teaching concerning the believer's
participation in the Saviour's redemptive acts. The Ephesians
passage appears to be the major source of the thought expressed in
Rheg. 45.27–28.

45.28–29 'Now if we are revealed . . .' Wilson and Zandee
translate the beginning of this clause, 'But if . . .' (*De Resurrectione*,
p. 62). Since no contrast is implied in the use of the Greek particle
ⲛ̄ⲁⲉ (δέ), however, we prefer a translation indicating only a simple
transition. The grammatical structure of the protasis indicates that
the condition is viewed as fulfilled (cf. Till, *Dial.*, par. 337, p. 79).
Also to be noted in this passage is the 'Conjugatio Periphrastica'

[20] A similar thought of having already gone to heaven but without the Christological reference is found in Heb. 12.22—'But you have come to the city of the
living God, the heavenly Jerusalem, and to innumerable angels in festal gather-
ing . . .'

construction in the clause ⲧⲙ̄ⳝⲟⲟⲛ ⲛ̄ⲁⲉ ⲉⲛⲟⲩⲁⲛ̄ⳅ ⲁⲃⲁⲗ (cf. Till, *Dial.*, par. 276, p. 61; *Sah.*, par. 332, p. 171). The presence of such a construction would seem to indicate a fair degree of sophistication on the part of the Coptic translator.

45.30–31 'wearing him' (. . . ⲉⲛⲣ̄ⳏⲟⲣⲉⲓ ⲙ̄ⲙⲁϥ). Compare with this descriptive phrase in the idea of 'wearing' or 'putting on' the Saviour in the *Odes of Sol.* VII.4; *Ev. Phil.* 123.22; The Gospel of Mary (Grant, *Gnos.*, p. 68); *Manich. PsB.* 38.22; 99.29–30. Interestingly, in *Manich. PsB.* 178.3–4 Christ is said to 'wear the believer'.

(27) As the editors have indicated (*De Resurrectione*, pp. 27–28),[21] there is probably an allusion in 45.30–31 to Paul's theme of 'putting on Christ', as found in Rom. 13.12–14 and Eph. 4.22–24. Cf., however, I Cor. 15.49: 'Just as we have borne the image (ⲉⲛⲧⲁⲛϥⲟⲣⲓ ⲛ̄ⲑⲓⲕⲱⲛ) of the man of dust, we shall also bear the image (ⲧⲛ̄ⲛⲁϥⲟⲣⲓⲟⲛ ⲛ̄ⲑⲓⲕⲱⲛ) of the man of heaven.'

45.31 'beams' (ⲛ̄ⲁⲕⲧⲓⲛ = ἀκτίς). Although this substantive appears not at all in the NT and only once in the Apostolic Fathers (Barn. 5.10), it is found in Philo, the Septuagint, and some early Christian writings. Lampe, for example, presents two texts (*Lexicon*, I, p. 68), in which the Gnostics have metaphorically spoken of Christ's 'rays' (Clem., *Exc. Theod.* 61; Hippolyt., *Ref.* VIII, 13.3), and one from Eusebius which speaks of the 'rays' of θεοσεβείας (*Laud. Const.* 8). Cf. also *Mand. PB.* 49 (where the believer is called 'a ray of the great radiance of life'); 73; 75 (Dr., pp. 77f.); 141; 198; 251; 254; 309; C.H. XVI.16; *Pist. Soph.* 96.4–7; 150.16ff. In the Apocalypse of Peter, just after a prayer by the Twelve that they might be shown the resurrected form of some righteous brethren who had died, we read the following description of two of these brethren:

> For there issued from their countenance a ray as of the sun, and their raiment was shining so as the eye of man never saw the like: for no mouth is able to declare nor heart to conceive the glory wherewith they were clad and the beauty of their countenance (James, p. 508, sec. 7).

(28) The editors (*De Resurrectione*, p. xvi) believe that the whole passage, 45.31–39, may draw inspiration from the early hymn quoted

[21] Actually, Zandee, *NTT*, 16 (1962), p. 366, was the first to point out this allusion.

by Paul in Eph. 5.14 and by Clement of Alexandria in a more
expanded form in *Protrept.*, IX, 84.2. Certainly, the passage may have
supplied some ideas to the author, but it has scarcely moulded his
language.

45.34–35 'until our setting, that is to say, . . .' The Coptic
substantive ϩⲱⲧⲡ seems to translate the Greek δυσμή, 'sinking' or
'setting' (Crum, 725a). In some Patristic texts the term is used
metaphorically to mean 'the close of life' (see Lampe, *Lexicon*, 2,
p. 393).

The phrase translated 'that is to say' (ⲉⲧⲉ ⲡⲉⲉⲓ ⲡⲉ) introduces an
explanatory addition to what precedes. On this construction and
translation see Till, *Sah.*, par. 464, pp. 227–8.

45.36 'We are drawn'. Literally: 'they draw us'. This is the
normal circumlocution for the passive in Coptic. Compare to the
idea of the Saviour's 'drawing' the faithful to heaven, the following:
Acts of Th. 117; *Mand. PB.* 81; C.H. XVI, 5.

(29) Parallel to 45.36–37: 'we are drawn to heaven by him'
(ⲉⲩⲥⲱⲕ ⲙⲙⲁⲛ ⲁⲧⲡⲉ)—is the Johannine motif of the Saviour and
the Father 'drawing men'. Compare John 12.32: '. . . and I, when
I am lifted up from the earth, will draw all men to myself (. . .
ϯⲛⲁⲥⲁⲕ' ⲟⲩⲟⲛ ⲛⲓⲙ ϣⲁ ⲁⲣⲁⲉⲓ)'; John 6.44a: 'No one can come
to me unless the Father who sent me draws him (ⲥⲱⲕ ⲙⲙⲁϥ).'

45.37 'like the beams' (ⲛⲑⲉ ⲛⲛⲓⲁⲕⲧⲓⲛ). The Coptic ⲛⲑⲉ most
likely translates the Greek particle of comparison ὡσεί (see Crum,
638b). Its usage here is comparable to that of ὡσεί in Acts 2.3a: 'and
there appeared to them tongues as of *(ὡσεί)* fire'. This, then, is
figurative language similar to that found in the *Odes of Sol.* XV.1–2
and Ign., *Rom.* 2.2; and such is the character of the whole of 45.28–
39. Contrast the literal interpretation of this passage offered by the
editors in *De Resurrectione*, pp. xiiiff.

45.36–39 'We are drawn to heaven . . . not being restrained
(ⲉⲛⲥⲉⲉⲙⲁϩⲧⲉ ⲙⲙⲁⲛ ⲉⲛ) by anything'.

(30) Cf. perhaps, Acts 2.24: 'But God raised him up, having
loosed the pangs of death, because it was not possible for him to be
held (ⲉⲧⲣⲉⲩⲁⲙⲁϩⲧⲉ ⲙⲙⲟϥ) by it.'

45.40 'the spiritual resurrection'. Cf. the view propounded in the
Naassene Exegesis reported by Hippolytus, *Ref.* V, 8.23–24:

. . . and again, 'the dead will come forth from the sepulchres',—i.e.,
from the earthly bodies, being regenerated as spiritual beings, not

carnal *(πνευματικοί, οὐ σαρκικοί)*. This is the resurrection which takes place through the gates of heaven.

(31) The passage 45.39–46.2 is permeated with Pauline terminology which our author utilizes in his own unique way:

This is the spiritual resurrection (ⲧⲁⲛⲁⲥⲧⲁⲥⲓⲥ ⲛ̄ⲡⲛⲉⲩⲙⲁⲧⲓⲕⲏ) which swallows up the psychic (ⲛ̄ⲧⲯⲩⲭⲓⲕⲏ) alike with the other fleshly (ⲧⲕⲉⲥⲁⲣⲕⲓⲕⲏ).

Unlike I Cor. 15.42–46 (the probable background of the author's thought), 'spiritual' and 'psychic' are not applied to the *type of 'body'* one may have in the resurrection, but to the *mode of the resurrection*.[22] Similarly, 'fleshly' is never used by Paul in any discussion of the resurrection or the resurrection body.[23] We also find echoed here for the third time (cf. 45.14, 19) Paul's expression, 'swallowing up' something. Instead of death being 'swallowed', as in I Cor. 15.54, however, it is the 'psychic' and 'fleshly' modes of the resurrection which are destroyed. The whole passage should be compared to I Cor. 15.42–46.[24]

46.1–2 'which swallows the psychic alike with the other fleshly (ⲧⲕⲉⲥⲁⲣⲕⲓⲕⲏ)'. The two attributive adjectives, 'psychic' and 'fleshly', both appear without the substantive they modify, but they obviously have reference to 'resurrection' (ⲁⲛⲁⲥⲧⲁⲥⲓⲥ) in 45.40. Such omission of the substantive is frequent in Greek style where it can be supplied from the sense and context provided through the attributives (cf. Blass-Debrunner-Funk, par. 480, pp. 253–4). This means that the 'spiritual resurrection' swallows up (or destroys) both the 'psychical' and the 'fleshly' types of resurrection. Wilson and Zandee leave the ('other, also') untranslated in ⲧⲕⲉⲥⲁⲣⲕⲓⲕⲏ.

---

[22] In support of this interpretation of the passage see our note to 46.1–2 just below, and *infra*, pp. 148f. By contrast, Schenke (*OrL*, 60 (1965), col. 473) seems to agree with the editors (see *infra*, p. 112, n.20) that 45.39–46.2 actually refers to the Valentinian trichotomous division of man's nature.

[23] The contrast of 'spiritual' and 'fleshly' men in I Cor. 3.1–3 refers instead to the capacity of believers to receive mature instruction in the faith; whereas, other occurrences of σαρκικός are not relevant to the comparison, viz. Rom. 15.27; I Cor. 9.11; II Cor. 1.12; 10.4; I Peter 2.11.

[24] We are well aware of the opinion of Walther Schmithals that Gnostic eschatology is both combated and adapted in I Cor. 15 by Paul. See *Die Gnosis in Korinth: Eine Untersuchung zu den Korintherbriefen* (*FRLANT*; N.F. 66, Heft 48; Göttingen: Vandenhoeck & Ruprecht, 1956), esp. pp. 240–2. But we think Robert M. Grant's criticisms of this view are sound. See Grant, *Gnosticism*, pp. 157–8.

46.4–5 'he does not have ((the capacity for)) persuasion (ⲘⲚ̄ⲦⲈϤ ⲘⲘⲈⲨ Ⲛ̄ⲡⲣ̄ⲡⲈⲓⲐⲈ)'. Wilson and Zandee (*De Resurrectione*, p. 63) translate this difficult, and in literal English nonsensical, clause rather freely. We attempt to remain as literal as possible by retaining the meaning of the negative existential verb ⲘⲚ̄ⲦⲈ⸗ (SAA²F pronominalis status of ⲘⲘⲚ̄- SAA², Crum, 166b) and by providing, as does Walter Till (*De Resurrectione*, p. 53), an explanatory addition in brackets. The context justifies such an addition since 46.5–8 makes obvious the contrast between faith and persuasion. 'Persuasion' here (the Coptic loanword seems to translate an articular infinitive, τὸ πείθειν) refers to some type of logical demonstration, and 'faith' is contrasted to it as trust and belief in the reality of something incapable of such demonstration. Cf. Ign., *Rom.* 3.3; *Asclep.* I.13 and 14. Contrast the positive view of philosophy in C.H., Excerpt II B, 2.

(33) Several NT themes and parallels have been detected in the passage 46.3–13, which reads:

> But if there is one who does not believe (πιστεύειν), he does not have ((the capacity for)) persuasion (πείθειν). For it is the place of faith (πίστις), my son, and not of persuasion (πείθειν). He who is dead shall arise. There is one who believes (πιστεύειν) among the philosophers (φιλόσοφος) who are in this world. At least he will arise. And let not the philosopher (φιλόσοφος) who is in this world be caused to believe (πιστεύειν) that he is a man who returns himself (and ((that))) because of our faith (πίστις)).

The futility of trying to 'persuade' men about the resurrection is also expressed in the NT: Luke 16.31: 'He said to him, "If they do not hear Moses and the prophets, neither will they be convinced (πεισθήσονται) if some one should rise from the dead." ' Cf. also II Cor. 5.1–9. By contrast, the 'persuasion' of men concerning the truth of the Resurrection and the Gospel is positively assessed in the mission work of Paul, e.g. in Acts 17.2–4; 19.8; 28.23–24; II Cor. 5.11.

The theme that those who 'believe', though dying, shall be resurrected (46.8–9) is found frequently in the NT, e.g. John 11.25–26: 'Jesus said to her, "I am the resurrection and the life; he who believes in me, though he die, yet shall he live, and whoever lives and believes in me shall never die." ' Cf. also John 6.40 and I Thess. 4.14. Other NT passages also relate faith to the reception of the resurrection, the theme appearing to be primarily Johannine: John 3.36; 5.24; 6.47; I John 5.13; Heb. 11.5, 35. 'Faith' is said to be essential for the salvation of the 'psychical' men in *Exc. Theod.*, 63 (cf. *Pist. Soph.* 107.11–12).

46.8–13 Our translation reflects changes from that of Wilson and Zandee (*De Resurrectione*, p. 62) which we think help to convey the sense of the passage better. First, ⲁⲩⲱ ('and') in 46.8 is omitted as being rather paratactic (cf. ⲛ̄ⲁⲉ in 46.3 and ⲅⲁⲣ in 46.5). Thus, the clause, 'He who is dead shall arise', is understood as a summation of the author's preceding discussion. Second, the 'but' (ⲁⲗⲗⲁ) in 46.10, we think, indicates a contrast between 'the philosophers who are in these places (i.e. the world)' (46.9) and that one philosopher who 'believes' (46.8) and thus 'shall arise' (46.10). The 'and' (ⲁⲩⲱ = καί) in 46.10 must then be understood as adding a new thought, viz. that the philosophers 'in this world' (spoken of in 46.9), who differ from that philosopher who 'believes and shall be saved' (46.8, 10), should not think that they return to their pre-existent state by their own power (46.12–13). Rather, salvation is possible only through faith (46.13-parenthetically). Contrast this interpretation with that offered by Puech (*De Resurrectione*, pp. 30–31).[25]

(33) The editors indicate (*De Resurrectione*, p. xix) that the opposition of 'faith' and 'persuasion' in 46.8–13 calls to mind that established by Col. 2.8 between 'plausible (but false) arguments' and 'faith'. By contrast, we believe that the opposition is between 'faith' and the possibility of logically persuading men concerning the Resurrection. But there is no doubt that Col. 2.8 evaluates philosophy rather negatively.

(34) If there is a denial in 46.10–13 that 'conversion' and the 'resurrection' resulting therefrom can occur without the aid of faith or 'grace', then the editors (*De Resurrectione*, p. 31) think that we should bear Eph. 2.4–10 in mind as a background.

46.14–15 'we have known . . ., and we have believed'. The parallels to this passage presented by the editors (*De Resurrectione*, p. 31) are only half-parallels. That is, while they emphasize the role of 'knowledge' (γνῶσις) in the salvation of the 'spiritual man', they make no mention of what seems equally important to the author of our Letter, viz. 'faith' (πίστις: 46.15, 20–21). Cf. the combination of γνῶσις and πίστις in Barn. 1.5 and The Gospel of Matthias (Clem. Alex., *Strom.* III, 4.26).

---

[25] Cf. also Barns' conjectures in *JTS*, N.S., Vol. XV (1964), p. 165. Schenke, *OrL*, 60 (1965), col. 476, offers a new translation of this passage which tends to support our interpretation.

(35) To the ideas of 'knowing' the Saviour and 'believing' in his resurrection (46.14–19), cf. possibly Phil. 3.10 and I Thess. 4.14.

46.16–17 '. . . that He arose from the dead'. It is most unusual for a Gnostic to make such a statement without qualification. Contrast *Ev. Phil.* 104.15–18, where the writer states that it is incorrect to say Christ rose from the dead; or, the view of Cerinthus (Iren., *Adv. Haer.* I, 26.1), who distinguished the Jesus who suffered from the spiritual Christ who remained impassible.

(36) In 46.16–17, 'he arose from the dead' (ⲁϥⲧⲱⲟⲩⲛ ⲁⲃⲁⲗ ϧⲛ ⲛⲉⲧⲙⲁⲟⲩⲧ), the author clearly echoes a NT expression: cf., e.g., Matt. 27.64c (ⲁϥⲧⲱⲟⲩⲛ ⲉⲃⲟⲗ ϧⲛ ⲛⲉⲧⲙⲟⲟⲩⲧ); Matt. 17.9 (par. Mark 9.9) (ⲡϣⲏⲣⲉ ⲙ̄ⲡⲣⲱⲙⲉ ⲧⲱⲟⲩⲛ ⲉⲃⲟⲗ ϧⲛ ⲛⲉⲧⲙⲟⲟⲩⲧ); cf. Rom. 10.9 and Matt. 28.7. There are also a number of NT confessions which affirm 'Jesus rising from the dead': Matt. 17.22–23; 20.18–19; Mark. 9.31; 10.33–34; Luke 9.22.

(37) In 46.17–19 we read: 'This is he of whom we say, "He became the destruction of death (ⲛ̄ⲃⲱⲗ ⲁⲃⲁⲗ ⲙ̄ⲡⲙⲟⲩ)." ' There may be an echo here of certain NT expressions about the 'destruction' or 'destroying' of death (so the editors in *De Resurrectione*, p. 31). If so, however, the Coptic NT uses a completely different phrase from our Letter for 'destruction' (46.17–ⲛ̄ⲃⲱⲗ ⲁⲃⲁⲗ). Cf. Heb. 2.14–15 ('destroy' = ⲉϥⲉⲟⲩⲱⲥϥ); and, less clearly, I Cor. 15.24, 26 and II Tim. 1.10.

46.19–21 'as He is a great One who is believed in. Among the im[mortal] are those who believe'. Our translation attempts to render the passive construction (ⲡⲉⲧⲟⲩⲣ̄ⲡⲓⲥⲧⲉⲩⲉ ⲁⲣⲁϥ = lit.: 'the one whom they believe him') more clearly, and thereby carries the corporate plural subject throughout the rest of this sentence, viz. in 46.14: ⲁϧⲛ̄ⲥⲟⲩⲛ; 46.15: ⲁϧⲛⲡⲓⲥⲧⲉⲩⲉ; 46.17: ⲛⲉⲧⲛ̄ϫⲟⲩ. Moreover, since the context gives it strong support, we accept Zandee's conjecture (*De Resurrectione*, p. 32) that a copyist or the translator has inadvertently omitted the substantive ⲙⲟⲩ ('death') after the privative prefix ⲁⲧ- in 46.21. But the preposition ϧⲛ- in 46.20 must assuredly be translated with ⲛⲁⲧ[ⲙⲟⲩ] (i.e., 'among the immortal') and not with what precedes. Thus, we reject Barns' ingenious emendation of ⲛⲁⲧ to ⲛⲁϭ, i.e. 'great are they who believe' (*JTS*, N.S., Vol. XV (1964), p. 165). Christ is called a 'Great One' in *Manich. PsB.* 52.9 and in the *Acts of Th.* 119.

(3) The editors (*De Resurrectione*, p. 31) suggest that we should possibly bear in mind Acts 8.6 as a parallel to 46.19–20. Obviously

they mean Acts 8.9, but it is still difficult to see any similarity of concepts between the two passages.

46.21–24 'Among the im[mortal] are those who believe. The thought of those who are saved shall not perish. The mind of those who have known him shall not perish.'

(39) It has been pointed out (*De Resurrectione*, p. 32) that 'knowledge' and 'immortality' are spoken of here as being interdependent, a phenomenon recalling John 17.30. Note, however, that 'immortality' (ⲁⲧⲙⲟⲩ = ἀθάνατος) is just as closely linked with 'belief' (πιστεύω) in 46.21–24. Further, it is doubtful whether 'eternal life' (αἰώνιος ζωή) in John 17.30 can be simply equated with ἀθάνατος. Cf., for an approximate parallel, the use of ἀθανασία in I Cor. 15.53–54; and, especially, II Tim. 1.10.

46.22 'the thought' (ⲡⲙⲉⲩⲉ). Although the editors (*De Resurrectione*, p. 32) state that ⲙⲉⲩⲉ translates 'sans doute' the Greek ἔννοια, Crum (200a) shows that it may be used to render any one of the following: λογισμός, διαλογισμός, νόημα, as well as ἔννοια. The choice among these is difficult since more than one of these terms are used in Gnostic texts, e.g. λογισμός is the Fifth Aeon in the Simonian system (Hippolyt., *Ref.* IV, 51.9; VI, 12.2; 13). To evaluate properly the parallels offered by the editors to 46.21–23, it should be recognized that ⲙⲉⲩⲉ always has reference to mental activity elsewhere in the Letter (cf. 43.31–32; 47.29; 48.10; 48.6–7).

46.23–24 'The mind (νοῦς) . . . shall not perish'. Cf., on the idea of the survival of the 'mind', Philo, *Ebr.* 99–103; C.H. I.18; X.9, 19.

(40) Although νοῦς is used in neither NT passage, it may be that the author has been inspired here by Rom. 8.6: 'To set the mind (φρόνημα) on the flesh is death, but to set the mind on the Spirit is life and peace'; or by Col. 3.2–3: 'Set your minds on (φρονεῖτε) things that are above, not on things that are on earth. For you have died, and your life is hid with Christ in God.'

46.25–26 'Therefore, we are elected to salvation and redemption.'

(41) As a background to the notion of 'election to salvation', we might compare I Thess. 5.9; II Thess. 2.13; I Peter 1.3–5. In conjunction with the concept 'redemption' (ⲡⲥⲱⲧⲉ = ἡ ἀπολύτρωσις), the editors (*De Resurrectione*, p. 32) suggest a study of Eph. 1.14. Certainly ἀπολύτρωσις is predominantly a Pauline term, seven of its ten occurrences appearing in the Apostle's letters. However, Paul closely links 'redemption' with 'justification' and 'forgiveness of sins'

(e.g. Rom. 3.24; I Cor. 1.30; Eph. 1.7; Col. 1.14), whereas the author of our Letter never mentions 'sin'. Instead, 'redemption' appears to have become a stock term, stripped of many of its earlier associations.

46.26–27 'since we are predestined (ⲉⲁϩⲟⲩⲧⲁϣⲛ̄) from the beginning'. Cf. Ignatius' comments on the predestination of the righteous in the Praescript of his Letter to the Ephesians. The pronominalis status form ⲧⲁϣ S^aAA²F, from the root ⲧⲱϣ, may be used to translate ὁρίζειν or, especially, προορίζειν (Crum, 449b).

(42) The expression 'to predestine' is also Pauline, e.g. Rom. 8.29–30a:

> For those whom he foreknew he also predestined to be conformed to the image of his Son, in order that he might be the first-born among many brethren. And those whom he predestined he also called . . .

46.28–29 'not to fall into the foolishness (ⲧⲙⲛ̄ⲧⲁⲑⲏⲧ)'. Here we translate the causative infinitive form ⲁⲧⲣⲏ̄ⲧⲙ̄ϩⲁⲉⲓⲥ as a simple infinitive, 'not to fall' (cf. Till, *Sah.*, par. 335, pp. 173–4). Normally the abstract noun ⲧⲙⲛ̄ⲧⲁⲑⲏⲧ translates the Greek ἀφροσύνη or ἄνοια (Crum, 715a), but it can translate μωρία. On the idea of separate destinies for the Elect and non-Elect, cf. *Apoc. Joh.*, Cod. II. p. 26.23–27.30. 'Ignorance' is viewed as a state of sinfulness in the *Acts of Th.* 59; Heracleon, *Frag.* 41; C.H. I.20, 27; VII.2; X.8b.

(43) Van Unnik (*JEH*, XV, No. 2 (1964), p. 166) suggests that the parable of the Wise and Foolish Virgins (Matt. 25.1–13) may be applied here (46.28–32) to the fate of the Elect and non-Elect. The contrast between wisdom and folly, however, is native to Jewish Wisdom Literature, the more probable source of the author's concepts.[26] Some other NT passages for comparison include: (with μωρία) I Cor. 1.18, 21; 2.14; (with ἀγνοία) Eph. 4.17–21; (with σοφία) I Cor. 1.24; 2.6–7; Col. 1.9, 28; 2.3; James 3.13–17.

46.32–34 'Indeed the truth which they keep (ⲉⲧⲟⲩⲣⲁⲉⲓⲥ ⲁⲣⲁⲥ) cannot be abandoned, nor has it been'. Wilson and Zandee take the cited Coptic clause as a passive construction (*De Resurrectione*, p. 63), while we translate it as active since it seems to carry further the meaning of 46.30–32. The passage appears to mean that the 'Truth' which the Elect have 'known', and which is the predetermined possession of those who 'believe', is, for the Elect at least, that which cannot be let go. Possession of this 'Truth' and conviction by its

[26] See *infra*, p. 150, n.151.

content are part and parcel of election. Contrast the editors' interpretation of this passage in *De Resurrectione*, p. 33.

46.36-37 'that which broke loose ((and)) became'. Here the substantized relative, ⲡⲉⲛⲧⲁϩⲃⲱⲗ ⲁⲃⲁⲗ, is not reflexive, such as Wilson and Zandee translate it. Moreover, although they translate 'and' without brackets, no conjunction appears in the Coptic. Since the sense of the passage calls for an ⲁⲩⲱ ('and') before the I Perfect, we include it between double parentheses.

46.35-47.1 The logical connection between this passage and what precedes it is difficult to ascertain. Still, some clues may be derived from the form of the lines and from a key expression: The abruptness with which lines 35-38 are introduced raises the question of whether the author is inserting here something from another document. Moreover, a re-translation of the passage into what may be its Greek 'Vorlage' reveals a marked degree of parallelism in its lines:

ἰσχυρόν ἐστι τὸ σύστημα τοῦ πληρώματος,
μικρόν ἐστι τὸ ἀφορίσθεν [καὶ] ἐγένετο κόσμος·
τὸ δὲ Ὅλον ἐστι τὸ περιεχόμενον
καὶ ἦν πρὶν αὐτὸ γένεσθαι.

Despite interruptions, the basic parallelism of the first three lines is sufficient to suggest that this is a citation of a hymnic passage. Since the cosmogonic views expressed are Valentinian, it is reasonable to assume that we have here a fragment of an early Valentinian hymn. The first two lines affirm the eternity and power of the structure of the Divine, i.e. the 'Pleroma', in contrast to the weakness and corruptibility of the 'world' (46.35-38).

The 'All' (ⲡⲧⲏⲣϥ = τὸ Ὅλον) in line 38, we believe, refers to the total group of the Elect.[27] Such is the explicit definition given this expression in Rheg. 47.26-27. Thus, the meaning of 46.38-47.1 is that the 'All', who are of course members of the 'Pleroma', are encompassed by the Saviour (cf. 45.32-34). This elect group, the 'All', pre-existed in the Pleroma before its existence in the cosmic sphere (46.39-47.1).[28] Compare and contrast the meaning of 'All' in *CGT* I, 1-4; *Apoc. Joh.*, Cod. II, p. 22.8-30; and the teaching of Marcus found in Iren., *Adv. Haer.* I,13.

[27] Zandee (*NTT*, 16 (1962), p. 368) and Schenke (*OrL*, 60 (1965), cols. 473-4) also favour this interpretation.
[28] On the notion of the pre-existence of the Elect, see *infra*, pp. 111f. Schenke (*OrL*, 60 (1965), col. 474) concurs in this understanding of the 'All'.

(44) Because of the interpretation accepted in the preceding paragraph, we reject the editors' view (*De Resurrectione*, p. 33) that 46.38–47.1 means: '. . . before (the world) came into existence, it (the All) existed'. Thus, we also reject their efforts to seek parallels to the expression 'before (the world) came into existence' in John 17.24d and Eph. 1.4.

47.1 '(before) it came into being, it was existing ([ⲙ̅]ⲛⲉϥϣⲱⲡⲉ ⲛⲉϥϣⲟⲟⲛ)'. As our note to 46.35–47.1 indicates, we understand the subject of this sentence to be the 'All'. The verb [ⲙ̅]ⲛⲉϥϣⲱⲡⲉ, which possesses the third singular Temporalis prefix, refers to time prior to the cosmic existence of the 'All'. The following Imperfect Tense form plus the Qualitative (ⲛⲉϥϣⲟⲟⲛ) conveys the notion of this 'All's' pre-existence. Contrast with this the editors' 'Note Critique' in *De Resurrectione*, pp. 33–34. The verbal form ⲛⲉϥϣⲟⲟⲛ thus carries no durative meaning since the Coptic Imperfect is not the equivalent of the Greek Imperfect, for the former is used to describe a durative state or action now regarded as completed (see Plumley, par. 194, p. 88). The meaning of ⲛⲉϥϣⲟⲟⲛ is that once the members of the 'All' have come into existence, the 'All' no longer exists in its heavenly state but must be restored to it.

47.1–2 'Therefore, never doubt (ϩⲱⲥⲧⲉ ⲙ̅ⲡⲱⲣ ⲁⲣ̅ⲁⲓⲥⲧⲁⲍⲉ)'. The Greek loanword ϩⲱⲥⲧⲉ (ὥστε) introduces an independent clause, as opposed to expressing result (cf. Arndt-Gingrich, p. 908). Moreover, as opposed to Wilson and Zandee (*De Resurrectione*, p. 64), we take ⲙ̅ⲡⲱⲣ as a deprecatory interjection—'by no means! nay! never!' (cf. Till, *Sah.*, par. 409, pp. 204–5; Crum, 178b; and Till's Coptic Index in *De Resurrectione*, p. 70).

(45) As we shall show (*infra*, p. 131), 'to doubt' (διστάζειν) in our Letter is the opposite of 'to believe' (πιστεύειν), especially of 'belief' in the resurrection. It is probably no coincidence, then, that the author here uses the expression with a meaning similar to what it bears in one of the only two occurrences of διστάζειν in the NT, viz. Matt. 28.16–17:

> Now the eleven disciples went to Galilee, to the mountain to which Jesus had directed them. And when they saw him they worshipped him; but some doubted (ϩⲟⲉⲓⲛⲉ ⲁⲩⲁⲓⲥⲧⲁⲍⲉ).

47.4–8 'For if you did not exist in flesh (ϩⲛ̅ ⲥⲁⲣⲝ), you received flesh (ⲥⲁⲣⲝ) when you entered this world. Why ((then)) will you not receive flesh (ⲥⲁⲣⲝ) when you ascend into the Aeon (ⲁⲡⲁⲓⲱⲛ)?'

The Greek loanword ⲥⲁⲣⲝ̅ retained in this passage is also found frequently in the Sahidic and Bohairic New Testaments (see Böhlig, *GLW*, Register, pp. 96–97). Compare to the thought of believers entering the world—probably from a pre-existent state—the following: *Gos. Th.*, Log. 28.27; *Manich. PsB.* 181.19–24.

Other Gnostic texts also reflect the view that the ascended Elect will have some type of body or 'flesh', as opposed to being pure spirit. Cf., for example, *Pist. Soph.* 145.25ff.; 169.15ff.; *Ang. Rös.* IIIc.13; *Mand. PB.* 49; 379 (Drower, p. 302); and Celsus' description of an Ophite Diagram in Origen, *Con. Cels.*, 6.38.

The phrase 'when you ascend' (47.7–8) is expressed by means of the Conditionalis Tense, ⲉⲕϣⲁⲛ ⲃⲱⲕ. The Conditionalis conveys the meaning of a condition which will probably be fulfilled (cf. Steindorff, par. 492, p. 240). Note, also, that the Greek loanword ⲁⲓⲱⲛ denotes a heavenly sphere or domain to which the Elect ascend, as it does in *Ev. Phil.* 102.1–5 and *CGT* XXX, m.s.f. 112, c.s., p. 20. Cf., to the idea of ascension of the Elect, the following: *Mand. PB.* 54; 379 (Drower, p. 302); *Manich. PsB.* 65.13–14; 81.20–21; 87.3–4; C.H. I.24; *Apoc. Joh.*, Cod. II, p. 1., 26–27. The movement of the resurrection and thus of salvation is upward: ⲁϩⲣⲏ̈ⲓ ⲁϩⲟⲩⲛ ('upward into').

(46) On the basis of the interpretation offered in our note to 46.35–47.1, it would appear that the idea expressed in 47.4–8 is that whereas the Elect pre-existed in the 'All' without flesh, their entry into the world meant taking on flesh. The experience of the Elect thus seems to parallel that of the Saviour.[29] If so, then it becomes possible to see how Gnostic allegory could apply certain NT sayings about Jesus to the Elect, e.g. John 1.14a: 'And the Word became flesh and dwelt among us . . .'; I Tim. 3.16b: 'He was manifested in the flesh, vindicated in the Spirit, . . . taken up in glory.' Cf. also Phil. 2.5–8; Heb. 2.14; 5.7; I John 4.2; II John 7; Rom. 8.3–4.

The editors have argued (*De Resurrectione*, p. 34), and we agree, that the 'flesh' to be received by the Elect in their ascent to the Aeon (47.6–8) must be understood as a 'spiritual flesh'. They relate the concept to Paul's idea of a 'spiritual body' in I Cor. 15.44. But certainly, if that passage did inspire the author, he gave it a twist with the use of 'flesh' which is not Pauline (see below, pp. 148–9).

47.9–10 'What is better than the flesh is for it ((the)) cause *(αἴτιος)* of life'. The immediate context does not inform us as to what is the

---

[29] See *infra*, pp. 112f.

'cause' of life, although it does seem connected with the pre-existent state of the Elect (47.34–35). This 'cause' is definitely not the body (47.34–35), nor is it the visible members which are part of the flesh (47.38–39). Thus, there may be reference here to the inward spiritual man who seems indirectly alluded to in the expression 'living members' which exist within the visible (48.1–3). The spiritual nature of man appears, then, to be the 'cause' of his life. Contrast the view expressed in *Ev. Phil.* 105.11–19.

(47) On the assumption that 47.9–10 implies that the inner invisible 'spiritual' being of man animates his external 'flesh', any one of several NT texts could have been 'eisegeted' to arrive at this view. E.g. John 6.63a: 'It is the spirit that gives life, the flesh is of no avail'; Rom. 8.11: 'If the Spirit of him who raised Jesus from the dead dwells in you, he who raised Christ Jesus from the dead will give life to your mortal bodies also through his Spirit which dwells in you.' Cf. also I Cor. 5.5; 15.50; Phil. 1.21–24; I Peter 3.18; 4.6.

47.17–19 'the afterbirth (ⲡⲭⲟⲣⲓⲟⲛ) of the body is old age, and you exist in corruption'. 'Afterbirth' is a name given the placenta and membranes with which the foetus is connected, and which are expelled after delivery of the foetus. Metaphorically, then, it represents that which has had its useful purpose, but which ultimately is discarded. Thus, 'old age' (47.21–22) is a time of expulsion from life on this earth and in this corruptible 'flesh'. Cf. to this such ideas on the decay of mortal life as are found in *Asclep.* III.27e; the Gospel of the Egyptians (in Clem. Alex., *Strom.* III, 6.45); Philo, *Abr.* 55.

(48) The editors (*De Resurrectione*, p. 35) point out correctly that 47.17–22 reflects the same type of interpretation of Eph. 4.22–24 as we find in Tertullian's *De Resurrect.* xlv.1. Cf., as a background, also Col. 3.9–10. By contrast to 47.18, 'old age' is viewed in the OT as a blessing: Judg. 8.32; I Chron. 29.28; Job 5.26; 42.17. Moreover, 'corruption' (cf. 47.19) is most frequently used in the NT to describe the state of the dead, e.g. Acts 2.27, 31; 13.34–37; Gal. 6.8; and, especially, I Cor. 15.50.

47.19–22 'You have absence *(ἀπουσία)* as a gain (ⲛⲟⲩϩⲏⲩ). For you will not give up what is better (ⲙ̄ⲡⲉⲧⲥⲁⲧⲡ) if you should depart.' ἀπουσία, which is a hapax legomenon in the NT (Phil. 2.12), is synonymous here with departure from the corruptible body of old age. Such departure is a 'gain' for the Elect since he ascends with a new resurrection flesh (47.7–8).

On death as a 'departure' from this world, see II Clem. 8.3; *Ang.*

Rōs. VIIa, 11; *Acts of Th.* |21; 165; *Mand. PB.* 8; 17; 30; 31; 33; 48; 49; 52; 74 (Drower, p. 66); 94; 410 (Drower, p. 314); C.H. X.16.

(49) Zandee (*NTT*, 16 (1962), p. 371) has indicated that in the idea of departure from the body as a 'gain' we probably have an echo of Phil. 1.21, 23: 'For to me to live is Christ and to die is gain (ⲟⲩϩⲏⲩ). . . . I am hard pressed between the two. My desire is to depart and be with Christ, for that is far better (ⳡⲥⲟⲧⲡ̄).' Cf., similarly, II Cor. 5.8–9 and John 13.1a.

47.24 'but there is grace for it (ⲁⲗⲗⲁ ⲟⲩⲛ̄ ϩⲙⲁⲧ ⲁⲣⲁ ⳡ)'. The passage is exceedingly difficult to interpret. The preceding lines equate old age with corruption, describe departure from such corruption as a gain, and state that the 'worse part' of man (presumably the corruptible body) is destined gradually to diminish (46.17–23). However, with ⲁⲗⲗⲁ ('but') does the author indicate a transition to something new or a contrast with what precedes? The object suffix pronoun, -ⳡ of ⲁⲣⲁ ⳡ, shows by its gender that its antecedent is ⲡⲉⲑⲁⲩ ('that which is worse') in 47.22. Thus the author apparently intends a contrast between the diminution of the corruptible part of man and the blessing which still exists for that part. Zandee (*De Resurrectione*, p. 35) thinks that the clause alludes to the resurrection. In support of this, we might note that at his resurrection, the Saviour transformed himself, i.e. something already existent was changed (45.17–18). Moreover, the resurrected one will take on new flesh (47.6–8); and there is apparently a retention of personal identity in the resurrected state (48.6–10). While still unclear, then, there may be in 47.24 the idea that although in life there is a gradual shrivelling and dying of the worse part of man's nature, viz. his 'body', in the resurrection he will retain some of the identifiable characteristics of that corruptible body.

47.24–26 'Nothing therefore redeems us from this world'. This statement, of course, cannot mean that salvation is impossible, for that would be flatly contradicted by most of what has been said in the preceding three pages and by what follows in lines 26–28. Therefore, it must mean that despite the deliverance the Elect already have through Christ, they must still pass through the time of corruptible old age (cf. 48.21–22). This interpretation seems preferable to J. W. B. Barns' conjecture that this may actually be a question (see *JTS*, N.S., Vol. XV (1964), p. 165).

(50) The editors (*De Resurrectione*, p. 35) tell us to compare, 'en un

sens', Rom. 7.24 with 47.24–26; but there is no direct dependence here.[30]

47.26–30 On the meaning of 'All' in this passage see our note to 46.35–47.1; contrast the view presented by Puech (*De Resurrectione*, pp. 35–36). The elect are said to be members of the 'All' in *Pist. Soph.* 57.7–14; 123.6–17; 126.30–34. Compare and contrast the use of 'All' (ⲡⲧⲏⲣϥ) in *Ev. Phil.* 118.35–37; 119.4, 12–13; 124.33–34; *Gos. Th.*, Logia 67 and 77.

(51) Cf., as parallels to 47.29–30, the NT passages Phil. 4.8–9 and I Cor. 14.20.

47.31–36 'But there are some ((who)) wish to understand in the enquiry about those things they are looking into, whether he who is saved, if he leaves behind his body, will be saved immediately.'

For clarification, the relative pronoun 'who' has been added in brackets on the basis of the Coptic parallelism between ⲟⲩⲛ̄ ϩⲁⲉⲓⲛⲉ ⲟⲩⲱϣⲉ in 47.31 and ⲟⲩⲛ̄ ϩⲁⲉⲓⲛⲉ ⲉⲧⲱϣⲉ in 43.25.

The Coptic of 47.32–33, if literally translated, is very awkward in English: 'in the search concerning those things which they seek concerning them'. We, in our translation, have tried to avoid such awkwardness while still attempting to be more literal than the paraphrase offered by Wilson and Zandee.

The statement in 47.34–35, 'if he leaves his body behind', recalls the very common Gnostic theme of the departure of the 'self' from the corruptible body. See, e.g. *Ev. Phil.* |104.26–105.19; *Huw* I.58; VII.22; *Mand. PB.* 9; 96 (Drower, p. 99); 125 (Drower, p. 119); *CGT* XXX, m.s.f. 112, c.s.p. 20; *Asclep.* I.8; III.27; Basilides in Iren., *Adv. Haer.* I, 24.5; Marcion in Iren., *Adv. Haer.* I, 27.3; *Manich. PsB.* 21.12; 66.19–20; 70.28–31; 75.16–17; 98.14; the Sethian-Ophites in Iren., *Adv. Haer.* I, 30; *Apoc. Joh.*, Cod. II, p. 21.8–14; p. 25.19–26.4; p. 26.23–31; The Naassene Exegesis in Hippolyt., *Ref.* V, 8.22–24; Marcus in Iren., *Adv. Haer.* I, 21.5. Cf. also Philo in *Leg. Alleg.* i.107, 108; *Quaest. Gen.* iv.152; *Abr.* 2, 3, 4.

(52) The editors (*De Resurrectione*, p. 36) would compare 47.31–36 in a 'general way' with the questions raised by Paul in I Cor. 15.35–37. We, however, would note that whereas in Paul the questions are about the *kind* of resurrection body (it being assumed that there would be one), in our Letter Rheginos asks how an immediate, bodiless resurrection following death is possible. Consequently, the main

---

[30] In contrast to our Letter, the NT does speak of the possibility of salvation for the world, e.g. in II Thess. 2.13 and John 3.17.

similarity between our Letter and I Cor. 15.35–37 lies in the fact
that both contain questions about the state of the resurrected. Cf.,
instead, II Peter 1.13–14.

47.38–48.3 The opening words of this passage, as the editors have
indicated (*De Resurrectione*, pp. 36–38), present an insoluble difficulty.
We cannot accept the emendation of J. W. B. Barns which would
substitute ⲛ̄ⲛⲉϣ ⲛ̄ϭⲉ for ⲛ̄ⲛⲉⲥ ⲛ̄ϭⲉ, nor can we adopt his proposed
reconstruction of the passage in the form of a dialogue (*JTS*, N.S.,
Vol. XV (1964), p. 165). For, while the 's' sound of both ⲥ and ϣ
might confuse a scribe receiving dictation, it is not likely that such
confusion would arise for a scribe copying directly from or translating
another text. And it is doubtful that a text of this nature was dictated
to several scribes at a time. In accord with the editors, then, we leave
a blank space at the beginning of 47.38 where these words occur.
Even their translation, however, would not seem to alter the sense
materially, for the indirect question resulting would be simply a re-
phrasing or reiteration of the objection already rejected by the author
in 47.33–36.

(53) With regard to the NT and 47.36–48.3, three things are to be
noted: (1) Another occurrence of διστάζειν in 47.36–37 (cf. our note
to 47.1–3) recalls the Matthaean usage of that word in Matt. 28.16–
17. (2) After stating that the preceding context shows that in our
author's thought the body cannot be resurrected, the editors (*De
Resurrectione*, p. 37) ask us to compare I Cor. 15.50, which was often
used by the Gnostics to support this teaching.[31] (3) Mention in 47.38–
48.3 of the inward, invisible, and immortal members (μέλη) which
will be raised recalls the Pauline conception of the 'inner man' (e.g.
II Cor. 4.16—ὁ ἔξω ἡμῶν ἄνθρωπος contrasted with ὁ ἔσω ἡμῶν; and
Eph. 3.16—εἰς τὸν ἔσω ἄνθρωπον). In our opinion, the author has
developed an anthropological dualism out of this facet of the Apostle's
teaching. The key text for comparison is Rom. 7.21–25, where the
usage of μέλη should be especially noted.[32] Cf. to the idea of an 'inner
man' the striking parallels to be found in Plato (*Rep.* IX.589a: τοῦ
ἀνθρώπου ὁ ἐντὸς ἄνθρωπος); in Philo (*Plant.* 42, where 'mind' (νοῦς) is
identified with ὁ ἐν ἡμῖν πρὸς ἀλήθειαν ἄνθρωπος; and *Congr.* 97, where

---

[31] However, as we show below (pp. 146–9), our Letter does entertain the idea
of a type of 'spiritual' resurrection body.
[32] Paul actually interprets 'members' negatively in Rom. 7.21–25 as part of the
sinful flesh. The author of our Letter, however, evaluates 'members' positively!
A. Orbe (*Greg.*, 46 (1965), p. 172f.) also finds belief in an 'interior homo' reflected
in our Letter.

the νοῦς is called ὁ ἄνθρωπος ἐν ἀνθρώπῳ); in the Hermetica (I.18 and 21 : ὁ ἔννους ἄνθρωπος; XIII, 7—ὁ ἐνδιάθετος ἄνθρωπος); and, in Irenaeus' report on the views of the Marcosians (*Adv. Haer.* I, 21.5, where an 'interior homo' is said to ascend at death while the body remains in the world).

48.1–2 'living [members] which exist (ⲛⲙⲉ[ⲗⲟⲥ] ⲉⲧⲁⲁⲛⲅ ⲉⲧϣⲟⲟⲡ)'. The reconstruction of the Greek loanword ⲙⲉⲗⲟⲥ for the lacuna of 48.1 (*De Resurrectione*, p. 37) is supported by the immediate context; for contrast seems implied between the visible, dead 'members' (ⲙⲉⲗⲟⲥ) in 47.38–48.1 and something which is 'inward' and 'living' in 48.2–3. An alternative reconstruction, ⲙⲉⲣⲉ, would have to draw its support from as remote a passage as 46.22. Further, on the meaning of the expression 'living members' see the editors' comments in *De Resurrectione*, pp. 37f.; and, compare the following parallels: *Huw* I.51 (the 'limbs' of those in heaven); *Gos. Th.*, Logia 70 and 80; *Odes of Sol.* XXI.4; C.H. I.15; XIII.14; *Asclep.* I.7b; III.22; C.H. Frag. from Tert., *De Anima* 33; *Manich. Ps.B.* 173.19; *Pist. Soph.* 32.11–12; 45.7–8. Irenaeus, *Adv. Haer.* II, 28, 29, reports that the Valentinians distinguish between an 'indwelling man' and the soul of the individual. Similar views are found in the teaching of Basilides, who speaks of an 'inner man' (Hippolyt., *Ref.* VII, 27.6); of Marcus (Iren., *Adv. Haer.* I, 13.2); and of Ptolemaeus, who teaches of a 'spiritual man' within man (*Adv. Haer.* I, 6.1). In Irenaeus' report of Marcosian worship (*Adv. Haer.* I, 14.4; I.187 Harvey) we find this interesting description of the abandonment of the initiate's earthly body and the ascent of his invisible 'inner man' at death:

> *Alii sunt qui mortuos redimunt ad finem defunctionis, mittentes eorum capitibus oleum et aquam, sive praedictum unguentum cum aqua, et cum supradictis invocationibus . . . ut superascendat super invisibilia interior ipsorum homo, quasi corpus quidem ipsorum in creatura mundi relinquatur, anima vero projiciatur Demiurge.*

48.3–6 'Then, what is the resurrection? It is always the disclosure of those who have arisen'. The substantive ⲡϭⲱⲗⲛ̄ may translate the Greek ἀποκάλυψις or ἐμφάνεια (Crum, 812b). We translate it, 'the disclosure', in order to distinguish it from ⲟⲩⲱⲛⲅ̄, 'revelation' in 48.34. Moreover, in the Sahidic OT the phrase ⲛ̄ⲟⲩⲟⲉⲓϣ ⲛⲓⲙ is used to translate διαπαντός in the underlying LXX text. διαπαντός means 'always, continually, constantly' (cf. Crum, 225a). Thus, the passage means that the resurrection entails making manifest the resurrected form or 'body' of the believer, presumably in the heavenly Aeon to which he ascends. The proof of such manifestation is offered in the following lines through a citation of details from the Marcan Transfiguration pericope.

(54) In connection with 48.3–6, Zandee points to I John 3.10 where φανερός is applied to the manifestation of the children of God. He rules out Rom. 8.19 as a parallel on the grounds that it refers to a future 'eschaton'; he prefers Gal. 1.16: 'was pleased to reveal his Son in me', as referring to a revelation of the Resurrected One 'in the present'. In sum, Zandee wishes to understand 48.4–6 as applying to the manifestation *in the present* of the 'pneumatics' through their acquisition of knowledge (see *NTT*, 16 (1962), pp. 363–4). We completely disagree with this interpretation because of (*a*) the faulty translation of ⲡⲟⲩⲁⲉⲓϣ ⲛⲓⲙ that it presupposes (cf. our immediately preceding note); (*b*) the failure to grasp the real movement of the argument here which it reflects.[33] We would recall, instead, those NT passages where the person who has been or will be resurrected has been or will be made manifest in an identifiable, resurrected, 'spiritual body'. Cf., e.g., Acts 10.40; Rom. 8.19; Col. 3.4; also I Clem. 50.3–4.

48.6–10 'For if you remember reading in the Gospel that Elijah appeared and Moses with him, . . .' Despite the presence of the form ⲟ̅ⲏⲗⲉⲓⲁⲥ (='Ηλίαs) in the text, we see no need to retain the German translation, 'Elias', as do Wilson and Zandee (*De Resurrectione*, p. 65); we prefer the more normal English, 'Elijah' (cf. Arndt-Gingrich, p. 345). Contrast the examples of resurrected man, viz. Moses and Elijah, in this passage with the Philonic conception of the re-absorption of the individual's 'spirit' (πνεῦμα) into the Divine in *Cher.* 113–18; *Det.* 75; *Mut.* 38, 79, 80; *Quaest. Gen.* i.86; *Mos.* ii.288.

(55) As noted earliei (*supra*, pp. 18–20), the passage 48.6–11 contains a fragmentary citation of Mark 9.2–8. Here we present the relevant texts which form the basis of our decision:

Rheg. 48.6–11 (A Re-translation into Greek)

(6) . . . εἰ γὰρ (7) μιμνήσκεις ἀναγιγνώσκων ἐν τῷ (8) εὐαγγελίῳ ὅτι Ἡλίας (9) ὤφθη καὶ Μωϋσῆς (10) σὺν αὐτῷ, μὴ νομίσῃς τὴν (11) ἀνάστασιν ὅτι (ἐστι) φαντασία.

---

[33] See our analysis of this passage and its context, *supra*, pp. 44f.

Matt. 17.3	Mark 9.14	Luke 9.30–31a
καὶ ἰδοὺ ὤφθη αὐτοῖς Μωϋσῆς καὶ Ἠλίας συλλαλοῦντες μετ᾽ αὐτοῦ.	ὤφθη αὐτοῖς Ἠλίας σὺν Μωϋσεῖ, καὶ ἦσαν συλλαλοῦντες τῷ Ἰησοῦ.	καὶ ἰδοὺ ἄνδρες δύο συνελάλουν αὐτῷ, οἵτινες ἦσαν Μωϋσῆς καὶ Ἠλίας, οἱ ὀφθέντες ἐν δόξῃ ἔλεγον τὴν ἔξοδον αὐτοῦ, . . .

COPTIC TEXTS

Rheg. 48.6–11

(6) . . . ⲉⲓϣⲡⲉ ⲁⲕⲣ̄- (7) ⲡⲙⲉⲧⲉ ⲛ̄ⲥⲁⲣ ⲉⲕⲱϣ ϩⲙ̄ (8) ⲡⲉⲧⲁⲅⲅⲉⲗⲓⲟⲛ ⲝⲉ ⲁ̄ϩⲏⲗⲉⲓⲁⲥ (9) ⲟⲩⲱⲛϩ ⲁⲃⲁⲗ· ⲁⲧⲱ ⲙⲱⲧⲥⲏⲥ (10) ⲛ̄ⲙ̄ⲙⲉϥ ⲙ̄ⲡⲱⲣ ⲁⲙⲉⲧⲉ (11) ⲁⲧⲁⲛⲁⲥⲧⲁⲥⲓⲥ ⲝⲉ ⲟⲩϥⲁⲛⲧⲁⲥⲓⲁ.

Matt. 17.3	Mark 9.14	Luke 9.30–31a
ⲉⲓⲥ ϩⲏⲏⲧⲉ ⲁⲧⲟⲩⲱⲛϩ̄ ⲛⲁϥ ⲛ̄ϭⲓ ⲙⲱⲧⲥⲏⲥ ⲙ̄ⲛ̄ ϩⲏⲗⲉⲓⲁⲥ ⲉⲧϣⲁ- ⲝⲉ ⲛ̄ⲙ̄ⲙⲁϥ.	ⲁⲧⲱ ⲁϥⲟⲩⲱⲛϩ̄ ⲉⲣⲟⲟⲩ ⲛ̄ϭⲓ ϩⲏⲗⲓⲁⲥ ⲙ̄ⲛ̄ ⲙⲱⲧⲥⲏⲥ ⲉⲧϣⲁ- ⲝⲉ ⲙ̄ⲛ̄ ⲓ̄ⲥ̄.	ⲉⲓⲥ ϩⲏⲏⲧⲉ ⲝⲉ ⲛⲉⲣⲉ- ⲣⲱⲙⲉ ⲥⲛⲁⲩ ϣⲁⲝⲉ ⲛ̄ⲙ̄- ⲙⲁϥ. ⲉⲧⲉ ⲛⲁⲓ ⲛⲉ ⲙⲱ- ⲧⲥⲏⲥ ⲙ̄ⲛ̄ ϩⲏⲗⲓⲁⲥ. ⲛⲁⲓ ⲉⲛⲧⲁⲧⲟⲩⲱⲛϩ̄ ⲉⲃⲟⲗ ϩⲛ̄ ⲟⲩⲉⲟⲟⲩ. ⲛⲁⲓ ⲉⲛ- ⲧⲁⲧⲝⲱ ⲛ̄ⲧⲉϥϩⲓⲏ.

One cannot but wonder how influential on the author's mode of argumentation may have been Paul's demonstration of Christ's resurrection by appeal to the appearances of the Risen One (cf. I Cor. 15.3–8).

48.16–19 '. . . than the resurrection which came into being through our Lord the Saviour, Jesus Christ'.

(56) There may be a vague echo in this passage of such NT expressions as I Cor. 15.21: 'For as by a man came death, by a man has come also the resurrection of the dead'; or Acts 4.2.

48.21–22 'Those who are living shall die'. As we try to demonstrate below (pp. 114–16) the verb translated 'living' here, i.e. ⲛⲉⲧⲁⲁⲛϩ̄, is always used of the Elect (cf. 47.10; 48.2, 23). Thus, the statement means that the Elect, just as the Saviour himself (cf. 45.19; 45.24–26; 46.14–17), must suffer death (cf. 45.24–26; 45.34–35; 46.7–8; 47.33–36). Such is the natural consequence of life in this world, a life which subjects even the Elect to the corruption of old age (47.17–18). However, the immortal, spiritual nature of the Elect makes death for them only a transitional stage to their ascension into heaven (45.34–46.2).

(57) In the idea that believers must also die (48.21–22), our author would find an affinity in—though probably not direct stimulus from —several NT passages: Rom. 14.8: 'If we live, we live to the Lord, and if we die, we die to the Lord; so then, whether we live or whether we die, we are the Lord's'; I Cor. 15.21–22; II Cor. 7.3; Phil. 1.21; Heb. 9.27.

48.22–23 'How do they live in an illusion?' Here, too, those under discussion are the Elect. Thus, this is not an exclamatory remark, as Wilson and Zandee translate it (*De Resurrectione*, p. 65), but it is a rhetorical question introduced by the particle πῶς (cf. Arndt-Gingrich, p. 739; Böhlig, *GLW*, Register, pp. 94–95). Cf. this picture of earthly existence to that described in C.H., Excerpt IIA, 18.

48.24–27 'The rich have become poor (ⲁⲩⲣ̅ ϩⲏⲕⲉ) and the kings have been overthrown (ⲁⲩϣⲣ̅ϣⲱⲣⲟⲩ), everything is wont to change (ϣⲁⲣⲉⲃ̅ϣ̅ⲃⲉⲓⲉ).' Our translation tries to convey the past tense meaning of the I Perfect verbs more strongly than does that of Wilson and Zandee (*De Resurrectione*, p. 65). Moreover, the verbal prefix ϣⲁⲣⲉⲃ̅- is the Praesens Consuetudinis I, conveying the idea of habitual, repeated action, e.g. 'is accustomed to, is wont to', etc. (cf. Till, *Sah.*, par. 304, p. 155). The agent suffix of this prefix, -ⲃ, does pose a problem. It is either a scribal error in which -ⲃ has been accidentally written for -ⳇ; or, more probably, as was the practice since the period of 'Old Coptic', -ⲃ is exchanged with -ⳇ (cf. Till, *Sah.*, par. 12, p. 40).

(58) There are no literal parallels to 48.24–26 in the NT, but the transitoriness of wealth and the temporariness of earthly rule are common biblical themes. On the former, see Ps. 52.7; Prov. 11.28; Job 15.29; 27.19; Luke 16.19–22; I Tim. 6.17; James 1.10–11; 5.1–4. As a point of comparison for the whole passage the editors (*De Resurrectione*, p. 39) offer Luke 1.52–53:

> He has shown strength with his arm, he has scattered the proud in the imagination of their hearts, he has put down the mighty from their thrones, and exalted those of low degree; he has filled the hungry with good things, and the rich he has sent away empty.

48.28–30 'so that I should not rail at things exceedingly (ϫⲉⲕⲁⲥⲉ ⳓⲉ ⲛ̅ⲡ̅ⲣⲕⲁⲧⲁⲗⲁⲗⲉⲓ ⲥⲁ ⲛ̅ϩⲃⲏⲩⲉ ⲁⲡⲉϩⲟⲩⲟ)'. Although the conjunction ϫⲉⲕⲁⲥⲉ (=ἵνα) normally introduces a final clause, it is difficult to see how this could be construed as the logical conclusion to the preceding, i.e. 48.27–28. Also, in the light of other statements made about the world (e.g. 44.35–36; 45.16–17; 46.10–11, 35–38, and especially 48.15, 23–28), we cannot interpret this statement as a softening of the author's attitude toward the 'world'. Rather, 48.28–30 appears to be a parenthetical remark in which, having just repeated the point he is trying to make (48.27–28), the author concludes that he has said enough on the matter. The Greek verb καταλαλεῖν, which probably lies behind the Coptic here, has the meaning of 'to slander, talk down, rail at' (cf. Liddell-Scott, I, p. 897). Cf. Herm., *Mand.* 2.3 where καταλαλεῖν is denounced as a practice. Finally, the Coptic adverb ⲁⲡⲉϩⲟⲩⲟ probably translates περισσῶς, meaning 'exceedingly, beyond measure, very' (Crum, 736a).

(59) The implied bad connotation given the verb καταλαλεῖν in 48.28–30 may be paralleled from its uses in the NT, e.g. in James 4.11; I Peter 2.12; 3.16; and, especially from its occurrences in the Apostolic Fathers (Herm. *Mand.* 2.2, 3; 8.3; *Sim.* 9.23.2, 3; I Clem. 30.1, 3; 35.5, 8; Polyc., *ad Phil.* 4.3; 2.2; Barn. 20.2).

48.32–33 'for it (the Resurrection) is the Truth, *that which stands firm* (ⲡⲉⲧⲁϩⲉ ⲁⲣⲉⲧϥ̄)'.

(60) As the Coptic of the following phrases will show, the author definitely seems to echo a NT phrase in his expression 'to stand firm': Rom. 11.20b: '. . . but you stand fast (ⲉⲕⲁϩⲉⲣⲁⲧ̄ⲕ̄) only through faith'; I Cor. 16.13b: '. . . stand firm (ⲁϩⲉⲣⲁⲧ ⲧⲏⲩⲧⲛ̄) in your faith'; Phil. 4.1c: 'stand firm (ⲁϩⲉⲣⲁⲧ ⲧⲏⲩⲧⲛ̄) thus in the Lord'. We could also add II Cor. 1.24c; Gal. 5.1; Phil. 1.27; I Thess. 3.8; I Peter 5.12; all of which use similar Coptic constructions for this phrase.

48.34–38 '. . . it (the resurrection) is the revelation of that which exists, and the transformation of things, and a transition (μεταβολή) into newness'. The 'revelation' is similarly linked to an eschatological goal in *Ev. Phil.* 133.18–21.

Cf. to the concept of 'transformation' in 48.35–36 the 'transformation' of the Elect and their souls in the following Gnostic texts: *Odes of Sol.* XVII.13–14; *Acts of Th.* 37; C.H. X.7; C.H. Excerpt XXIII, Sec. 41.

To the idea of 'transition' in 48.37, compare especially C.H. XI.15b. Moreover, on the abstract feminine noun ⲁⲩⲙⲛ̄ⲧⲃ̄ⲣⲣⲉ ('to newness'), which probably translates the Greek καινότης (Crum, 43a), see the *Odes of Sol.* XXXVI.5.

(61) Several clear NT echoes seem present in 48.34–38. First, by the statement that the 'resurrection . . . is the revelation of that which exists . . .' we are reminded of such passages as Rom. 8.19 and I Peter 1.3–5, the latter reading:

> Blessed be the God and Father of our Lord Jesus Christ! By his great mercy we have been born anew to a living hope through the resurrection of Jesus Christ from the dead, and to an inheritance which is imperishable, undefiled, and unfading, kept in heaven for you, who by God's power are guarded through faith for a salvation ready to be revealed in the last time.

Second, we agree with the editors (*De Resurrectione*, pp. xxi and 39) and van Unnik (*JEH*, XV, No. 2 (1964), p. 151) that the expression 'the transformation (ⲛ̄ϣⲃⲉⲓⲉ)[34] of things' in 48.35–36 distinctly echoes the Pauline theme of the 'change' or 'transformation' of the resurrection body. The key text for comparison is I Cor. 15.51–52:

> Lo! I tell you a mystery. We shall not all sleep, but we shall all be changed (ⲧⲛ̄ⲛⲁϣⲓⲃⲉ), in a moment, in the twinkling of an eye, at the last trumpet. For the trumpet will sound, and the dead will be raised imperishable, and we shall be changed (ⲧⲛ̄ⲛⲁϣⲓⲃⲉ).[35]

Third, the term μεταβολή ('transition') in 48.37 appears neither in the NT nor in the Apostolic Fathers. But might we perhaps compare Col. 1.13: 'He has delivered us from the dominion of darkness and transferred us to the kingdom of his beloved Son'?

Finally, the concept of 'newness' (ⲁⲩⲙ̄ⲧⲃ̄ⲣⲣⲉ =καινότητα) in 48.38 seems also to be drawn from Paul. Cf. Rom. 6.4:

> We were buried therefore with him by baptism into death, so that as Christ was raised from the dead by the glory of the Father, we too might walk in newness of life (ϩⲛⲟⲩⲙⲛ̄ⲧⲃ̄ⲣⲣⲉ ⲛⲱⲛϩ̄).

See also Ign., *Eph.* 19.3; *Magn.* 9.1.

48.38–49.4 'For imperishability (ⲧⲙ̄ⲛ̄ⲧⲁⲧⲧⲉⲕⲟ) de[scends]

---

[34] The substantive ϣⲓⲃⲉ may translate ἀλλαγή, ἀλλοίωσις, μεταμόρφωσις, or παραλλαγή (Crum, 551). It most probably translates ἀλλαγή here, as this would have been the form most easily derived from the verb ἀλλάσσω utilized in I Cor. 15.51–52, the most probable source of our author's comment.

[35] The verb ϣⲓⲃⲉ is also used of the 'transformation' of Christ in the Transfiguration pericope, Mark 9.2c: 'he was transfigured (ⲁϥϣⲃ̄ⲧϥ̄) before them' (par. Matt. 17.2).

([ϭⲟⲉϯⲉ]) upon the perishable (ⲡⲧ[ⲉⲕ]ⲟ)'. The substantives ⲁⲧⲧⲉⲕⲟ and ⲧ[ⲉⲕ]ⲟ probably translate the Greek ἀφθαρσία and φθορά, respectively (see Crum, 405b and 405a). Cf., to the passage, the following: Heracleon, *Frag.* 37; *Frag.* 40; *Odes of Sol.* XV.8 ('I have put off corruption by His Name, and I have put on incorruption by His grace'); XXXIII.12; XL.6. Moreover, we accept the editors' conjecture (*De Resurrectione*, p. 40) of ϭⲟⲉϯⲉ for the lacuna occurring at the beginning of 49.1. This is supported by an identical construction in 49.2–3, the balancing clause in this compound sentence.

(62) In the use of the technical terms 'imperishable' (ⲧⲙⲛ̄ⲧⲁⲧⲧⲉⲕⲟ) and 'perishable' (ⲡⲧ[ⲉⲕ]ⲟ), as the editors have shown (*De Resurrectione*, p. 40), the author definitely echoes the language of I Cor. 15.53–54:

> For this perishable nature must put on the imperishable (ⲉⲧⲣⲉ ⲡⲁⲓ ⲉϣⲁϥⲧⲁⲕⲟ ϯ ϩⲓⲱⲱϥ ⲛ̄ⲟⲩⲙⲛ̄ⲧⲁⲧⲧⲁⲕⲟ), and this mortal nature must put on immortality. When the perishable (ⲡⲧⲁⲕⲟ) puts on the imperishable (ⲟⲩⲙⲛ̄ⲧⲁⲧⲧⲁⲕⲟ), and the mortal puts on immortality, then shall come to pass the saying that is written: 'Death is swallowed up in victory.'[36]

49.2–4 '. . . and the light flows down upon the darkness, swallowing it up'. On the victory of 'light' over 'darkness', cf. *Ang. Rōs.* VI.63; *Mand. PB.* 31; 66; 75; and 103. The 'downward' movement of salvation also finds expression in C.H. Excerpt XI.40.

(63) There are no close parallels to 49.2–3 in the NT. However, in several passages 'light' as the element or person of the Divine does enter the darkness of this world for redemption, e.g. John 1.5–9; I John 2.8; Matt. 4.16; Col. 1.12–13; I Peter 2.9.

In 49.3–4 we have a fourth occurrence (cf. 45.14, 19; 46.1) of the Pauline expression 'to swallow up', as it is found in I Cor. 15.54 and II Cor. 5.4.

49.7 'the images (ⲛ̄ⲧⲁⲛⲧⲛ̄) of the resurrection'. The substantive ⲧⲁⲛⲧⲛ̄, as predicate nominative in the non-verbal clause found in 49.6–7, is preceded by the plural definite article, ⲛ̄-. Thus, as opposed to Wilson and Zandee (*De Resurrectione*, p. 66), we translate the article. Moreover, while the editors (*De Resurrectione*, p. 40) think

---

[36] Zandee would have us compare, instead, I Cor. 15.42: 'So it is with the resurrection of the dead. What is sown is perishable (ϩⲛ̄ⲟⲩⲧⲁⲕⲟ), what is raised is imperishable (ϩⲛ̄ⲟⲩⲙⲛ̄ⲧⲁⲧⲧⲁⲕⲟ).' See *NTT*, 16 (1962), p. 372. Cf. also *Diognetus* 6.8; I Peter 1.23.

that ⲦⲀⲎⲦⲚ renders the Greek εἰκών, three matters tend to undercut their view: (1) Crum (420b) shows no instances of εἰκών being translated ⲦⲀⲎⲦⲚ; rather, the Coptic noun normally translates ὁμοίωμα, ὁμοίωσις, or ἀναλογία. (2) The Greek word εἰκών is retained as a loan-word in all twenty passages in which it occurs in both Sahidic and Bohairic Versions of the NT, remaining thus untranslated (cf. Böhlig, *GLW*, p. 312). (3) Even the indigenous Coptic writer Schenute uses εἰκών in its untranslated form (cf. Böhlig, *GLW*, Register, pp. 34–35).

49.8–9 'He (ⲚⲦⲀϤ) it is who makes the good'. All three translations in *De Resurrectione* (pp. 15, 56, and 66) translate ⲚⲦⲀϤ as 'this'. Certainly, the immediate context (48.30–49.9) makes no clear allusion to any individual, but speaks only of the 'symbols' and 'images' of the resurrection. Doubly curious, then, is the use of the third, masculine, independent *personal* pronoun as subject of this non-verbal sentence: (1) it is masculine, not feminine as we should expect if its antecedent were the 'resurrection' (ⲦⲀⲚⲀⲤⲦⲀⲤⲓⲤ); (2) it is a personal, not a demonstrative pronoun. Indeed, none of the major Coptic grammars (Till's, Plumley's, Steindorff's) show any instance of the personal pronoun being used as a demonstrative. Thus, we conclude that ⲚⲦⲀϤ should be translated 'he', probably referring to the Saviour. In defence of this translation it may be pointed out that much of the imagery in 48.32–49.5 is descriptive of the Saviour's work, work which was outlined earlier (e.g. 48.35–38/45.16–19). The 'good' in 49.8–9 must then be understood as referring to the whole process of salvation brought about through the Saviour. Cf. the affirmations that Jesus is he who 'does' and 'proclaims' the Good in *Apoc. Joh.*, Cod. II, pp. 4, 6–7 and in Baruch, cited by Justin in Hippolyt., *Ref.* V, 26. 34.

49.9–16 'Therefore, do not (10) think in part (μερικῶς), O Rheginos, (11) neither live (πολιτεύεσθαι) (12) in conformity with (κατά) this flesh (σάρξ) for the sake of (13) unanimity, but flee (14) from the divisions (μερισμός) and the (15) fetters, and already (ἤδη) you have (16) the resurrection.'

A brief section of exhortation begins here (49.9–16). As opposed to the editors' efforts (*De Resurrectione*, pp. 40–42) to find in this section a number of rather cryptic references to such technical Gnostic ideas as partial 'gnosis' versus full 'knowledge', 'unity' (ἕνωσις) with the Pleroma versus 'divisions' (μερισμοί) of the carnal condition, etc., we believe the text must be understood in the light of the whole context of the Letter. That is, if we are correct in detecting throughout the

Letter objections raised by others concerning the resurrection, objections which Rheginos has shared with his teacher, then this passage must be viewed as the teacher's exhortation to Rheginos to avoid the thought of those who seek to lead him astray. Of course, as in the case of many Gnostic texts, there could be both metaphysical and literal levels of meaning in the passage. Our preference, however, is to try to understand such exhortations in the context of a disciple-teacher dialogue in which the disciple's erroneous thoughts are being rebutted by correct teaching (cf., e.g., 44.3–6; 44.39–45.13; 46.30–37; and especially 47.28–30). The admission of Puech (*De Resurrectione*, p. 42), in the midst of a huge collection of parallels to demonstrate the contrary, that one of these expressions has no metaphysical but rather a more literal meaning is much to be commended.

To continue the preceding discussion, the editors (*De Resurrectione*, p. 41) appear to favour ἕνωσις as the Greek underlying ⲧⲙⲛ̄ⲧⲟⲩⲉⲉⲓ ('unanimity') in 49.13. However, the same abstract Coptic noun is used to translate ἑνότης and ὁμόνοια (Crum, 470a). ἑνότης and ἕνωσις are used in Ignatius (cf. *Philad.* 4; 7.2; 8.2; *Magn.* 1.2; *Polyc.* 5.2; *Eph.* 3.2; 4.2; 5.1; 14.1) to denote mystical union with Christ or the unity of Christians with God or Christ; however, both terms are also used like ὁμόνοια to express 'unity' or 'oneness' of mind, thought, etc. We favour ὁμόνοια since the meaning of 'unanimity, oneness of mind, concord' (e.g. in I Clem. 30.3; Ign., *Philad.* 11.2; Herm., *Mand.* 8.9) suits best the context described in the preceding paragraph. Cf. *Philad.* 8.1, where ἕνωσις, μερισμός, and ἑνότης are utilized together.

The term μερισμός ('divisions'), used as a Greek loanword in 49.14, is frequently used in Ignatius with reference to schisms precipitated by heretical thinkers (cf. *Philad.* 2.1; 3.1; 7.2; 8.1; *Smyrn.* 7.2). The first of these provides an informative parallel to our passage: 'Therefore, as children of the light of truth, flee from division (μερισμόν) and wrong teaching.'

'Fetters' (ⲛⲙⲣⲣⲉ) in 49.15 is probably a Coptic rendering of δεσμός (Crum, 182a), a term which in the NT refers either to burdens imposed by illness (Mark 7.35; Luke 13.16) or to literal fetters of imprisonment (cf. Phil. 1.7, 13f.). Here the concept seems to bear a metaphorical meaning, i.e. the entanglements of false thought. Cf., as approximate parallels, Ign. *Eph.* 19.3; *Philad.* 8.1.

Finally, to the idea of the present possession of the resurrection stated in 49.15–16, compare: *Mand. PB.* 29; C.H., X.9; the Epilogue to *Asclep.* III; also the immortality conferred by Menander's baptism

(Iren., *Adv. Haer.* I, 23.5); *Manich. PsB.* 25.12–14; *Ev. Phil.* 104.18–19; 121.1–5.

(64) There are several possible points of contact between 49.9–16 and the NT: The editors (*De Resurrectione*, pp. 40–41) point to the concept of 'imperfect' or 'partial knowledge' (ⲉⲃⲟⲗ ϩⲛ̄ⲟⲩⲙⲉⲣⲟⲥ or ⲉⲃⲟⲗ ϩⲙ̄ⲡⲙⲉⲣⲟⲥ=ἐκ μέρους) in I Cor. 13.9a, 10, 12 as a source of the author's exhortations 'not to think in part (ⲙⲉⲣⲓⲕⲱⲥ)' in 49.9–10. However, whereas our author treats 'partial thinking' as an evil which can be overcome, Paul recognizes 'partial knowledge' as a lamentable but intrinsic part of finite existence. Cf., rather, II Cor. 1.13b–14a.

(65) The phrase 'to live in conformity with this flesh' (ⲙ̄ⲡⲣ̄ⲡⲟⲗⲓⲧⲉⲩⲉⲥⲑⲁⲓ ⲕⲁⲧⲁ ⲧⲉⲉⲓⲥⲁⲣⲝ) is most likely taken from such Pauline expressions as to 'walk . . . according to the flesh' (ⲉⲧⲉⲛ̄ⲥⲉⲙⲟⲟϣⲉ ⲁⲛ ⲕⲁⲧⲁ ⲥⲁⲣⲝ Rom. 8.4b; II Cor. 10.2); 'to live according to the flesh' (ⲕⲁⲧⲁ ⲥⲁⲣⲝ Rom. 8.5a, 12b, 13). Cf. also Diog. 5.8b and the editors' comments (*De Resurrectione*, p. 41).

(66) There are no significant NT parallels to the concepts of 'unanimity', 'divisions', and 'fetters' in 49.11–15. The editors' attempt (*De Resurrectione*, p. 41) to adduce John 17.23 for comparison is, in our opinion, completely erroneous since the author of our Letter views the 'unity' discussed here not positively but negatively.

(67) As the editors have indicated (*De Resurrectione*, p. 42), the closest NT parallel to the statement in 49.15–16 concerning the present possession of the resurrection by the Elect is found in II Tim. 2.18: '. . . who have swerved from the truth by holding that the resurrection is past already'. Still, it is not difficult to see how a Gnostic interpreter utilizing a tendentious exegesis could deduce such a view from passages like Rom. 6.9–11; Eph. 2.3–6; Col. 3.1–4; John 11.25. Most NT scholars are agreed that Gnostics are combatted in II Timothy.

49.16–30 The editors' 'Note Critique' to 49.28 (*De Resurrectione*, p. 42) begins rather misleadingly by stating that 'two classes of men' are under discussion in this passage. In point of fact, however, the progression of the argument in this section (see our analysis in Chapter II) and the teaching of our Letter on the subjects mentioned[37] show that actually only one class of men is under discussion, viz. the Elect. What is being discussed are the two ways in which the Elect should or should not regard his death and resurrection. The change of

[37] See *infra*, pp. 139–43.

person from second singular to third singular and vice versa in lines 16–30 is a stylistic device used for emphasis. Rheginos is addressed as representative of the whole of the Elect throughout. Clarity for the English reader may be afforded by the substitution of 'you' for 'he'.[38]

(68) On the theme of the inevitability of death even for the Elect, see the biblical parallels we have earlier adduced in our note to 48.21–22. To these parallels we may add Eccles. 3.3; 9.2; John 11.25b. In Eccles. 6.3–6 and 11.8 we find a theme similar to that in Rheg. 49.12–21, viz. that death will come despite one's longevity.

(69) Stressed in the question raised in 49.22–24 is the view that death has already occurred (i.e. 'this'='death'). Such a view could echo several NT statements, e.g. Col. 2.20a: 'If with Christ you died to the elemental spirits of the universe'; Col. 3.3: 'For you have died, and your life is hid with Christ in God'; II Tim. 2.18b: 'If we have died with him, we shall also live with him'. Dr van Unnik (*JEH*, XV, No. 2 (1964), p. 151) would add also Rom. 6.11 ('. . . to be dead to sin . . .'). If such be accepted as a parallel, one could also include Col. 2.11ff. and II Cor. 5.14.

(70) Mentioned again in 49.22–24 is the idea of having already been raised. Cf. on this our treatment of parallels to 49.15–16.

(71) In 49.28 and its immediate context, the editors (*De Resurrectione*, pp. 42–43) find, as noted earlier, two classes of men or modes of existence, viz. 'the living' and 'the dead'. As instances of related terms they adduce the following: Matt. 8.22 and par.; John 5.25; 11.25–26; II Cor. 4.11; Col. 2.13; I Tim. 5.16. Since, as argued earlier, we believe that only one class of men is under discussion, viz. the Elect who need to possess a proper perspective on death and the resurrection, more relevant parallels would be those cited in Section 67 just above.

49.28–33 '. . . why then do I ignore your lack of exercise (-γυμνάζεσθαι)? It is right for each one to practise (ἀσκεῖν) in a number of ways, and he shall be released from this Element (στοιχεῖον)'.

The expressions 'lack of exercise' and need of 'practice' in this passage recall strikingly the theme of 'practising for dying' as it is set forth by Socrates in the *Phaedo*.[39] The same theme makes its

---

[38] The parallels offered by Puech in *De Resurrectione*, p. 43, seem to show that he, too, despite his opening words, supports the view that only one class of men is under discussion here. Zandee's interpretation, *NTT*, 16 (1962), pp. 375–6, agrees with ours.

[39] See, for example, B. Jowett, tr., *The Dialogues of Plato* (Oxford and New York, 1937), Vol. I, pp. 447f., 451f. Against Schenke (*OrL*, 60 (1965), col. 476), we agree

appearance in Philo, *Gig.* 13, 14 and in II Clem. 20.2, 4. Contrast the *Odes of Sol.* XXVI.9: 'Or who can train his soul for life, that his soul may be saved?'

To the idea of release from 'this element' in 49.33, compare the thought of Basilides (Iren., *Adv. Haer.* I, 24.4), who maintains that knowledge of the saving work of Christ and the Father frees one 'from the world-making principalities'.

(72) The substantive ἀγυμνασία, which seems to be the underlying Greek for 'lack of exercise' in 49.28–31, appears nowhere in the NT; although both γυμνάζω and γυμνασία occur. The closest parallel found to the thought of 'practising' for one's eschatological reward is in II Clem. 20.2:

> Let us then have faith, brothers and sisters: we are contending in the contest of the living God, and we are being trained *(γυμναζόμεθα)* by the life which now is, that we may gain the crown in that which is to come . . .

The change from γυμνασία to ἄσκησις in 49.28–31 may be done simply for stylistic reasons, as is apparently the case in II Clem. 20.2–4.

(73) The editors (*De Resurrectione*, p. 44) think that πολυτρόπως in Heb. 1.1 is the 'equivalent' of the expression 'in a number of ways (ⲡⲟⲧⲁⲛ︤ⲧ︥ ⲛ̄ⲣⲉⲉⲥ)' in 49.32. However, the Coptic of Heb. 1.1a (ⲟ̄ⲛ̄ϩⲁϩ ⲙ̄ⲙⲉⲣⲟⲥ ⲁⲧⲱ ϩⲛ̄ϩⲁϩ ⲛ̄ⲥⲙⲟⲧ = 'in many and various ways') offers no support for direct citation.

(74) Whereas in 49.33–34 'element' *(στοιχεῖον)* is singular, in the NT and Early Christian literature the noun always appears in the plural (cf. Arndt-Gingrich, *Lexicon*, pp. 776–7). Thus, we agree with the editors (*De Resurrectione*, p. 44) that Gal. 4.3, 9 and Col. 2.20, 22 are not especially helpful for clarifying our passage. Actually, στοιχεῖον seems to be identified with 'the world' *(κόσμος)* in our Letter, a usage apparently borrowed from the metaphysics of a Gnostic cosmology.

49.36–37 'what at first was'. Literally: 'this which first was'. It is difficult to see how Wilson and Zandee arrive at the translation, 'as he was at first', for the phrase ⲡⲉⲉⲓ ⲉⲧϣⲣⲡ̄ ⲛ̄ϣⲟⲟⲡ without considerable interpretative paraphrase. The expression seems to mean the Gnostic's 'return to his own self' (*De Resurrectione*, pp. 44–45), or it may mean that the Elect receives again that pre-existent state which was his before he came into the 'world'.

---

with Orbe (*Greg.*, 46 (1965), p. 173) that the 'practice' mentioned here has nothing to do with 'sufferings' or martyrdom.

49.38 'trust (ⲦⲘⲚ̄ⲦⲀⲦⲢ̄ϥⲟⲟⲛⲉⲓ).' The underlying Greek here, probably |ἀφθονία, seems contrasted to φθονέω (Ⲙ̄ⲠⲢ̄Ⲣϥⲟⲟⲛⲉⲓ) in 50.8–9. This play upon words in the underlying Greek seems to support strongly the case for viewing 'Rheginos'' text in its present form as translation Coptic. The sense of the passage may be paraphrased: 'as my Lord Jesus Christ trusted me with this information, so you (Rheginos) should not be distrustful of anyone who is with you'.

(75) Dr van Unnik (*JEH*, XV (1964), p. 167) has suggested comparing James 1.5 to the idea of a generous gift of knowledge from the Divine (49.37–50.1). The Christological title 'Lord Jesus Christ' in 50.1 is clearly Pauline.

50.1–4 '[I have] taught you and your broth[ers], my sons, concerning them, while I have not at all omitted any of the things suitable for strengthening you*.'

The probable use of the I Perfect Tense prefix in the lacuna in 50.1 does not make clear whether the author refers here to instruction given previous to this Letter or to that offered in this document alone. We believe both are meant since the teaching of this Letter can hardly be 'everything fitting for the confirmation' of Rheginos and his brethren (50.3–4); yet, the author obviously considers the content of this Letter to be an important supplement to earlier instruction. Certainly, several passages make clear a former relationship between the author and Rheginos: (1) References to Rheginos as 'my son' (43.25; 46.6; 47.3) and to his brethren as 'my sons' (50.2–3) point to a teacher-disciple relationship of prior existence. Rheginos reflects confidence in the author as one whose teaching he trusts and whose further instruction he is willing to seek. Moreover, the author-teacher does not doubt the sincerity of Rheginos' inquiry (44.3–6). (2) Passing allusion is made in 46.8–10 to a 'philosopher' who is so well-known to Rheginos that he need not be named. (3) Only instruction given prior to this Letter makes intelligible the parenthetical rebuke of Rheginos for his 'lack of exercise' (49.28–30).

In 50.2 the expression 'my sons' (ⲚⲀϢⲎⲢⲉ) must be understood as being in apposition to ⲤⲚ[ⲎⲨ], not as a vocative plural. Wilson and Zandee (*De Resurrectione*, p. 67) translate it as the latter. However, our translation: (*a*) eliminates the problem of plural, direct address at this point;[40] (*b*) shows that the phrase 'my sons' actually identifies those in the company of Rheginos; (*c*) finds grammatical support

---

[40] See *supra*, p. 9.

from similar constructions in Coptic (cf. Till, *Sah.*, par. 110, p. 65).

In 50.3 the literal meaning of ⲉⲙⲡⲓⲕⲉ ⲗⲁⲧⲉ ⲛ̄ⲥⲱⲉⲓ is: 'I have not left *anything after me* of . . .' But, since the preposition ⲛ̄ⲥⲁ- is sometimes used to intensify the meaning of a preceding verb, we translate it: 'omitted at all any of . . .' Cf. Crum, 314a.

The phrase 'for strengthening (ⲁⲡⲧⲁⲝⲣⲉ) you' in 50.4 seems to refer, as the editors indicate (*De Resurrectione*, p. 46), to the 'confirmation' of Rheginos and his brethren in the faith, knowledge, and practice of the doctrine. Such a statement may have been conventional for teachers of this period. Cf., e.g., Barn. 17.1. Finally, the author's mention of his other 'sons' (50.2–3) has now led him to a wider circle of reference, viz. 'you' (plural). Rheginos, however, still remains the primary addressee.

(76) The editors (*De Resurrectione*, p. 46) correctly propose that the Greek underlying ⲧⲁⲝⲣⲉ ('strengthening') in 50.4 is probably στηρίζω, which often appears in the NT with the figurative meaning of 'to confirm, establish', or 'strengthen'. Cf. Luke 22.32c; Acts 16.5; 18.23; Rom. 1.11; 16.25; I Thess. 3.2, 13; II Thess. 2.17; Col. 2.5; I Peter 5.10; II Peter 1.12; 3.17.

50.6–7 'my exposition (*ἀπαγγελία*) of the Word (*λόγος*)'.

In the form ⲧⲁⲡⲁⲅⲅⲉⲗⲓⲁ the possessive article, feminine singular, first person ⲧⲁ- has been elided with the initial ⲁ- of the following substantive (cf. Till, *Dial.*, par. 128, p. 30). Thus we translate: 'my exposition'.

Whereas the translators of the official edition understand ⲗⲟⲅⲟⲥ in 50.7 to refer to the 'subject' or 'discussion' contained in this Letter,[41] we would maintain that it refers to the 'Word of Truth' mentioned earlier in 43.34 and 45.3. For the meaning of the phrase see our note to 43.34 and *infra*, p. 131, n. 85.

50.7–8 'for you* when you* ask'. The plural 'you's' here do not indicate a large group of readers; they seem simply a continuation of the plural used in 50.2–4 (cf. our note to that passage). That is, the author informs his addressee, Rheginos, that he will be happy to offer any further instruction or clarification needed by him or his brethren. The plural 'you' denotes the circle of reference of his comment, but is not a form of direct address.

50.9 'who is in your number (ⲉⲧⲏⲡ)'. The Qualitative verbal form ⲏⲡ normally translates λογίζειν='to reckon, count, number'. Since the Qualitative implies a state resulting from the action of the

---

41 See *De Resurrectione*, p. 17 (Malinine and Puech), p. 50 (Till), and p. 67 (Wilson).

verb, the reference seems to be to the other disciples of the teacher who are with Rheginos. Cf. Crum, 526a.

50.10–11 'when it is possible for him to help'. The editors (*De Resurrectione*, p. 47) interpret this sentence to mean that Rheginos should share this Letter with his fellow-disciples '. . . because it can help' (Wilson and Zandee, p. 67)—presumably with their own difficulties concerning the resurrection. This interpretation encounters problems, however, since these same editors have understood the phrase 'my sons' in 50.2–3 as a direct form of address. Is it not strange, on this basis, that in 50.9–11 Rheginos is told to share with his fellow-disciples a letter which apparently (50.2–3) they are already reading? We, on the contrary, find the more natural and grammatical meaning of the sentence to be that Rheginos should not be jealous of the more mature knowledge of some of the brethren who are with him. By discussing his difficulties in understanding the 'Word of Truth' or the teacher's exposition of it with a co-disciple, he may find such a one of help to him. This interpretation also avoids the need for any mental gymnastics in trying to find the antecedent to the suffix pronoun in ⲙ̅ⲙⲁϥ ('for him').

(77) Our author could have found precedent for his view that the strong and more mature should help the weak (cf. 50.10–11) in such a NT passage as I Thess. 5.14. We reject Wilson's offer of Matt. 10.8b as a parallel (*De Resurrectione*, p. 47), however, since it is based on an erroneous translation and interpretation of 50.10–11.

50.11 'Many may look at (into)'. Although the German, French, and English translations offered in the first published edition of our Letter all translate this passage as meaning 'look forward to' in the sense of anticipation and expectation (*De Resurrectione*, pp. 17, 57, and 67), none of the Greek words of which the Coptic phrase ϭⲱϣⲧ̅ ⲁϩⲟⲩⲛ ⲁ- is a translation ever carry this meaning: παρακύπτω, ἐμβλέπω, or εἰσβλέπω (Crum, p. 838). Rather, the fundamental meaning of these verbs is to 'look at' or 'upon' something already present. Since a literal translation of this phrase would imply that many in the *author's* circle are at that moment looking at what he has written, however, the intention of the statement seems best conveyed by use of the subjunctive mood: 'may look into'. Coptic grammar is not prohibitive of such a translation, the subjunctive having no special verbal forms (cf. Till, *Sah.*, p. 164). Thus, unlike the editors, we interpret 50.11–13 not as a command that Rheginos share this letter with his fellows, but as a suggestion that others may desire to see it.

50.13 'to these I say' (ⲛⲉⲉⲓ ϯⲧⲁⲙⲟ).

The demonstrative pronoun ⲛⲉⲉⲓ, which refers to those who may chance to read this letter, is actually the indirect object of ⲧⲁⲙⲟ, the direct objects being 'peace' and 'grace' in the next line. Thus, we translate, 'to these'.

The Coptic verb ⲧⲁⲙⲟ followed by the preposition ⲁ- is generally the equivalent of such Greek verbs as ἀναγγέλλω, γνωρίζω, δείκνυμι, διδάσκω, εἶπον, and παρατίθημι. The general meaning is 'to tell, say, inform, show or point out'. Thus, we think the simple translation 'I say' with the addition in brackets of the verb 'to be' (which must often be supplied in translation of Coptic or Greek) is clearer than Wilson's and Zandee's rendering: 'These I teach concerning peace among them . . .' (*De Resurrectione*, p. 67).

(78) In the valediction found in 50.13–14, '. . . I say, "Peace ((be)) among them and grace",' the editors (*De Resurrectione*, p. 47) say that our author utilizes an epistolary formula found frequently in the Pauline Epistles. While conceding that the terms 'peace' and 'grace' may both be Pauline, we, however, have shown (*supra*, pp. 11f.) that our author does not consciously imitate the Pauline style here. This conclusion is further strengthened by a comparison of the Coptic text of Rheg. 50.14 with the typical Pauline formula:

Rheg. 50.14—ⲁϯⲣⲏⲛⲉ ⲛ̄ϩⲏⲧⲟⲩ ⲙⲛ̄ ⲧⲉⲭⲁⲣⲓⲥ
Rom. 1.17 —ⲧⲉⲭⲁⲣⲓⲥ ⲛⲏⲧⲛ̄ ⲙⲛ̄ ϯⲣⲏⲛⲏ ϩⲓⲧⲙ̄ⲡⲛⲟⲩⲧⲉ

50.15 'I greet you' (ϯϣⲓⲛⲉ ⲁⲣⲁⲕ). As the editors (*De Resurrectione*, pp. 47–48) have shown, the underlying Greek here, ἀσπάζομαι, occurs frequently as an epistolary formula at the end of Paul's letters: Rom. 16.22 (the only occurrence of the first person singular); Rom. 16.16; I Cor. 16.20; II Cor. 13.12; I Thess. 5.26. Cf. also I Peter 5.14; Titus 3.15; III John 15. The Coptic text of Rom. 16.22 supports the probability of a Pauline echo here: ϯϣⲓⲛⲉ ⲉⲣⲱⲧⲛ̄.

50.16 'you*' (ⲙ̄ⲙⲱⲧⲛ̄). The plural 'you' has the collective sense of 'both you (Rheginos) and you other disciples of mine'. Thus, the greeting is extended through Rheginos as primary addressee to those friendly towards the circle of disciples—quite a wide greeting, to say the least! Nevertheless, it is probably not possible to attribute this to an error in translation from the Greek, for throughout the Epilogue the translator has very carefully distinguished between the singular and the plural.

(79) The editors' conjecture (*De Resurrectione*, p. 48) that ⲙ̄ⲙⲁⲉⲓⲥⲁⲛ in 50.16 translates the Greek φιλάδελφος ('fraternal love')

is probably correct. The Greek word appears as a hapax legomenon in the NT, viz. in I Peter 3.8. However, close to our passage is the use of φιλαδελφία in the NT, which denotes love towards a brother in the Christian faith. Note the Coptic texts of the following passages where φιλάδελφος and φιλαδελφία appear: I Peter 3.8—ⲉⲣ̄ⲙⲁⲓⲥⲟⲛ; I Peter 1.22—ⲉⲩⲙⲛ̄ⲧⲙⲁⲓⲥⲟⲛ; Rom. 12.10—ϩⲛ̄ⲧⲙⲛ̄ⲧⲙⲁⲓⲥⲟⲛ; I Thess. 4.9—ⲉⲧⲃⲉ ⲧⲙⲛ̄ⲧⲙⲁⲓⲥⲟⲛ; Heb. 13.1—ⲧⲙⲛ̄ⲧⲙⲁⲓⲥⲟⲛ; II Peter 1.7—ⲧⲙⲛ̄ⲧⲙⲁⲓⲥⲟⲛ. Cf. also I Clem. 47.5; 48.1.

IV

THE TEACHING OF THE LETTER

IN THE FOREGOING CHAPTERS we have established the translation upon which our interpretation of the Letter to Rheginos must be based, we have analysed the movement of thought within that translation, and we have supported the translation with critical and exegetical notes. Our objective in this chapter is to present an exposition of the teaching of the Letter, teaching which has eschatology as its focal concern.

Before proceeding to the exposition, however, it is important to make explicit several controlling presuppositions. First of all, it would seem that in a Letter which is both didactic and argumentative in style a reasonable degree of consistency might be expected in its author's use of key terms, such as 'resurrection', 'body', 'flesh', and 'faith'. Study of these terms, therefore, should provide a sound basis for understanding the Letter's teaching. Second, although we accept the first editors' demonstration of the Valentinian provenance of the Letter to Rheginos,[1] it appears that the only manner in which the uniqueness of its teaching may be discerned over against what has previously been known of Valentinian Gnosticism is to attempt to understand the author's teaching within the framework of the Letter itself. This is to say that although some expressions in the Letter cannot be fully explicated without recourse to parallels from other Valentinian texts, the teaching generally is not so esoteric as to demand constant appeal to such parallels. Rather, careful attention to terminology, explicit statements, implicit ideas, and turns of argument by the author yields, we believe, nuances glossed over by the first editors in their 'parallel hunt' in other Valentinian texts. And these nuances, as we shall show more fully in Chapter V, pose a serious challenge to the Puech-Quispel hypothesis that our Letter was penned by Valentinus himself.

[1] See *supra*, p. ix, and n. 9 on that page.

Finally, the full comprehension of any eschatological system demands attention to four of its facets. To begin with, only when one is cognizant of the state of man and of cosmos presupposed in the system does he properly understand the context in which eschatology is realized. Thus, initial attention will be given to the cosmology and anthropology of the Letter. Secondly, given this context, consideration must be directed to the means by which eschatological goals are achieved, whether these be the activities of a Saviour or the responses of the individual believer. Thirdly, at the heart of any eschatology are the goals toward which an individual, nation, or universe is tending. Therefore, examination of these goals must be part of our investigation. And, fourthly, within any eschatology is an implicit or explicit understanding of time. Therefore, we shall conclude this chapter with a discussion of the temporal dimensions reflected in the Letter.[2]

A. THE SPHERE OF ESCHATOLOGY

1. *The Cosmological Context*

(a) *The 'Pleroma' and the 'All'*

It is evident from the author's scattered comments that he presupposes a certain cosmogonic theory, though this is never fully articulated. Two of the key terms echoing this theory are 'Pleroma' (ⲡⲡⲗⲏⲣⲱⲙⲁ = πλήρωμα) and 'the All' (ⲡⲧⲏⲣϥ = τὸ "Ολον). Although the first of these is never defined in the Letter, several passages provide clues as to its meaning.

The first most important passage is one which we have identified as a stanza from a Valentinian hymn, 46.35–38:[3]

[2] The four facets of eschatology mentioned here are ones which have been determinative of the format of several recent studies bearing on Gnostic eschatology. See, e.g. Robert Haardt, 'Das universaleschatologische Vorstellungsgut in der Gnosis', *Vom Messias zum Christus: Die Fülle der Zeit in religionsgeschichtlicher und theologischer Sicht*, herausgegeben von Kurt Schubert (Wien, 1964), pp. 315–36; Jan Zandee, 'Gnostische Eschatologie', *X. Internationaler Kongress für Religionsgeschichte. 11–17 September, 1960 im Marburg/Lahn*, herausgegeben vom Organisationsausschuss Kommissionsverlag (Marburg, 1961), pp. 94–95.

[3] See our note to this passage, *supra*, pp. 81f. Generally, cross-references of this nature will not be given in the notes of this chapter. When support for an interpretation offered is sought, the reader should consult the analysis in Chapter II, the critical notes in Chapter III, or the Index of Passages at the back of this volume.

Strong is the system of the
Pleroma; small is that which
broke loose ((and)) became ((the))
world.

From this stanza it may be inferred that: (1) the 'Pleroma' existed prior to the world (cf. 44.33–36); (2) the 'Pleroma' stands in opposition to the world, i.e. its 'strength' is contrasted with the world's 'smallness', a condition apparently due to the world's 'breaking loose' from the 'Pleroma', and (3) the 'Pleroma' is a 'system' (σύστημα). Since σύστημα in other classical and later texts means a 'whole compounded of several parts or members' (see Liddell-Scott, *Lexicon*, II, p. 1735), the expression here probably refers to the members constitutive of the 'Pleroma'.[4] Aeons which are called 'Spirit' and 'Truth' (45.11–13)[5] appear to be some of the divine members found in this 'system' of the 'Pleroma'.

Of two other important allusions, the first, 49.4–5—'the Pleroma fills up the deficiency'—indicates that a state of incompleteness (пєϣⲧⲁ = ὑστέρημα, Crum 593a) exists as a result of the breaking off of the world. This thought is elaborated in the second passage, 44.30–33:

. . . through the Son of
Man the restoration (ἀποκατάστασις)
to the Pleroma
might occur, . . .

Clearly implied here is the incompleteness and disjuncture of the 'Pleroma' prior to the Saviour's completion of his work of restoring something (probably the Elect) to it.

The second concept providing insight into the author's underlying cosmology is 'the All'. In the concluding lines of 46.38–47.1 we read:

---

[4] σύστημα appears neither in the NT nor in the Apostolic Fathers, and none of its nine occurrences in the Septuagint are parallel to our text. Moreover, it is not listed as a term peculiar to Valentinian Gnosticism by F. M.-M Sagnard, *La gnose Valentinienne et le témoignage de Saint Irénée* (*Études de Philosophie Médievale*, Directeur Etienne Gilson, XXXVI; Paris, 1947), p. 655.

[5] This interpretation rests on an earlier conjecture that προβολή ('emanation') in 45.12 is descriptive of both the Saviour produced and the activity of production by 'Spirit' and 'Truth'. See *supra*, pp. 66f.

. . . But the 'All' is
what is encompassed. ((Before))
it came into being, it was existing.

Then, in 47.26–29 is found:

. . . But the 'All' which
we are—we are saved. We have received
salvation from ((one)) end of it
to the other.

Though the first editors of our text identify the 'All' in 46.38 with the 'Pleroma',[6] we have argued that the term refers instead to the total number of the Elect, as it seems to in 47.26–27.[7] If so, this would indicate that the whole of the Elect pre-existed within the 'Pleroma' prior to their coming into existence in the world.

One further text is of importance, viz. 48.13–19:

. . . It is more
suitable to say, then, that
the world is an illusion,
rather than the resurrection which
came into being through
our Lord the Saviour,
Jesus Christ.

Since the Saviour brought the resurrection into existence, which as 'truth' is opposed to the 'illusion' of this world (48.10–13), then we must certainly conclude that he has neither been instrumental in nor the instrument of the world's creation.

(b) *The World*

Five rather synonymous expressions are utilized to refer to the earthly sphere: (1) 'place' or 'earthly plane of existence' ($\tau \acute{o} \pi o \varsigma$—44.18);[8] (2) 'world order' or 'world' ($\pi \kappa o c \mu o c = \kappa \acute{o} \sigma \mu o \varsigma$ in 45.16, 30; 46.38; 47.6; 48.15, 28);[9] (3) 'element' or 'fundamental prin-

---

[6] See *De Resurrectione*, p. 33.

[7] See *supra*, pp. 81f. Cf. also the supporting views of Zandee, *NTT*, 16 (1962), p. 368; Schenke, *OrL*, 60 (1965), col. 474.

[8] Cf. Liddell-Scott, *Lexicon*, II, p. 1806; Arndt-Gingrich, *Lexicon*, p. 830. On the long usage of this term in Greek philosophical cosmology, see Helmut Köster, '$\tau \acute{o} \pi o \varsigma$', *TWNT*, VIII: Lieferung 3 (Januar 1966), pp. 191–2.

[9] Cf. Liddell-Scott, *Lexicon*, II, p. 985; Arndt-Gingrich, *Lexicon*, pp. 446–7; Lampe, *Lexicon*, 3, p. 771.

ciple' embodied in this world (στοιχεῖον in 49.33);[10] (4) the 'structure' or 'composition' of this world (σύστασις in 44.36);[11] (5) 'these places', a designation probably denoting the mortality and perishability of the world'[12] (ⲛⲓⲙⲁ, possibly ἐπίκηρος)[13] in 46.9, 11; 47.14, 26. Drawing together passages in which these terms appear, we are able to discern several characteristics of the author's world-view.

The first thing to be noted is the antithetical nature of the world. It stands in opposition to the 'Pleroma' (as we have seen in 46.35–38), to the 'Aeon' (47.7–8), and to the reality and stability found in the truth of the resurrection (48.13–28). The first two contrasts imply the existence of a heavenly realm positioned above and separated from the world, a conception reappearing in 47.4–8 where the 'Aeon' is spoken of as a heavenly sphere within the Pleroma:

> For if you did not exist
> in flesh, you received flesh when
> you entered this world (κόσμος). Why ((then))
> will you not receive flesh when you
> ascend into the Aeon?[14]

A second characteristic of the world is its negative character. Indeed, in a few passages, such as 45.30; 44.17–20; 44.18–19, the earthly sphere is assessed rather neutrally. But this neutral view is offset by a considerable number of negative allusions. As we have seen, because the 'world' has come into being through a disjuncture in the pre-existent 'Pleroma' (44.36–38), it is viewed in 46.36–38 as being 'small' (= insignificant). Moreover, 'these places' (ⲛⲓⲙⲁ) are the locale of faithless philosophers (46.9, 11), and the Elect experience an incomplete existence in them (47.14–15). More significant is the fact that the 'world' is the sphere of the 'flesh' (47.5–6), where old age and corruption are the inevitable fate of all its inhabitants (47.17–26). The 'cosmos' is perishing (45.16–17); it is an illusory place

---

[10] Cf. Liddell-Scott, Lexicon, II, p. 1647; Arndt-Gingrich, Lexicon, pp. 776–7.
[11] Cf. Liddell-Scott, Lexicon, II, p. 1735; Arndt-Gingrich, Lexicon, p. 802.
[12] Cf. Liddell-Scott, Lexicon, I, p. 638.
[13] Crum, Coptic Dictionary, p. 153a, notes that ⲙⲁ with the singular demonstrative ⲛⲉⲓ has been used to translate ἐπίκηρος with reference to life in this world. The editors think that ⲛⲓⲙⲁ translates ἐνθάδε, De Resurrectione, p. 30.
[14] The conception of αἰών in our Letter has basically spatial (as here) and personified (as in 45.18) connotations rather than temporal. It is possible, of course, that spatial and temporal conceptions may be blended in 47.8, but the basic meaning is spatial. On the mingling of these conceptions, see Herman Sasse, 'αἰών, αἰώνιος', TWNT, I (1933), p. 206.

(φαντασία—48.13–16, 27–28) marked by transitoriness and change (48.22–28). It lies in darkness, in need of redemption by the Light (49.2–4).

Finally, several passages imply that the world has an almost active evil character. Although not explicitly stated, the association of many 'dominions' and 'deities' with the 'system' of this world (44.37–38) gives them an evil connotation. One might infer, then, that these powers exercise some evil sway over men. Certainly, divisive teachings of this world seduce and bind the Elect, presumably to existence in this 'cosmos' (49.13–15). But the world's inimical character is made explicit in 49.30–36 where Rheginos is informed of the need to practise diligently in order to free himself from that 'Element' (στοιχεῖον) which seeks to imprison him.

(c) The Cosmogonic Process

From the preceding investigation the major outlines of the author's cosmogony have begun to appear. Prior to the world's creation there existed a 'Pleroma', a system of divine beings, two of whom are named 'Spirit' and 'Truth'. Also within this 'Pleroma' were the whole number of the Elect ('the All') and the Saviour. A disjuncture occurred—how is not described, although it is clear that the Saviour Christ had no part in it—whereby an insignificant part of the 'Pleroma' became detached and formed the world. Apparently this rupture also involved the coming into existence of the Elect. The 'cosmos' into which these Elect are thrust is characterized by its temporariness, fallenness, illusory nature, and binding inimical power. It is understood as being completely antithetical to the divine sphere of the 'Pleroma' and the heavenly 'Aeon', thus a cosmic dualism is presupposed. As a result of the creation of the 'cosmos' and the coming into existence of the Elect, a deficiency (ὑστέρημα) in the 'Pleroma' occurred which can only be overcome through a 'restoration' by the Son of Man.

Although we shall return in Chapter V to a comparison of these ideas with the cosmogony and cosmology of Valentinianism, it may be noted here that they correspond to that type of Gnostic speculation which Hans Jonas has described as the 'Syrian-Egyptian'.[15] In this form of the Gnostic myth, creation and the emanation of inferior deities result from an initial split in the Godhead. The first fundamental movement ('Grundbewegung') of the myth is a fall downward

15 Gnosis, I, pp. 255ff.; The Gnostic Religion, pp. 236f.

from a former state of perfection and the resultant enslavement of man and the cosmos.[16] As a result, human existence is viewed as a mistake, worldly life an illusion, and the world a prison.[17] Some striking differences are evident in our Letter, however, including the facts that nothing is ever said about the cause of this fall, and no 'dramatis personae' are named. Especially noticeable are the omissions of any mention of the highest Deity or of the agent (whether male Demiurge or female Sophia) of creation.

2. The Anthropological Context

(a) The Pre-Existence of the Elect

Presupposed in the author's view of the nature of the Elect is an understanding of their pre-existence. This is clear from an allusion treated earlier (p. 108) to the pre-existence of the 'All', viz. the total number of the Elect. (46.38–47.1). It is also assumed, it seems, in the author's assurance to Rheginos in 47.4–6:

> For if you did not exist
> in flesh, you received flesh when
> you entered this world.

If this interpretation be correct, then the previous existence of the Elect may be seen to parallel that of the Saviour, as mentioned in 44.34–36:

> originally He (the Saviour) was from above,
> a seed of Truth,[18] before
> this structure had come into being.

This view makes intelligible two other passages. The first of these, 46.10–13, points up the erroneous attitude of the philosopher who believes that he is able to 'return himself' by his own effort. The second, 49.30–36, indicates that by practice the Elect man may secure release from this worldly 'element, so that he . . . shall receive himself again what at first was'. The idea of 'return' conveys the notion of a prior existence which has been lost and is sought again; whereas,

[16] *Gnosis*, I, p. 5.

[17] Cf. the general Gnostic view of the world and man as presented by Hans Jonas, 'Gnosticism', *A Handbook of Christian Theology*, eds. Marvin Halverson and Arthur A. Cohen (New York, 1958), pp. 144–7; by Jan Zandee, 'Gnostic Ideas on the Fall and Salvation', *Numen*, Vol. XI, Fasc. 1 (January 1964), pp. 13–74.

[18] A number of striking Valentinian parallels to the phrase '. . . from above, a seed of the Truth' are collected by the editors in *De Resurrectione*, p. 24.

that which may be 'received again' is most probably the original, pre-existent state of the Elect.[19]

(b) The Dualistic Nature of Man

Since the conception of man's physical, spiritual, and mental make-up held by the author was apparently already familiar to his pupil, Rheginos, no explicit anthropology is set forth in our Letter. Consequently, it is only through careful consideration of certain fundamental concepts, again, that we are able to discern something of that anthropology. These concepts include: 'flesh' (ⲧⲥⲁⲣⲝ = σάρξ); 'body' (ⲡⲥⲱⲙⲁ = σῶμα); 'members' (ⲛ̄ⲙⲉⲗⲟⲥ = μέλη); 'thought' (ⲡⲙⲉⲩⲉ = ἔννοια?); 'mind' (ⲡⲛⲟⲩⲥ = νοῦς). The three concepts, 'spiritual' (πνευματική), 'psychic' (ψυχική) and 'fleshly' (σαρκική) are also used in the Letter (45.39–46.2) and are interpreted by Puech and Quispel as referring to the exclusion of soul and flesh by the 'spiritual resurrection'.[20] However, as we have shown earlier (pp. 74f.), the underlying Greek syntax of this passage (45.39–46.2) makes clear that the author speaks here of three types of resurrection rather than three aspects of man's nature. These three we shall consider later under our treatment of the resurrection.

'Body' and 'Flesh'

The manner in which the terms 'body' and 'flesh' are utilized indicates that for the author of our Letter they denote the external, corruptible nature of man. The 'body', for example, is said to encompass the 'visible, outward members' (47.17–20) and presumably the 'flesh', as well. Life in this 'body' has as its inevitable result 'old age' and 'corruption' (47.11–13, 17–19). Its inherent mortality seems referred to in 48.38–49.2:

> For imperishability
> de[scends] upon the
> *perishable.*

Further, the 'redeemed' leaves the 'body' behind at death (47.33–36), and the resultant 'absence' (ἀπουσία) from the 'body' is considered a 'gain' (47.17–20). Thus, it is obviously not the 'better part' of the Elect man's nature (47.21–22).

The 'flesh', too, is viewed negatively. It characterizes the temporary earthly mode of existence shared by both the Saviour and the

---

[19] See our notes to 46.8–13 and to 49.36–37 in Chapter III.
[20] See *De Resurrectione*, pp. xx and xxiv.

Elect. For, as we have seen, neither of these possessed 'flesh' in their pre-existent state (see above, p. 111), although earthly life for both the Saviour (44.13–15) and Rheginos (47.4–6) entailed the 'taking on' of 'flesh'. Thus, in 44.24–26, we read of the Saviour that:

> He embraced both of them,
> possessing the
> *humanity* and the divinity.[21]

And, just as with the 'body', so also this earthly 'flesh' is abandoned at death (47.6–8), to be replaced by a new, resurrection 'flesh' (47.7–8).

Two other texts underscore the corrupt and evil nature of the 'flesh'. The first of these, 47.9–10, makes clear that 'flesh' is not only an inferior portion of man's nature but also a part without life in itself, for something else animates it:

> What is better than the flesh *(σάρξ)* is
> for it ((the)) cause *(αἴτιος)* of life.

In the second passage, 49.9–16, Rheginos is warned against living 'in conformity to the flesh', the implication being that life κατὰ σάρκα is—as in Rom. 8.4–5, 12–13; II Cor. 10.2—unredeemed life.[22] Thus, the 'flesh' represents both the outward, corruptible nature of man, as well as the sphere of error and death.

'Members', 'Mind', and 'Thought'

Three other important concepts in the Letter give evidence of the author's understanding of a second nature in man which stands in opposition to 'body' and 'flesh'. 'Members', 'mind' and 'thought' are representative of an inward, incorruptible nature. The clearest expression of this dualism is found in 47.38–48.2:

> . . . indeed, the visible members *(μέλη)*
> which are dead shall
> not be saved,

[21] It is difficult in the light of such passages to see how the editors could conclude that our Letter presents a thorough-going docetic Christology. The overwhelming desire to identify the Letter with the Oriental School of Valentinianism has apparently led the editors' interpretation here. See, e.g., *De Resurrectione*, pp. xxiiiff. What our text does support is a Christology which maintains that the Saviour used a body of flesh only temporarily while on earth.

[22] For the parallelism between the expression 'in conformity to the flesh' (or, 'according to') in our Letter and in Paul, see section 65 of the New Testament echoes, *supra*, p. 97.

((only)) the living [members] which exist within
them would arise.

Here the invisible, inward members—probably to be identified with
the 'spiritual nature' to be redeemed (45.39–46.2)—are retentive of
immortality.[23] Such a nature is probably also alluded to in 45.19–21
where the Saviour by his resurrection is said to have 'swallowed up
(i.e. destroyed) the visible by the invisible'.[24]

But in addition to these 'members', the 'mind' and its 'thought'
also survive after death.[25] Saving 'belief' in and 'knowledge' about
the Saviour are the functions of this 'mind' (46.15–17, 24).

(c) The Events of Life and Death

For a full understanding of the anthropology presupposed by the
author of our Letter, two other concepts of consequence remain to be
considered, viz. 'life' and 'death'. Because of certain subtleties over-
looked in previous interpretations, we shall treat each separately.

'Life'

The Coptic translator of the Letter to Rheginos uses two words for
the concept 'life' as it appears in his Greek original: πεειβιος (οὖτος
ὁ βίος) in 45.35 and 49.20; πωωνϩ (probably = ζωή) in 47.10;
48.2, 21 and 23.[26] More than being synonyms utilized for stylistic
reasons, however, these two expressions actually seem to denote two
qualitatively different types of life in the author's thought.[27] The
reasons for such a conclusion are as follows:

(1) The Sahidic New Testament, probably the most influential
factor in the shaping of early Coptic Christian vernacular,[28] normally retains the Greek loanword βιος, e.g. in Mark 12.44; Luke
8.14; II Tim. 2.14; I John 2.16; 3.17. Never, however, is βίος translated by the Coptic ωνϩ.[29] On the other hand, various forms of the
Coptic ωνϩ are predominantly translations of the Greek ζάω or ζωή:

[23] The editors have assembled numerous Gnostic parallels to the expression
'living members'. See De Resurrectione, pp. 37f. Of course, our summation here rests
on the supposition that the reconstruction of μελος for the lacuna in 48.2 is correct.

[24] On the meaning of the phrase 'to swallow up', see infra, p. 121.

[25] The idea of an immortal νοῦς, distinct from soul and body, which survives is
an Aristotelian teaching, as well. See Erwin Rohde, Psyche: The Cult of Souls and
Belief in Immortality among the Greeks, Translated from the Eighth Edition by W. B.
Hillis (London, 1925), pp. 493ff.

[26] The last three passages all utilize the Qualitative form ανϩ.

[27] See our note to 48.21–22, supra, pp. 90f.

[28] Cf. Arthur Vööbus, Early Versions, p. 214.

[29] See, on this, René Draguet, Index Copte et Grec-Copte, 16 (CSCO, 1960), p. 68.

(*a*) the verb ⲱⲛ̅ϩ̅ (of 63 occurrences, 46 translate some form of ζῆν);
(*b*) the Qualitative ⲟⲛ̅ϩ̅ (of 92 occurrences, 90 translate ζῆν, the other
two ζωή); (*c*) the substantive ⲱⲛ̅ϩ̅ (of 136 occurrences, 128 translate
ζωή).[30] It would appear, then, that these two words, ⲃⲓⲟⲥ and ⲱⲱⲛ̅ϩ̅,
as used by the author of our Letter point to two different Greek
words. The balance of probability is against considering them as
synonyms.

(2) The contexts of both passages in which βίος occurs place it in
association with physical death and the κόσμος. Thus, in 45.35 βίος is
said to be terminated in the 'setting', i.e. the death of the faithful
(cf. 45.28ff.). And, in 49.20 this βίος, despite the extent of its longevity, is still ended by death. From the larger contexts of these passages we learn that βίος is that plane of existence out of which the
Elect passes into the heavenly Aeon through his 'spiritual resurrection' (45.35ff.); βίος is also that sphere of being over against which
one is to live as though it were already passed and completed (49.17–
24). βίος thus derives its essential quality from its association with
death; it is that type of life characterized by a limited duration. Such
a view shows affinity with uses of βίος in the New Testament and
Early Christian literature where it denotes the earthly life and its
duration, e.g. I Peter 4.3; II Clem. 20.2.

Moreover, both occurrences of βίος are preceded by the demonstrative pronoun ⲡⲉⲉⲓ, which probably translates οὗτος. The demonstrative may have a note of contempt in it, such as we find to be the
case in the New Testament (Matt. 26.61; John 9.28; I Cor. 6.11).[31]

(3) The Coptic ⲡⲱⲱⲛ̅ϩ̅, however, which we have shown to be a
probable translation of ζωή, appears to represent life as especially
qualified by its association with the spiritual and hence redeemed
nature of believers. Two passages make this clear, viz. 47.9–10 and
47.38–48.3:

> What is better than the flesh is
> for it ((the)) cause of life (ⲡⲱⲱⲛ̅ϩ̅).
>
> . . . indeed, the visible members
> which are dead shall

[30] Michel Wilmet, *Concordance du Nouveau Testament Sahidique. II. Les Mots
Autochtones. 2.* ⲟ -ⲱ (*CSCO*, Vol. 183, Subsidia, Tome 13; Louvain: Secretariat du
Corpus *CSCO*, 1958), pp. 1138–45.
[31] See William Douglas Chamberlain, *An Exegetical Grammar of the Greek New
Testament* (New York, 1954), p. 47. Also, cf. Arndt-Gingrich, *Lexicon*, p. 601,
1.b., ζ.

not be saved,
((only)) the living (ⲁⲁⲛ̅ϩ̅) [members] which exist within
them would arise.

In the first of these, ⲡⲱⲱⲛϩ̅ is that which animates the 'flesh', but
the real 'cause' of this 'life' resides in the better, spiritual nature.[32]
The second text makes this more explicit, i.e. 'life' is the special
quality of the inward, invisible 'members' (i.e. the spiritual nature
which shall arise).

Two other passages making use of forms of the root ⲱⲱⲛϩ̅ are
apparently understood in a negative way by the first translators of
the Letter. That is, their rendering of 48.22–23 as an exclamation
instead of a question introduced by πῶς seems to convey the translators' view that those spoken of there and in 48.21 are not the Elect
but the unspiritual men.[33] But if our analysis is correct, we may
understand these lines as referring instead to the Elect. Thus we read
in 48.21–23:

> . . . Those who are
> living (ⲛⲉⲧⲁⲁⲛ̅ϩ̅) shall die. How *(πῶς)*
> do they live (ⲉⲧⲁⲛ̅ϩ̅) in an illusion?

Understood on this basis, the passage means that those possessing ζωή,
the 'life' of the redeemed spiritual nature of believers, must themselves anticipate death (cf. 45.34–35; 49.16–30). The question then
follows: How is that world an illusion in which these ζωή-possessors
live? In sum, the possession of ζωή (ⲡⲱⲱⲛϩ̅) does not insure against
death, the inevitable fate of Elect and non-Elect alike; but it does
guarantee immortal 'life' following death. Death, then, becomes only
a necessary entrance way into the resurrected state.

If the foregoing be correct, then our author speaks of two types of
life which are both possessed by the believer, but which are qualitatively different: (1) that life (ⲃⲓⲟⲥ) bound up with earthly existence
which is especially qualified by the death that terminates it; (2) that
life (ⲡⲱⲱⲛϩ̅) associated with the redeemed, spiritual nature of the
Elect which is especially qualified by the resurrection proceeding
from it. This latter type shows some close affinities with the Johannine
view of ζωή (e.g. John 5.40; 10.10; 11.25f.; 20.31).[34]

---

[32] Cf. our note to 47.9–10, *supra*, pp. 83 f.

[33] See *De Resurrectione*, p. 13 (French), p. 55 (German), and p. 65 (English).

[34] Cf. the comments of C. H. Dodd on 'eternal life' in his *The Interpretation of the
Fourth Gospel* (Cambridge, 1954), pp. 144–50.

'*Death*'

Death, then, is the cessation of earthly 'life' (βίος), that which is diametrically opposed to 'life' (ζωή). Its primary expression in our document is through various forms of the Coptic root ϻⲟⲩ ('death'), although there are several metaphorical usages which also indicate dying. The most important texts are those in which ϻⲟⲩ appears as an intransitive verb (ἀποθνῄσκειν)—48.22; 49.17, 19, 27, 28; as a Qualitative form of the verb (probably νεκρός)—46.7, 17; 47.39; and, as a masculine substantive (θάνατος)—44.21, 28; 45.15, 35; 46.19.[35] In addition, there are relevant metaphorical expressions: 'departure' (47.22), 'absence' (ἀπουσία—47.20), 'to leave the body behind' (47.34–35), 'suffering' (45.25), and 'release' (49.33).

The first thing to note about our author's view of death is that he considers it the inevitable destiny of both Elect and non-Elect and that the Saviour, too, participated in it! This is made plain in 45.32–35:

> . . . and we are
> enclosed by
> him (the Saviour) until our setting, that is to say,
> our death in this life.

Use of the first person plural, 'we', here makes clear that the author is affirming that he and others redeemed by the Saviour must experience death. The same idea appears elsewhere: 48.21–22 ('they', i.e. the faithful who possess ⲱⲱⲛϩ̄); cf. 47.23–25. The Son of Man, too, has 'arisen from among the dead' (46.16–17), the clear implication being that he has also participated in death.[36] Such experience is a possible corollary to his possession of 'humanity' (44.26) and 'flesh' (44.14–15). A similar inference may be drawn from the statement in 45.25–26 that the Elect '. . . suffered with Him (the Saviour)'. 'Suffered', which is most likely a translation of συνεπάθομεν, seems to be a euphemistic way of indicating the Saviour's death.

A crucial but exceedingly difficult passage for understanding the nature of death occurs in 44.17–21. It is necessary to give it con-

---

[35] Our citations of the Greek underlying these various forms of ϻⲟⲩ are based upon probabilities derived from the usage of translators of the Sahidic New Testament. Thus, the verb ϻⲟⲩ translates ἀποθνῄσκω 112 out of 171 occurrences of the Greek verb; the Qualitative ϻⲟⲟⲩⲧ translates νεκρός 116 out of 119 occurrences of the Coptic verb; the substantive ϻⲟⲩ translates θάνατος 116 out of 120 occurrences of the Coptic verb. Cf. Wilmet, *Concordance*, (*CSCO*), Tome II, pp. 337–48.

[36] See our exegetical comment on this passage, *supra*, p. 78.

siderable attention. The passage, whose subject is Christ, runs as
follows:

> . . . He lived
> in this place where you
> remain, speaking
> about the Law *(νόμος)* of Nature *(φύσις)*. (But I
> call it 'Death'.)

As noted earlier, the official edition of the Letter gives the appearance
of a 'house divided against itself' in its interpretation of this passage.
We, however, have argued on the basis of Coptic syntax that the
words—'But I call it "Death" '—are actually the author's own
parenthetical remark, qualifying what he states to have been part of
the Lord's teaching.[37] Important to consider in the interpretation of
the passage are the following matters:

(1) Puech and Quispel are correct in stating that it is 'vain' to
seek a parallel to this saying in the Synoptic tradition.[38] Neither in
the eighteen occurrences of 'Law' in Matthew and Luke (there are
none in Mark) nor in the thirteen occurrences of it in John do we
find mention of a 'Law of Nature' or anything comparable. Nor do
we find anything like it in those passages in which 'Law' is not expressly mentioned, but is obviously under discussion.[39] Moreover,
while Christ's teaching on the 'Law' in the Synoptics reflects an
ambiguity between criticism (e.g. Luke 16.16; Matt. 11.11–13) and
affirmation (e.g. Matt. 5.17ff.; Luke 22.15–16), the parenthetical
remark in our Letter indicates that the author understood Jesus'
teaching on the 'Law of Nature' to be strictly negative.

(2) Another suggestion by the editors could be correct, i.e. that
the author has here been influenced by certain Pauline views. But if
this were the case, his attitude would reflect an incomplete understanding of Paul's position on the Law. That is, by failing to note
what Paul says positively about the Law (e.g. Rom. 3.31; 7.12, 14;
8.7) and by attention only to his very negative views (e.g. Gal.
3.10ff.; Rom. 3.20–21; 4.15), the author could have concluded that

---

[37] The conflicting interpretations of 44.20–21 offered by the editors are quoted
supra, p. 59. Our arguments for the interpretation offered here are presented in our
note to 44.21, pp. 58f.

[38] See *De Resurrectione*, p. 22.

[39] These passages are dealt with by Walter Gutbrod in his article, 'νόμος',
TWNT, IV (1942), pp. 1051–7.

Paul spoke of the Law in a completely negative way. This interpretation would then have been attributed to Jesus.

(3) We do find ourselves in disagreement, however, with another of the first Editors' suggestions, viz. that the 'Law of Nature' may be related to Philo's conception of a natural Law assimilated to the Mosaic. We are able to find no reference whatsoever in Philo relating the 'natural law' to man's death.[40] Rather, the 'Natural Law' is always positively assessed by Philo.[41]

(4) The difficulty of finding clear parallels to our author's expression in 44.20–21 raises the question of whether the reference really is to the Mosaic Law. For, if such were the case, it would seem that a libertine ethic might be taught in the Letter in contradiction to such a Law; however, we seem to find just the opposite in 49.28–36. Also, if the Mosaic Law were meant, one would expect an allusion somewhere to the inferior God who created this Law. But, in fact, there is no allusion whatsoever to God, either negative or positive. This raises the further question of whether the context provided by the subject matter of the Letter as a whole might not help illuminate the meaning of the phrase 'Law of Nature'. To this consideration we now turn.

From beginning to end the author's concern in our Letter is with one single theme: the nature and reality of the resurrection. It seems reasonable, therefore, to infer that 'Law of Nature' has something to do with this theme. A 'Law of Nature' which could be interpreted as a 'Law of Death' must pertain to the inevitable fate in which either man's 'nature' or that 'nature of things' in which man finds himself has involved him. That is, it is by some 'natural condition' that man is destined for death, a condition from which only the resurrection can bring release. Indeed, such a condition is spoken of by Josephus who says in his *Antiquities*, 4.322, that one should not grieve himself over death:

[40] See those passages cited by Joannes Leisegang, *Philonis Alexandrini Opera Quae Supersunt* (Vol. VII, *Indices ad Philonis Alexandrini Opera*; Berolini: Pars I, 1926; Pars II, 1930), p. 551.

[41] See Erwin R. Goodenough, *By Light, Light* (New Haven, 1935), pp. 49–58, 69–71, 349–50. The editors of *De Resurrectione* in their allusion to the treatment of 'Natural Law' as identified with the Mosaic in Harry A. Wolfson's volume, *Philo. Foundations of Religious Philosophy in Judaism, Christianity, and Islam* (2 Vols.; Cambridge, Mass., 1947), have apparently cited the pages given in the Index of Wolfson's work (see p. 522) without checking the passages themselves. This Index contains a typographical error referring the reader to Vol. I instead of Vol. II where the discussion actually appears. The editors have reproduced this error, referring the reader to Vol. I. See *De Resurrectione*, p. 23.

ὡς κατὰ βούλησιν αὐτὸ πάσχοντας θεοῦ καὶ φύσεως νομῷ.[42]

And from the Christian sphere we find Tertullian saying about Christ in his *Adversus Marcionem*, III.8:

> Porro, si caro eius negatur, quomodo mors eius adseueratur, quae propria carnis est passio, per mortem reuertentis in terram, de qua est sumpta, secundum legem sui auctoris?[43]

The same sort of idea is expressed in several of the parallels offered by the editors from various Gnostic texts,[44] although for the reasons we have just reviewed, we do not think it probable that the reference in 'Rheginos' is to the Mosaic Law.

If the preceding line of argumentation be followed, then there is less reason to conjecture that an apocryphal gospel saying of Jesus may be reflected in Rheg. 44.20–21. As we have seen earlier (pp. 18–21), our author never exactly cites the New Testament, and he often imparts his own ideas to whatever citations he makes. It seems likely, therefore, that in this passage, the author has attributed to Jesus a philosophical teaching derived from another sphere. This teaching would be that every man is subject by his very humanness to a 'Law of Nature', i.e. a Law of increasing corruption and decay. The author sums it up in a word: it is a Law of 'Death'! Such an interpretation would be quite in harmony with the teaching of our Letter on death.[45]

The second thing about death is that it involves the extinction of life in the body and entails separation from it. Both of these ideas appear in 47.30–48.1:

> But there are some ((who)) wish to
> understand in the enquiry about
> those things they are looking into, whether
> he who is saved, if he leaves behind

---

[42] The passage is cited by Gutbrod, *TWNT*, IV, p. 1043. Josephus makes a distinction here between the Mosaic and the 'natural' Law.

[43] The text is cited from Aemilii Kroymann, *Quinti Septimi Florentis Tertulliani Opera* (*Corpus Scriptorum Ecclesiasticorum Latinorum*, Editum Consilio et Impensis Academiae Litterarum Caesareae Vindobonensis, Vol. XXXXVII, Pars III; Lipsiae, 1906), pp. 389–90, lines 29–32.

[44] Cf. *De Resurrectione*, pp. 22–23. The parallels cited are mainly from the *Excerpta ex Theodoto* and Heracleon's *Commentary on John* preserved by Origen.

[45] See *supra*, pp. 117f. A. Orbe, *Greg.*, 46 (1965), p. 172, also interprets 44.20–21 as referring to a physical law rather than the Mosaic.

his body *(σῶμα)*, will
be saved immediately? Let
no one be given cause to doubt concerning this,
. . . indeed, the visible members
which are dead shall
not be saved, . . .

From this passage it is clear that death involves disengagement from the corruptible body (cf. 47.17–22), and that the body from which one is separated is recognizable by its dead, visible members (47.38–39).

But third, and most important for understanding our author's view, is the affirmation that death is no longer to be feared. It has lost its power, having been conquered by the Saviour as Son of Man (44.27–29). This was accomplished by his rising from among the dead, becoming thereby 'the destruction of death' (46.15–19). Another way of expressing it is that 'the Saviour swallowed up death' (45.14–15), an expression undoubtedly drawn from Paul (e.g. I Cor. 15.54 and II Cor. 5.4) and having a long Old Testament usage denoting divine punishment or natural destruction, often by earthquake (cf. Ps. 21.9; Prov. 1.12; Ex. 15.12; Num. 16.32; Deut. 11.6; Job 37.20; Isa. 9.16; Jer. 51.34, 44). Isaiah 25.8, which is used by Paul in I Cor. 15.54, is especially similar to our author's thought. Confidence in death's final defeat is reflected in the firm declaration: 'He who is dead shall arise' (46.7–8). Consequently, we must understand that although death is the expected lot even of the Elect, it has been made nothing more than a transitional stage to the spiritual resurrection.

The fourth aspect of the author's teaching on death is the recognition that its defeat by the Saviour carries with it the demand for a new attitude. It is necessary to be cognizant of death's inevitability, to know that it must come regardless of one's longevity (49.17–24). But knowledge of the Saviour's victory should provide incentive to practise diligently the things that will free one from the inimical power of the world (49.25–33). Finally, the goal of such living is 'release' from this 'worldly power' (49.30–36), 'release' being a metaphorical expression for death.[46] It involves 'departure' and 'absence' from the body (47.19–22).[47]

[46] Crum, *Coptic Dictionary*, pp. 326–33a, notes that the Coptic which here means 'release', i.e. ⲃⲁⲗ ⲁⲃⲁⲗ, often translates the Greek ἀναλύειν in the sense of 'being released by death'.
[47] As the editors have indicated in *De Resurrectione*, p. 35, the idea of ἀπουσία as a

In his views on death, then, the author of our Letter reveals two decisive differences from the Apostle Paul whose language he echoes and cites. In the first place, whereas Paul can speak of death as 'the last enemy to be destroyed' (I Cor. 15.25f.), our author holds that it has already been destroyed and has lost all threat for the Elect. Consequently, for the author there can be no thought of an interim period or 'sleep' (cf. I Cor. 15.51)[48] for the dead preceding the resurrection. But, second, and perhaps of greater importance, the author says nothing comparable to the Apostle's affirmation that the real 'sting of death is sin' (I Cor. 15.56). Thus, Christ's defeat of death has nothing to do with his nullifying its power by taking upon himself the sin of the world.[49] The author uses Pauline terms, but he knows nothing—or at least says nothing—of the Saviour's defeat of that death which is the 'wages of sin' (Rom. 6.21, 23; 7.5; 8.6, 13; Gal. 6.7f.; James 1.15; etc.). Consequently, the Cross is mentioned nowhere in our Letter, and salvation has to do with flight from a corruptible world rather than with the reconciliation of man to God.

B. THE MEANS OF ESCHATOLOGY

1. *The Saviour and his Work*

Our analysis of the Letter in Chapter II has shown that for the author the reality and realization of eschatological hopes are rooted in Christology. That is, the resurrection of believers, the destruction of death, and the restoration of the heavenly Pleroma are all accomplished through the work and teaching of the Saviour. In this section we shall attempt to summarize these functions as they appear in the Letter.

It should be noted at the outset that there are three groups of titles utilized by the author in referring to the Saviour. First, there are

---

'gain' seems parallel to Paul's expression in Phil. 1.21—'. . . to die is gain'. Cf. *supra*, p. 85, section 49. Also, on 'depart' (ⲃⲱⲕ) in 47.22 used as a metaphorical expression for 'death', cf. Crum, *Coptic Dictionary*, p. 29a.

[48] A convenient summary of Pauline passages containing the idea of an interim is found in Oscar Cullmann, *Immortality of the Soul or Resurrection of the Dead?* (New York and London, 1958), pp. 48–57.

[49] Cf. the discussion of this aspect of Paul's thought in Rudolf Bultmann, *Theology of the New Testament*, tr. Kendrick Grobel, Vol. I (New York and London, 1951), pp. 246–9, 345–52.

simple New Testament titles, including: 'Saviour' (ⲡⲥⲱⲧⲏⲣ = σωτήρ) in 45.14; 'Lord' (ⲡⲁⲁⲉⲓⲥ = κύριος) in 44.13; 'Son of God' (ⲡϣⲏⲣⲉ ⲙ̄ⲡⲛⲟⲩⲧⲉ = υἱὸς τοῦ θεοῦ) in 44.16–17, 22, 29; 'Son of Man' (ⲡϣⲏⲣⲉ ⲙ̄ⲡⲣⲱⲙⲉ = υἱὸς τοῦ ἀνθρώπου) in 44.23, 30–31; 46.14–15. Second, there are composite titles, only one of which may be exactly paralleled from the New Testament:[50] 'our Saviour, our Lord Christ' (ⲡⲛ̄ⲥⲱⲧⲏⲣ ⲡⲛ̄ⲁⲁⲉⲓⲥ ⲡⲉⲭ̅ⲣⲏⲥⲧⲟⲥ = ὁ σωτήρ, ὁ κύριος ἡμῶν Χρηστός) in 43.37; 'our Lord the Saviour, Jesus Christ' (ⲡⲉⲛⲁⲁⲉⲓⲥ ⲡⲥⲱⲧⲏⲣ ⲓ̅ⲥ̅ ⲭ̅ⲣⲏⲥⲧⲟⲥ = ὁ κύριος ἡμῶν ὁ σωτὴρ Ἰησοῦς Χρηστός) in 48.18–19; 'my Lord Jesus Christ' (ⲡⲁⲁⲁⲉⲓⲥ ⲓ̅ⲥ̅ ⲡⲉⲭ̅ⲣⲏⲥ[ⲧⲟⲥ] = ὁ κύριος μου Ἰησοῦς Χρηστός) in 49.38–50.1. Third, there are three designations, none of which may be paralleled from the New Testament: 'the solution', as applied to both Christ and the explanation he brings to certain problems (ⲡⲃⲱⲗ = ἡ λύσις) in 45.4–5; 'Great One' (ⲟⲩⲛⲁϭ = μέγας) in 46.19–20;[51] 'He who makes the Good'[52] (ⲛ̄ⲧⲁϥ ⲡⲉ ⲉⲧⲧⲁⲙⲓⲟ ⲙ̄ⲡⲡⲉⲧⲛⲁⲛⲟⲩϥ = ὁ κατασκευάζει τὸ ἀγαθόν) in 49.8–9.

Although New Testament usage has contributed directly or indirectly the titles in the first two of the preceding groups, some of the connotations they possess in Scripture are missing from 'Rheginos'. Thus, 'Saviour', 'Lord', 'Christ', 'Son of Man', and 'Son of God' are never used as in the New Testament, with respect to an expected second coming of the Saviour.[53] Moreover, the title 'Son of God' carries no overtones of pre-existence,[54] and 'Lord' does not denote

[50] The first two of these titles are most nearly paralleled in II Peter. 1.11; 2.20; 3.18. See our note to 43.35–37, Section 4, supra, p. 54. The third title, 'Lord Jesus Christ', is eminently Pauline, occurring forty-nine times in the Epistles (including Ephesians and II Thessalonians), but not once in the Synoptics or John. On the use of the unusual form of the name χρηστός for χριστός in Marcionite, Manichaean, and early Christian literature, see the parallels and secondary literature cited by Puech and Quispel in De Resurrectione, p. 20.

[51] In several NT passages we find the adjective 'great' used with certain substantives as a designation of Jesus, e.g. Luke 7.16: '. . . great prophet'; Titus 2.13: '. . . our great God and Saviour Jesus Christ'; Heb. 13.20: '. . . the great shepherd of the sheep'. Never, however, is 'great' used in the absolute, as here.

[52] Our arguments for taking the pronoun in this title to be personal instead of demonstrative are presented supra, p. 95.

[53] On the futuristic eschatological overtones of the titles given here, see the following: on 'Saviour', Oscar Cullmann, The Christology of the New Testament, tr. by Shirley C. Guthrie and Charles A. M. Hall (London and Philadelphia, 1959), p. 238; on 'Lord' and 'Christ', Ferdinand Hahn, Christologische Hoheitstitel: Ihre Geschichte im frühen Christentum (Zweite, durchgesehene Auflage; Göttingen, 1964), pp. 95–112, 179–89; on 'Son of Man', Vincent Taylor, The Names of Jesus (London and New York, 1953), p. 30f.; Hahn, Christologische Hoheitstitel, pp. 32–42; on 'Son of God', Hahn, ibid., pp. 287ff.

[54] Contrast to our document's usage the pre-existence postulated of the 'Son

the expected exaltation or glorification of Jesus.[55] In most other instances, however, the titles occurring in our Letter carry meanings similar to those which they possess in the New Testament. Indeed, the titles given the Saviour in our Letter, like those conferred upon him in the New Testament, are in part synonymous and to a degree interchangeable. In fact, so much is this the case that we have refrained from independent study of each title and offer instead a summary of the Letter's teaching about the Saviour's activity.[56]

The primary functions of the Saviour in our Letter are two. The first, whose frequent occurrence attests to its priority, is that eschatological function of destroying death and conferring immortality. The second, which we should expect to find emphasized in a Gnostic text, is the function of teaching the 'Truth' or communicating 'knowledge'. Both functions are to be understood against the background sketched earlier in this chapter, including the conceptions of a ruptured heavenly sphere or 'Pleroma'; a perishing world fallen in darkness; and a decaying, bound-for-death race of men.

The first, or eschatological function, falls into three acts. The opening centres in the 'Son of Man's' pre-existence as a pre-cosmic 'seed of Truth' (44.21–36). As such, he was the 'emanation' ($\pi\rho o\beta o\lambda\acute{\eta}$)[57] of the pleromatic deities 'Truth' and 'Spirit' (45.12–13), and he was presumably without 'flesh'.[58] Certainly, he had nothing to do with the disruption of the 'Pleroma' or the creation of the illusory world.[59] The second act of the Saviour's eschatological work finds him 'in mediis rebus'. That is, the scene opens with the 'Lord' living in this worldly 'place' ($\tau\acute{o}\pi os$), having taken on a body of 'flesh' (44.13–17).[60]

---

of God' in Gal. 4.4; Rom. 8.3; Phil. 2.5–11. See also Sherman E. Johnson, 'Son of God', *IDB*, Vol. IV (1962), p. 412; Hahn, *Christologische Hoheitstitel*, p. 316.

[55] See Cullmann, *Christology*, pp. 195, 203f., 218–30, for the relevant texts and discussion.

[56] Independent study of each title was undertaken in the writer's original dissertation, 'The Epistle to Rheginos: A Study in Gnostic Eschatology and Its Use of the New Testament' (Yale University, 1966), pp. 259–70. The ensuing section rests on that study.

[57] 'Emanation' is, as we have shown, *supra*, pp. 66f., a Valentinian '*terminus technicus*'. It is the Saviour as the 'Solution' who is identified as such an 'emanation'. From the context in 45.4–13 it is plain that the revelation he gave, as well as what he did, included the 'solution' to two problems of existence, viz. the presence of evil, and the fate of believers at death.

[58] See *supra*, pp. 111, 112f.

[59] See *supra*, pp. 108 and 110.

[60] This use of the title 'Lord' is similar to its oldest appearances in the primitive, Palestinian tradition. In that stratum of the tradition the title refers to the Saviour's

From certain adverbs and prepositions in the Letter we may gather that his entrance into the 'world' has involved a descent.[61] By taking on 'flesh' (44.13–15), the 'Son of Man' participates representatively in the 'humanity' of mankind (44.21–29), including the experience of death (46.16–17; cf. 45.25–26). The third and final act, however, reveals that death is no real threat to him, for as 'Saviour' he destroyed it by 'swallowing it up' (45.14–15) and 'conquered' it through his divine nature as 'Son of God' (44.27–29; cf. 45.4–11).[62] The 'Saviour' accomplished this by disassociating himself from the 'perishing world', by transforming himself into an immortal deity, by destroying his visible nature through his invisible, and by ascending (45.16–21). As 'Son of Man' he arose from among the dead, being called 'great' because of his destruction of death (46.14–20).[63] Through the 'Lord and Saviour, Jesus Christ', then, the resurrection was brought into being (48.16–19), the 'way of immortality' was opened (45.14–39), 'rest' was conferred on the faithful (43.35–38) and the Elect were revealed (45.10–11). This opening of the 'way of immortality' for the Elect is a basic part of the 'Son of Man's' cosmic role of restoring the 'Pleroma' (44.30–32). And, in the accomplishment of this dual eschatological function of giving the way of 'resurrection' to the Elect and consummating the 'restoration' of the 'Pleroma', the Saviour is said to 'make the Good' (49.8–9).[64]

---

humanity and earthly life without any reference to his resurrection, expected return, or exaltation. On this, see Hahn, *Christologische Hoheitstitel*, pp. 74–95. Cf. also Werner Foerster and Gottfried Quell, 'κύριος', *TWNT*, III (1938), pp. 1089f.

[61] For example, we may infer from the statement 'originally He was from above' (ⲁⲃⲁⲗ ϩⲙ ⲡⲥⲁ ⲛ̄ⲧⲡⲉ) in 44.34–35 a downward movement which has brought the Saviour into the 'cosmos'. Also, in such comments as 'He raised himself up' (ⲁϥⲧⲟⲩⲛⲁⲥϥ̄—45.19) and 'we arose with Him, and we went to heaven with Him' (45.26–28) we find implied an upward movement out of a temporary existence in the lower sphere. Cf., for passages from which similar inferences may be drawn, 45.36–38; 48.38–49.2; 49.2–3. The last two of these may be figurative allusions to the Saviour's ascent.

[62] Cf. this association of the title 'Son of God' with his conquest of death to Romans 1.4: '. . . and designated Son of God in power according to the Spirit of holiness by his resurrection from the dead'.

[63] See our note to 46.19–21, *supra*, pp. 78f. In the Patristic literature of the period, the comparative of μέγας ('great') was used in its masculine form as a substantive to denote the Son in relation to the Holy Ghost. See the texts offered in Lampe, *Lexicon*, 3, p. 837, B.4.a.

[64] An interesting comparison to this use of 'good' may be made with the Old Testament idea that what God performs for his people's salvation—the Exodus, the entry into the Promised Land, and the protection he grants his people—is described as the 'Good' (Exod. 18.9; Num. 10.29f.).

The second major function of the 'Saviour, the Lord Christ' is the communication of knowledge. This seems indirectly referred to in 43.35–44.3, where the 'Truth' which believers come to know and which has given them 'Rest' is probably to be understood as having been brought by the Saviour. 'Truth' in our Letter carries several shades of meaning,[65] but at least one of these refers to a knowledge of man's corruptible condition and the Saviour's work. Such is the content of the 'Solution' brought by the Saviour to the problems of existence (45.4–11).[66] Finally, it appears that our author considers much of what he has taught Rheginos to be 'knowledge' given him by the 'Lord Jesus Christ' (49.37–50.1).[67]

In conclusion, while being fully conscious of its hypothetical nature,[68] but considering it a helpful outline, we find that a comparison of Rudolf Bultmann's sketch of the so-called Gnostic 'Redeemed-Redeemer myth' with the view of the Saviour in our Letter yields some important insights.[69] The similarities are as follows: (1) In both the 'myth' and our Letter, the Saviour-Redeemer descends from a higher, heavenly sphere into a corruptible and decaying world. (2) In both, a type of 'knowledge' is communicated by the Saviour to his Elect which reveals their state of decay and his own work in providing a route of escape. (3) In both, the Saviour-Redeemer provides a way to immortality through his resurrection and ascent. (4) In both, the Redeemer restores the disrupted Pleroma by

[65] On the various meanings of 'Truth', see infra, p. 131, n.85.

[66] The term 'Solution' actually seems to refer to both the Saviour and his teaching. Cf. our analysis, supra, p. 39; De Resurrectione, p. 25. In Eusebius' Fragmenta ex Opere de Theophania 3 (p. 8.5) Christ's work of destroying death is referred to as 'the solution' (ἡ λύσις).

[67] Still, the contents of this Letter do not have an esoteric nature comparable to that found in the Pistis Sophia or the Apocryphon of John. And, there are no clear exhortations to keep secret its contents. See further on this, infra, p. 162.

[68] Carsten Colpe, Die religionsgeschichtliche Schule, passim, has amply demonstrated that the so-called 'Redeemed-Redeemer Myth' is a modern and often inaccurately used construction that cannot be directly derived from the Iranian Gayomart myth of the 'Primeval Man'. Indeed, although there may have been other 'Redeemer figures' in systems developed outside of Christianity, there was no 'Redeemer Myth' apart from contact with the Christology of the early Christian Kerygma. See Colpe's further statements on this question in his article, 'Gnosis', RGG, II³ (1958), col. 1652; also in his study, 'Zur Leib-Christi-Vorstellung in Epheserbrief', in Judentum, Urchristentum, Kirche: Festschrift für Joachim Jeremias, herausgegeben von Walther Eltester (Beiheft für die neutestamentliche Wissenschaft und die Kunde der Älteren Kirche, 26; Berlin, 1960), esp. pp. 186–7.

[69] Rudolf Bultmann's presentation of the 'Redeemed-Redeemer' myth is found in his Theology, I, pp. 166–7; and in his Primitive Christianity in Its Contemporary Setting, tr. by R. H. Fuller (London and New York, 1956), pp. 163–4.

leading the Elect back to it. The points of dissimilarity, on the other hand, are as follows: (1) In Bultmann's sketch, the Redeemer is 'sent' by a supremely transcendent Deity; but no mention is made in our Letter either of such a Deity or of the Saviour's having been 'sent'. (2) In the 'Redeemer-myth', stress is placed on the deceptive descent of the Saviour past a number of inimical divine powers; our Letter makes no mention of these. (3) In Bultmann's outline, the 'knowledge' the Redeemer brings consists mainly of a reminder to the 'pneumatics' of their origin in the realm of Light and of a number of magical passwords and sacraments designed to assist the 'pneumatic' in his heavenly ascent. (4) In our Letter, 'knowledge' consists also of a cognizance of man's nature, but there is no appeal to his heavenly origin.[70] Rather, 'knowledge' in 'Rheginos' centres in the comprehension of what the Saviour has already accomplished for the Elect, and it nowhere contains any magical passwords or incantations. (5) Moreover, not just the bare spirit of the 'pneumatic' is redeemed in our Letter, but rather the invisible, spiritual man with his inner limbs, immortal 'mind', and new flesh. (6) The most significant difference is that whereas in the Myth the Redeemer himself must be redeemed by a higher Deity (cf. Hippolytus' version in *Ref.*, V.6–11), in our Letter the Saviour saves himself. This is clear from a passage like 45.14–23:

> The Saviour swallowed up
> death. (You are not reckoned as being ignorant.)
> For He put aside the
> world which is perishing. He transformed
> [himself] into an imperishable Aeon
> and raised himself up, having
> swallowed the visible
> by the invisible,
> and He gave us
> the way of our immortality.

Thus, it is not God (whether the highest, transcendent Deity or the more orthodox Father) who is saving men through Christ, but it is Christ saving them through himself! This is Christocentrism emphasized to the exclusion of theology!

---

[70] As seen earlier, *supra*, pp. 111f., in our Letter the Elect are thought of as having been pre-existent. But at no point does the author argue for immortality or the resurrection on the basis of the heavenly origin of the Elect's 'spirit'.

2. *The Believer and his Response*

Though the work of the Saviour provides the basis for eschatological hopes, the author of our Letter plainly indicates that full realization of the resurrection is contingent upon the human responses of 'faith' (*πίστις*), 'knowledge' (*γνῶσις*), and 'practice' (*ἀσκήσις*). Such responses, however, seem confined to an Elect few. In this section we investigate these 'human means' of eschatological fulfilment and their context of Election.

(a) 'Election'

One passage in our Letter states explicitly the author's view of Election, while others become more intelligible when read in its light. The passage is 46.20–34:

> 20 . . . Among
> the im[mortal] are those who believe. The
> thought of those who are saved shall
> not perish. The mind of
> those who have known him shall not perish.
> 25 Therefore, we are elected to
> salvation and redemption,
> since we are predestined from the beginning
> not to fall into the
> foolishness of those who are without knowledge,
> 30 but we shall enter into the
> wisdom of those who have known
> the Truth. Indeed, the Truth which they keep
> cannot be abandoned,
> nor has it been.

To be noted in connection with the foregoing are the following matters: (1) The expressions 'elected to' (ⲧⲛ̅ⲥⲁⲧⲡ = *ἐκλέκτος*)[71] and 'predestined' (ⲁϩⲟⲟⲩⲛⲧⲁⲩϣⲛ̅ = *προορίζειν*)[72] in lines 25 and 27 indicate that the author considers both himself and his addressee to be among those chosen for salvation. (2) Since there is no mention of the Deity who might have predestined the Elect, it appears that as in the Fourth Gospel (John 6.65; 13.18; 15.16), Paul (Eph. 1.5–7), and

---

[71] *ἐκλέκτος* is most frequently translated in the Sahidic New Testament by the Qualitative form of ⲥⲱⲧⲡ̅. See, on this M. Wilmet, *Concordance* (*CSCO*), II, p. 843.

[72] On this expression, see our note to 46.27, *supra*, p. 80.

I Peter (2.4, 6, 9) our author's main interest is in the working out and confirmation of election in Christ. Such is certainly the case in 45.4–13, where we read that Christ as the 'Solution' made manifest just who the 'bound-for-resurrection' Elect were, the presumption being that prior to his coming the Elect were known neither to themselves nor to their fellows (cf. 44.13–17; 45.28–31; 48.6–11, 34–35). Similarly, the statement that the Elect are '. . . enclosed by him (the Saviour)' until their death (45.28–35)[73] probably implies an especially close and protective relationship between these parties during the Elect ones' earthly existence. Nevertheless, in our Letter election is resolutely more Christocentric than in the New Testament as a whole. (3) The statement that the Elect 'are predestined from the beginning' (ϫⲓⲛⲛ ϣⲁⲣⲡ̄ = ἀπ' ἀρχῆς in 46.27) probably points to the Election of believers before the creation of the 'cosmos'[74] when they were pre-existing as the 'All' in the heavenly Pleroma.[75] We base this conclusion upon the fact that the only other occurrence of ϣⲁⲣⲡ̄ in our Letter (44.33–34) clearly refers to the Son of Man's pre-existence 'Above'. (4) Finally, 46.28–34 indicates that the Elect are destined to share in the 'wisdom of the Truth', the resurrection being thereby identified with the acquisition of knowledge. A similar identification was made by Tertullian's Gnostic opponents mentioned in *De Resurrectione Mortuorum* (xxii.1).[76] Presumably such 'wisdom' involves perfect knowledge of the Divine and of the nature of one's self.

Other passages make clear the 'limited' scope of this Election. From 44.8–10 we learn that only a minority are chosen for resurrection:

> To be sure, many are
> lacking faith in it (i.e. the resurrection), but
> there are a few who find it.

[73] This passage also includes the expression 'wearing him', which may echo—as has been noted in *De Resurrectione*, pp. 27–28—the Pauline image of 'putting on Christ', as in Rom. 13.12–14 and I Cor. 15.49. If this be true, however, whereas Paul roots the Christian imperative ἐνδύσασθε in the kerygmatic indicative of what Christ has already accomplished, our author turns that imperative into another indicative—'we are revealed . . . wearing him' (46.28–31). See further on this indicative-imperative relationship, Albrecht Oepke, 'ἐνδύω', *TWNT*, II (1935), pp. 320–1; Bultmann, *Theology*, I, pp. 101, 332f.; II, pp. 79–82.

[74] If this is so, the passage shows some similarity to Eph. 1.4, the only place in the New Testament where election is explicitly said to have its roots in eternity.

[75] On the meaning of 'All', see *supra*, pp. 81 and 108.

[76] The passage from Tertullian has been cited in *De Resurrectione*, 'Note Critique' to 46.31–32, on pp. 32–33. Cf. also our study of the meaning of 'Truth' in our Letter, *infra*, p. 131, n.85.

The majority, including most of the 'philosophers of this world' (46.8–10), are not among the Elect. They do not possess the 'faith' held by the Elect, and no amount of logical argumentation ('persuasion') can bring them to belief in the resurrection (46.3–7).[77] Not all, then, are elected to salvation, for many are destined to 'fall into the foolishness of those who are without knowledge' (46.25–29).

(b) 'Faith' and 'Knowledge'

Interestingly, although the resurrection is said to be possible only for the Elect, the author of our Letter stresses the importance of 'faith' (πίστις) and 'knowledge' (γνῶσις) in appropriating the benefits of Christ's saving work. However, these responses were probably understood by the author more as characteristics of than as conditions for Election. At any rate, there is certainly no antithesis between 'believing' and 'knowing', for in our Letter the two complement and shade into one another as in the Fourth Gospel.[78] For example, we read in 46.14–17:

> For we have *known* the Son of
> Man, and we have *believed*
> that He arose from among the
> dead.

Nevertheless, some nuances do exist between 'faith' and 'knowledge' in our Letter, nuances that we shall need to examine more closely.

'Faith'

Apart from a single privative form (ἄπιστος) in 44.9, all occurrences of verbs and nouns denoting 'faith' (πίστις and πιστεύω) are found in the passage 46.3–24. From that passage we learn that 'faith' has a twofold meaning. It is both (a) an acceptance of the reality of Christ's resurrection from the dead (cf. 45.14–46.4, 14–17, 20) and (b) trust in the surety of that same 'spiritual resurrection' for those who believe in him (cf. 46.8–13).[79] This focus on the resurrection anchors 'faith' to a particular historical occurrence and person. At the same time,

[77] See our note to 46.4–5, *supra*, pp. 76f.

[78] See Bultmann's comments on John's usage in Rudolf Bultmann and Arthur Weiser, 'πιστεύω, κτλ.', *TWNT*, VI (1959), pp. 228–30.

[79] Such a meaning shows similarity to what Rudolf Bultmann has called the 'specifically Christian usage' of 'faith', viz. the reception of the Christian Kerygma as the saving belief, involving recognition of God's work of salvation in Christ. See Bultmann, *TWNT*, VI, p. 209. The main differences are that (1) in our Letter there is no mention of the 'Kerygma', though it is surely understood; (2) in our Letter there is no reference at all to God working through Christ.

'belief' and 'immortality' are said to be inextricably woven together, so that to have 'faith' is to be immortal (46.20–21).[80] Unfortunately, such 'faith' is held only by the Elect few, for many are without it (ἄπιστος—44.8–10). In sum, 'faith' in our Letter is Christocentrically defined and eschatologically oriented.

The opposites of faith are 'persuasion' (πείθειν) and 'doubt' (διστάζειν). No amount of logical demonstration can 'persuade' one to accept the resurrection, for acceptance is solely a matter of faith (46.3–7). But especially is one not to 'doubt' the resurrection (47.1–3) or its 'spiritual' mode (47.36–48.3).[81] It should remain a matter of confident hope.

'Knowledge'

A comparison of our Letter's use of the verb 'to know'[82] with what has elsewhere been shown to be the distinctive Gnostic usage of that term yields some fruitful insights. The first characteristic of Gnostic usage is that 'knowledge' (γνῶσις) has as its primary object a dualistically-conceived God, the unknown Father.[83] In our Letter, however, 'knowing' consists not in the apprehension of a transcendent Deity, but in the cognizance of the Son of Man and belief in the historical event of his resurrection (46.13–17).[84] Such 'knowing' has as its main object the 'Truth' (44.1–3; 45.3–11; 46.30–32), the proclamation of the resurrection in the Christian Gospel.[85] The transcendent Father of the Saviour is never mentioned.

[80] This recalls the linkage of 'faith' with 'eternal life' in the Johannine literature: John 3.36; 5.24; 6.47; 11.25–26; I John 5.13.

[81] This opposition of 'faith' and 'doubt' is found also in Matt. 14.31; 21.21; Mark 11.23; James 1.6; Rom. 14.23; I Clem. 11.2. On the interpretation of 47.36–48.3, see *supra*, pp. 113f.

[82] The noun 'knowledge' (ⲥⲟⲟⲩⲛ̄ = γνῶσις) never appears in our Letter. There are, however, seven occurrences of the verb 'to know', including: ⲥⲁⲩⲛⲉ (44.39; 49.17, 27); ⲥⲟⲩⲱⲛ (44.1; 46.31); ⲥⲟⲩⲛ (46.14); ⲥⲟⲩⲱⲱⲛ (46.24). These verbal forms translate either the Greek γινώσκω or οἶδα. See Wilmet, *Concordance* (CSCO), II, pp. 848–60. Neither γινώσκω or οἶδα are retained as loanwords in the Sahidic or Bohairic Versions of the Bible.

[83] So, Rudolf Bultmann, 'γινώσκω', *Theological Dictionary of the New Testament*, Vol. I, p. 693.

[84] On the uniqueness of such an historical interest in a Gnostic writing, see *infra*, p. 151, n.156.

[85] Actually, ⲙⲏⲉ (ἀλήθεια) in our Letter has three basic meanings: first, in 43.34 and 45.4, the phrase 'the Word of Truth' seems to echo Col. 1.5 or Eph. 1.13. 'Truth', as the 'Christian gospel', is related to the 'Solution' which came through Christ (45.3–11). The same idea seems present in 44.2 and 46.32. Second, 'truth' refers to what is real, what possesses enduring reality, as opposed to 'illusion' (cf. 48.13 and 33). And, third, 'Truth' appears to be the name of a divine Aeon of the

A second characteristic of Gnostic 'knowledge' is that it is under-stood as a 'gift', not as the result of any rationalistic process. It comes through mystical and ecstatic illumination and is markedly esoteric.[86] In our Letter, however, 'knowledge' is bound up with the process of 'thought' which originates in the 'mind' (νοῦς—cf. 46.22; 47.29; 48.10). Thus, one can be said to 'know', in the sense of self-recognition, one's own shortcomings as a teacher (44.39). And, one should 'know' of the inevitability of one's own death (49.16–19). Moreover, despite some mystical traces to be discussed in the next section, we find no indication that it is through ecstatic experience that such 'knowledge' is acquired. There is nothing highly esoteric in our Letter, although allusions to the Pleroma and Emanations (e.g. 44.31–32; 45.12–13; 46.35–36) might indicate the presence of such 'knowledge' in earlier teaching by the author.

The third characteristic of Gnostic 'knowledge' is that it 'invests the Gnostic with the divine nature, and therefore in the first instance with immortality'.[87] The apotheosis of the Gnostic occurs from his ecstatic vision; he is granted 'power' (ἐξουσία) and freedom from 'fate' (εἱμαρμένη).[88] This is the closest point of contact with the conception of 'knowledge' in our Letter, for it is through 'knowledge' that one should consider his impending death as already passed (49.25–28). Through perception of the 'Truth', one receives the eschatological 'Rest' in the present (44.1–3), as well as in the future (46.30–32). The 'mind' (νοῦς) of those who 'have known' the Saviour is considered immortal (46.23–24). Nevertheless, the fact that even the Elect must experience death before ascending to heaven[89] gives a slightly different meaning to the power of γνῶσις to make the knower divine.

(c) 'Practice'

In addition to 'faith' and 'knowledge', our author believes that another type of response is required of the Elect if he is to appropriate the full benefits of Christ's resurrection, viz. 'practice'. The key passage is 49.25–36:

> 25 If you have the
> resurrection, but continue as if

Pleroma, a deity who has begotten Christ (cf. 44.35 and 45.12). In sum, though overtones of the second meaning may be present in 44.1–3 and 46.30–32, these passages seem best explained as having reference to the 'Word of Truth', i.e. the 'Christian Gospel'.

[86] So Bultmann, *Theological Dictionary*, I, pp. 694–5.
[87] *Ibid.*, p. 696.   [88] *Ibid.*   [89] See *supra*, pp. 117ff.

you will die (and yet that one
knows that he has died), why then
do I overlook your
30 lack of exercise *(-γυμνάζεσθαι)*? It is right for
each one to practise *(ἀσκεῖν)*
in a number of ways, and
he shall be released from this element *(στοιχεῖον)*.

The 'practice' and 'exercise' involved in the Elect's extrication of himself from the inimical power of the 'cosmos' (i.e. 'this element') are only vaguely defined by the phrase 'in a number of ways' *(πολυτρόπως?)*.[90] Nevertheless, the immediate context (49.25–30) implies that the 'lack of exercise' in line 30 refers to Rheginos' mental attitude toward death, the attitude reflected throughout the Letter in his questions, problems, and doubts about the resurrection. It would seem that the 'exercise' called for entails eradication of such doubt (47.2–3; cf. 47.36–48.3); avoidance of divisive opinion (46.10–17; 49.9–16) and holding correct thought about salvation (47.26–30; 48.10–11). As opposed to external behaviour, 'exercise', then, appears to mean a type of internal or mental training designed to give confidence about the resurrection (cf. I Tim. 4.7–8).[91]

Still, because the verb 'to practise' *(ἀσκέω)* early came to mean a self-denying withdrawal from the world's contamination,[92] the passage 49.30–34 may encourage an ascetic ethic. Certainly, the author viewed negatively the world's transience and illusory nature (e.g. 48.13–16, 27–28), and the 'practice' he encourages is designed ultimately to free one from the στοιχεῖον of this world (49.32–33). No passage of the Letter, however, makes such an ascetic ethic explicit.

3. 'Unio Mystica'

As noted earlier, [93] the first editors of our Letter maintain that 45.24–

[90] On the possibility of πολυτρόπως as the Greek underlying the Coptic ⲛ̄ⲟⲩⲁϩⲥ ⲛ̄ϩⲣⲉⲉⲥ, see the 'Note Critique' to 49.32 in *De Resurrectione*, p. 44. Contrast, however, section 73, *supra*, p. 99.

[91] Such a meaning may be paralleled from the use of γυμνάζε in I Tim. 4.7–8. γυμνάζε in this passage implies a 'concentration on what is an inward instead of an externally dualistic asceticism'. So Albrecht Oepke, 'γυμνάζω', *TWNT*, I (1933), p. 775.

[92] Cf. especially the passages from Epictetus and Philo cited by Hans Windisch, 'ἀσκέω', *TWNT*, I (1933), pp. 492–3. Certainly, the Apostle Paul's attitude is not identical with the advanced asceticism of later ecclesiastical development, but it does contain some of the rudiments of that development.

[93] *Supra*, p. viii, n.7.

28 is a most important witness to the reception of 'Pauline mysticism' in Valentinian circles at a time when this teaching was almost without echo in more orthodox ecclesiastical writing. Further, 45.28–39 is viewed as an interpretative amplification of this mysticism, an amplification making use of a pagan solar theology which emphasized the consubstantiality of divine nature between Saviour and believers.[94] Since these conclusions are of considerable importance both for the history of Christian thought and for our understanding of the 'means of eschatology', we have reserved consideration of this passage until now. As a basis for our study, we quote these passages in their larger context of 45.14–46.2:

> 45.14 The Saviour swallowed up
> death. (You are not reckoned as being ignorant.)
> For He put aside the
> world which is perishing. He transformed
> [himself] into an imperishable Aeon
> and raised himself up, having
> 20 swallowed the visible
> by the invisible,
> and He gave us
> the way of our immortality.
> Then (τότε) indeed, as the Apostle
> said, 'We suffered
> with him, and we arose
> with him, and we went to heaven
> with him.' Now (δέ) if we
> are revealed in
> 30 this world wearing
> him, we are that one's beams,
> and we are
> enclosed by
> him until our setting, that is to say,
> 35 our death in this life.
> We are drawn to heaven
> by him like the beams
> by the sun, not being restrained
> by anything. This is
> 40 the spiritual resurrection

---

[94] See *De Resurrectione*, pp. xivf. Cf. also Puech, *CRAIBL* (1964), p. 318.

46.1   which swallows up the psychic
        alike with the other fleshly.

Several passages in the critical edition of *De Resurrectione* make
manifest the fact that by 'Pauline mysticism' Puech and Quispel
mean the dying and rising of believers 'in', 'by', and 'with' Christ in
the sacrament of baptism.[95] Such a definition, however, oversimplifies
the meaning of the very ambiguous term 'Pauline mysticism'.[96] To
illustrate, in New Testament study such 'mysticism' has been defined
from a Hellenistic frame of reference (A. Deissmann, R. Reitzenstein,
and W. Bousset), in Jewish-eschatological terms (A. Schweitzer and
A. Wikenhauser), or it has been denied altogether.[97] Consequently,
for an evaluation of the first editors' hypothesis, we must compare and
contrast this so-called 'mysticism' of our Letter with other studies of
it, such as Albert Schweitzer's.[98]

Similarities between 45.24–46.2 and New Testament assertions of
Paul's mystical thought are as follows: (1) The language of 45.25–31
is close to certain expressions commonly held to reflect Paul's
'mysticism'. The clause in 45.26–27, 'we suffered with him' ($\sigma\upsilon\nu\epsilon\pi\acute{a}\theta o\mu\epsilon\nu$
$a\mathring{\upsilon}\tau\tilde{\omega}$) parallels closely Rom. 8.17— '. . . and if children, then heirs,
heirs of God and fellow heirs with Christ, provided we suffer with
him ($\sigma\upsilon\nu\pi\acute{a}\sigma\chi o\mu\epsilon\nu$) . . .'[99] In both 'Rheginos' and Romans the expression 'suffer' seems to refer to the manifestation of dying in this
life.[100] However, while for Paul such 'dying' is continually recurrent

[95] *De Resurrectione*, pp. xiii–xiv, xxxi.

[96] On the ambiguous nature of the term as used in modern scholarship, see
Rudolf Schnackenburg, *New Testament Theology Today*, tr. by David Askew (New
York, 1963), p. 84.

[97] On the current debate over Paul's 'mysticism', see *ibid.*, pp. 83–87; Alfred
Wikenhauser, *Pauline Mysticism*, tr. by Joseph Cunningham (Based on the Second
German Edition of 1956; New York, 1960), pp. 13–15; and E. Earle Ellis, *Paul
and His Recent Interpreters* (Grand Rapids, Michigan, 1961), pp. 24–26, 32–34.

[98] *The Mysticism of Paul the Apostle*, tr. by William Montgomery (Reprint of
the Second Edition; London, 1956). We choose Schweitzer's study because it
presents the major features of the Apostle's mystical thought which have been the
concern of most subsequent studies. However, this choice does not mean that we
subscribe to some of the questionable aspects of Schweitzer's interpretation, e.g.
his theory of two resurrections in Paul's thought, or his failure to give due consideration to the change of 'aeons' presupposed by Paul. On this latter point, see
Robert C. Tannehill, *Dying and Rising with Christ: a Study in Pauline Theology*
(*Beihefte ZNW*, 32; Berlin, 1967), pp. 70ff.

[99] The only other occurrence of $\sigma\upsilon\mu\pi\acute{a}\sigma\chi\omega$ in the New Testament, viz. I Cor.
12.26a, shows no similarity to the thought of our Letter.

[100] Schweitzer, *Mysticism*, Chapter VII, pp. 141–59; Wikenhauser, *Pauline
Mysticism*, pp. 154–62.

in the present life (Rom. 8.17 and I Cor. 12.26a), our Letter's use of
the I Perfect tense to refer to this experience indicates it is considered
a past and completed act. (2) Moreover, both Paul (Eph. 2.6) and
our Letter (45.26–28) affirm in similar language that the resurrection
and ascension of the faithful have already occurred, while both also
consider these events to be not fully actualized in the present (cf.
Rheg. 45.34–39; 47.30–48.1 to I Cor. 15.51–55; II Cor. 4.14; I
Thess. 4.15–17). The resurrection and ascension are, for both Paul
and the author of our Letter, those saving events in Christ's experience which serve as the firm basis and anticipatory promise of the
believers' own hope of arising and going to heaven.[101] (3) The
'Pauline mysticism' of the New Testament is a 'Christ mysticism' and
not a 'God mysticism'.[102] In the passage under consideration, as
throughout the whole of our Letter, there is a distinctly Christocentric orientation.[103] (4) Two expressions imply an especially close
relationship between the Elect and Christ. In 45.30–31 believers are
said to 'wear Christ', an idea which may derive stimulus from the
Pauline figure of 'putting on Christ' (cf. Gal. 3.26–29). If so, then
45.30–31 may indicate that by 'wearing' Christ believers enter a new
world, receiving thereby a new, ontological relationship to the
Saviour.[104] A second expression—'we are encompassed by him'
(45.32–33)—may indicate that believers, as the Elect, stand within
the protection and oversight of Christ during this earthly life. Paul's
mystical thought also has associations with his teaching on Election.[105]

Despite these striking similarities, the differences between our
Letter and New Testament expressions of 'Pauline mysticism' are
no less and perhaps even more important. (1) The characteristic New
Testament language of such mysticism is almost non-existent in our
Letter. The formula 'with Christ' (σὺν Χριστῷ) appears only in the
three lines of 45.25–28; the formula 'in Christ' (ἐν Χριστῷ—cf. I Cor.
5.17; Phil. 3.7–9; 4.13; Rom. 6.11; Gal. 2.17; Col. 2.6) is completely
absent from the Letter;[106] and there is no usage of the genitive case

[101] Cf. the interpretation of Eph. 2.5–6 offered by Dahl in Nils Alstrup Dahl,
Hermann Dietzfelbinger, Martti Simojoki, Edmund A. Steimle, and Martin Haug,
Kurze Auslegung des Epheserbriefes (Göttingen: Vandenhoeck & Ruprecht, 1965),
pp. 27–28.
[102] See Schweitzer, *Mysticism*, pp. 4–13, 346–7; Wikenhauser, *Pauline Mysticism*,
pp. 70–71.
[103] See *supra*, p. 127.
[104] Cf. Wikenhauser, *Pauline Mysticism*, p. 32.
[105] Cf. Schweitzer, *Mysticism*, pp. 16, 90, 102–7, 116.
[106] Although subsequent scholarship has shown that he carried his thesis too

of Χριστός which might carry a mystical connotation.[107] (2) Ernst Lohmeyer has shown that Paul uses the phrase σὺν Χριστῷ to refer to his profound hope that he *will be clothed* in a spiritual body and *will be* forever with his Lord. The phrase ἐν Χριστῷ, on the other hand, always refers to life in this present world.[108] The consistent use of the I Perfect tense in the 'quotation' in 45.25–28, however, shows that the author of our Letter used Greek compounds with σύν- to refer to events of the past. (3) 'Dying and rising' in 'Pauline mysticism' is a recurring event in the believers' life, e.g. in II Cor. 4.11.[109] There is no such recurrence in our Letter. (4) Although the phrase 'dying and rising' was probably received by Paul from the baptismal liturgy inherited from the primitive Church, the use of a similar expression in a second-century text like 'Rheginos' cannot be taken as definitive proof of its sacramental basis, too. In fact, the almost complete absence of the formula from baptismal liturgies of the second-century Church tells against such a possibility.[110] (5) Finally, Paul's idea of the mystical union of believers in Christ is set within the framework of primitive Christianity's imminent eschatological expectation. 'Dying and rising with Christ' receives its final confirmation in the 'Parousia' when the dead in Christ shall be resurrected.[111] In our Letter, however, this orientation of eschatological hope has disappeared. Believers are to live as though 'already resurrected' (49.22–30), and death is only the portal to an immediate post-mortem ascension (45.34–39).

---

far in trying to find a mystical meaning in every occurrence of the formula, it is none the less striking that Adolf Deissmann found ἐν Χριστῷ 164 times in the Pauline literature, including the Pastorals. Of the formula in Paul, Deissmann says: 'it is really the characteristic expression of his Christianity'. See, *Paul: A Study in Social and Religious History*, tr. William E. Wilson (Second Edition; New York, 1957), p. 140.

[107] On this usage in Paul's mystical thought, see Wikenhauser, *Pauline Mysticism*, pp. 33–48.
[108] See Ernst Lohmeyer, 'ΣΥΝ ΧΡΙΣΤΩΙ', *Festgabe für Adolf Deissmann zum 60. Geburtstag. 7. November 1926*, herausgegeben von Karl Ludwig Schmidt (Tübingen, 1927), p. 220.
[109] On this theme of a repeated 'dying and rising' and the relevant texts, see Schweitzer, *Mysticism*, pp. 17f., 125–40.
[110] The editors themselves discuss the absence of this formula in the second century and cite relevant studies: *De Resurrectione*, pp. xiii and xxxi.
[111] The eschatological orientation of Paul's mysticism is, of course, the thesis of Schweitzer. See, for example, his comments in *Mysticism*, pp. 23–24, 37, 39, 65–66, 93–94, 100, 219, 342–3. Cf., also, Wikenhauser's espousal of the same framework, *Pauline Mysticism*, pp. 199–207.

Like Ignatius of Antioch, then, the author of our Letter echoes and expressly uses some of the mystical terminology of Paul, but in a very superficial manner.[112] Without grasping the depth of meaning in the Pauline expressions he employs, our author cites the Apostle to make a point, viz. that the way of 'immortality' has been opened for the Elect through their representative, Christ. Beyond making that point, however, the author displays no awareness of the eschatological context of Paul's thought; he never again uses the formulae characteristic of the Apostle's 'mysticism'; and he nowhere explicitly connects his 'quotation' from Paul with a sacramental practice. Thus, the fundamental thesis of Schweitzer seems vindicated: Pauline mysticism is completely missing from second-century Christian thought because of its change of perspective regarding the Eschaton.

A few concluding comments should be made on the Puech-Quispel interpretation of 45.28–39. These lines they believe to be an amplification of the Pauline mysticism found in 45.24–27, an amplification in which the Elect, as 'beams', are consubstantially identified with the Saviour, as the 'Sun'. The death and resurrection of the Elect entails their 're-absorption' into their spiritual source, the Christ.[113] The problems in so interpreting this passage are threefold. First, the ⲛ̅ϩⲉ (δέ or 'now') in 45.29 marks a transition in the author's thought to a statement of what is the 'spiritual resurrection' (45.39–40). This means that 45.24–28 is more closely connected with 45.17–23 in the author's thought than it is with 45.28ff. This, in turn, indicates that 45.28–39 is not an interpretation of the Apostle's thought which precedes it, but it is actually a figurative explanation of the 'spiritual resurrection'. Second, that the astrological imagery of 45.28–39 is to be understood in a figurative rather than a literal sense is shown by the use of the comparative particle meaning 'as' or 'like' (ⲛ̅ⲑⲉ = ὡσεί) in 45.37.[114] And, third, to argue for the meaning of consubstantiality between the Elect and the Saviour in 45.28–39 is probably to press the text beyond its intended meaning. For although Saviour and the Elect have come from the same Pleromatic Source, our author conceives of them as separate beings. He is able to do this because, like other Gnostics, he could think in terms of a 'hypostatic differentiation

---

[112] This has been abundantly shown by Schweitzer, *Mysticism*, pp. 38–39, 334–47. Cf. also Virginia Corwin, *St Ignatius and Christianity at Antioch* (New Haven, 1960), pp. 266–7.

[113] *De Resurrectione*, p. xiv. Cf., on the editors' view of the 'consubstantiality' of believers and Saviour, also pp. xvii–xviii, and xxi.

[114] See our note to 45.37, *supra*, p. 74.

of the One'.[115] Moreover, he is even capable of thinking of the retention of individual identity in the resurrected state, as opposed to reabsorption in the Divine and consequent loss of personality.[116] For these reasons we believe that there is no explicit assertion of the consubstantiality between the Elect and the Saviour in 45.28–39.

C. THE GOALS OF ESCHATOLOGY

From their investigation, Puech and Quispel have been led to the conclusion that eschatology in the Letter to Rheginos is 'realized', i.e. that eschatological goals are attained in the present experience of the Gnostic.[117] We could certainly agree that major stress is placed upon the view that 'the resurrection has already occurred'. At the same time, it has become evident in our study that certain eschatological hopes entertained by the author of the Letter are future and thus unrealized. To demonstrate this more clearly, we consider first the 'realized', and second the 'unrealized' aspects of the eschatological teaching.

1. Realized Eschatology in the Letter

(a) Already Dead

Two questions raised near the Letter's end, i.e. in 49.16–30, reveal that in the author's judgment the Elect should consider himself as being already dead:

> 16 . . . For if
> he who will die knows
> himself that he
> will die (even if he spends many
> 20 years in this life he is
> brought to this),
> why not consider yourself
> as risen and ((already))
> brought to this?

---

[115] The phrase and the insight it conveys into Gnostic thought are the contributions of Carsten Colpe in *Der Islam*, 32 (1957), pp. 208f.; *Die religionsgeschichtliche Schule*, pp. 94f., 115ff., and 185f.

[116] This will be shown below, pp. 146–9.

[117] See *De Resurrectione*, pp. x–xi.

25   If you have the
resurrection but continue as if
you will die (and yet that one
knows that he has died), why then
do I ignore your
30   lack of exercise?[118]

In the first question (49.16–24) death is clearly assumed to be the
inevitable, biological end of every man.[119] Yet, for the Elect who
believes that he proleptically shares in Christ's resurrection (49.22–
23), the event of death should be viewed as already experienced
(49.22–24; cf. 45.25–26).[120] The second question (49.25–30) shows
that the attitude toward death encouraged in 49.16–24 should have
as its corollary a mode of life and thought reflecting confidence in the
Saviour's victory over death. Presumably the author's rebuke—'If
you have the resurrection but continue as if you will die . . ., why
then do I overlook your lack of exercise?'—implies that his pupil's
questions have reflected a degree of anxiety about death which is
considered unworthy of a believer.[121] There is no room for dread,
anxiety, or doubt. The believer is 'already dead' through his full
participation in Christ's conquest of death (cf. 44.27–29; 45.14–15;
46.15–19). Thus death itself must be viewed as only an innocuous
transition stage to full participation in the resurrection—so innocuous,
in fact, that it should be considered as having already occurred!

(b) Already Resurrected and Resting
Just as he considers death to be already realized in the life of the
Elect, so our author maintains that the resurrection is also a present

---

[118] As shown earlier, *supra*, pp. 97f., both questions are addressed to Rheginos,
the change from third to second person being a stylistic device used for emphasis.

[119] That the Elect, the non-Elect, and the Saviour himself all experience biological death has been shown *supra*, pp. 117f. Our earlier discussion on the Letter's
teaching about death, *supra*, pp. 117–22, should be re-read as background for this
section.

[120] There is no similarity between this view and the NT teaching that a man
can be 'already dead' through his sinfulness, e.g. in Rom. 6.11, 13; Col. 2.13;
Eph. 2.1, 5; 5.14; I John 3.14. In fact, there is no connection whatsoever between
'death' and 'sin' in our Letter, such as we find in the NT (e.g. Rom. 1.32; 6.16, 21,
23; 7.5; 8.6; I Cor. 15.56) and in the Apostolic Fathers (e.g. Barn. 12.2, 5; I Clem.
3.4; Herm., *Vis, II*, 3.1; Did. 2.4).

[121] Rheginos' questions have raised such objections as the undemonstrable
nature of the resurrection, the paradox of a bodiless resurrection, and the illusory
character of the resurrection (cf. 46.3–49.9).

reality.[122] This is articulated most clearly in three passages contained in the section 49.9–30:

49.15–16   '. . . already you have
the resurrection'.

49.22–23   '. . . why not consider yourself
as risen . . .'

49.25–26   'If you have the
resurrection . . .'

On the basis of the positive teaching offered in 46.3–49.9, Rheginos should conclude that he already possesses the resurrection (49.15–16). And, to confirm this, a type of 'existential proof' is introduced: If it be correct to consider oneself already dead, then it may be surmised that one has also arrived at the post-mortem state of the Elect, viz. resurrection (49.16–26). Consequently, Rheginos should live as though already resurrected, i.e. free from all anxiety about death and the afterlife (49.25–27).

The state of being 'already resurrected' is also closely associated with election. The resurrection, we are told in 44.3–10, is a 'necessary' article of the believer's faith since it is a constituent part of his elec-

---

[122] The view that the 'resurrection has already occurred' has some affinity, of course, with that combated as heretical in II Tim. 2.18. Many commentators have understood this view to have arisen from a confusion of the resurrection of the body with the mystical resurrection 'in Christ' accomplished for the Christian in baptism. So W. Lock, *A Critical and Exegetical Commentary on the Pastoral Epistles* (The International Critical Commentary, Edinburgh and New York, 1924), p. 99; E. F. Scott, *The Pastoral Epistles* (The Moffatt New Testament Commentary, James Moffatt, ed.; London and New York, 1941), p. 56; Burton Scott Easton, *The Pastoral Epistles* (New York, 1947), p. 56; C. Spicq, *Saint Paul: Les Épîtres Pastorales (Études Bibliques*; Paris, 1947), pp. 354f.; J. N. D. Kelly, *A Commentary on the Pastoral Epistles* (Black's (Harper's) New Testament Commentaries, Henry Chadwick, General Editor; London and New York, 1963), p. 185. It seems that such confusion did exist among early Christians: see the comments about the Samaritan Menander in Iren., *Adv. Haer.* I.23. 5 (cf. Justin, *Apol.* I.26); about Nicolas, the proselyte of Antioch in Hipp., *Rep. VII*, 36; about Marcion in Justin, *Dial.* 80; Tert., *De Anima* 50, and the comment of Minucius Felix, *Octav.* 11. Nevertheless, other commentators are very cautious in their interpretation of this obscure passage since no further definition of the view of Hymenaeus and Philetus is offered in the Pastorals; as opposed to simple identification of this heretical view with one particular Gnostic group, it is pointed out that the author of the Epistle may have been warning against a variety of groups. See, on this, Martin Dibelius, *Die Pastoralbriefe (Handbuch zum Neuen Testament*, 13; 3. Auflage, neu bearbeitet von Hans Conzelmann; Tübingen, 1955), pp. 52ff. Moreover, in our Letter, there are no clear traces of any baptismal practices undergirding the author's view.

tion.[123] Such election gives assurance to the total group of believers, viz. 'the All', of having already been saved in the present (47.26–29). Thus, it may be said that believers are immortal by virtue of their election, their heavenly destination having been sealed before the 'cosmos' existed (so 46.20–32).

The election of believers is confirmed by Christ's work in this 'cosmos'; the surety of the present possession of the resurrection is founded upon his resurrection.[124] Christ, as Saviour, has destroyed death once and for all (46.14–20), giving the 'way of immortality' to believers by representatively anticipating their resurrection and ascension in his own dying and rising (45.22–28).[125] This is the Christological basis for the author's declaration: you already *have* the resurrection.

Still another aspect of the author's 'realized eschatology' is reflected in his use of the concept of 'rest'. This term early acquired eschatological overtones both in primitive Christianity[126] and in Gnostic circles,[127] and it has such meaning in our Letter. Thus, 'rest'

[123] The more one ponders the meaning of the phrase, 'that it is necessary', in 44.7, the stronger becomes the suspicion that our author may be drawing a logical conclusion to Paul's statement in I Cor. 15.13–14: 'But if there is no resurrection of the dead, then Christ has not been raised; if Christ has not been raised, then our preaching is in vain and your faith is in vain.'

[124] Such a view is not foreign to the NT: see Albrecht Oepke, 'ἀνίστημι, ἐξανίστημι', *TWNT*, I (1933), p. 372; John A. T. Robinson, 'Resurrection in the NT', *IDB*, IV, p. 51. The most striking difference between the teaching of 'Rheginos' and the NT is the latter's firm connection of the resurrection with the 'Parousia'. Also conspicuously absent from 'Rheginos' is the NT emphasis on the instrumentality of the Holy Spirit as the vital link between Christ's resurrection and ours, and between our present and future state (e.g., in Rom. 8.11; II Cor. 3.18; 5.4–5; 4.16; I Cor. 15.51–52; etc.).

[125] For our interpretation of the so-called 'Pauline mysticism' of this passage, see *supra*, pp. 133–9. Important to note in connection with this passage is that in our Letter Christ is always said to raise himself from the dead (e.g. 46.16 and 45.19). This contrasts sharply with the NT where, apart from John 2.19, it is always said that Christ 'was raised by God' (e.g. Matt. 14.2; 17.9; Mark 14.28; Luke 9.22; Acts 2.24; 5.30; Rom. 4.24; 7.4; 10.9; I Cor. 6.14; II Cor. 4.14; 5.15; Gal. 1.1; Eph. 1.20; Col. 2.12; I Thess. 1.10; I Peter 1.21; etc.).

[126] 'Rest' is especially used in Heb. 3.7–4.11 and Rev. 14.13 with reference to the anticipated state of the blessed. See, further, J. Y. Campbell, 'Rest', *IDB*, IV (1962), p. 38; Otto Bauernfeind, 'ἀναπαύω', *TWNT*, I (1933), p. 353.

[127] For the use of ἀνάπαυσις in Gnostic texts, the following provide numerous instructive parallels: Robert M. Grant with David Noel Freedman, *The Secret Sayings of Jesus* (London and Glasgow, 1960), pp. 115, 152, 173; Jacques E. Menard, *L'Évangile de Vérité: Rétroversion Grecque et Commentaire* (Paris, 1962), pp. 119–20, n.12; p. 128, n.29; Kendrick Grobel, *The Gospel of Truth*, pp. 79, 95, 193, and 199; Francois Sagnard, *La Gnose Valentinienne*, pp. 156–7; P. Vielhauer in *Apophoreta* (Beihefte ZNW, 30, 1964), pp. 281ff.

(ἀνάπαυσις) is related to and qualified by the 'resurrection' in 44.6. Such 'rest' seems to denote both a cessation of anxiety about death and the afterlife and a present anticipation of the fully-resurrected state. It is a gift conferred by the Saviour. This gift becomes actualized through knowledge of the 'Word of Truth' contained in Scripture (44.2) and of the 'Solution' embodied in Christ's work and word (45.3–11).

2. Unrealized Eschatology in the Letter

(a) Death As Inevitable Event

Rare indeed is that mystical piety which can maintain a point of view in the face of daily confrontation with facts of experience which contradict it. Such piety our author obviously did not have. For although he emphasized the believer's need to view death as a past event, he still conceded that this event had to be physically experienced. The biological inevitability of death is a necessary prelude to full participation in the resurrection.

This teaching of our author becomes clear from a brief summary:[128] Man, even Elect man, is subject by his very existence in this world to a 'law of nature', i.e. a law of physical death (44.17–21).[129] Consequently, the Elect who possess 'true life' (ζωή) must experience the cessation of life (48.21–22), and some of them have already expired (46.7–8). Indeed, the Saviour himself seems to have died (45.17–26; 46.14–17). The certainty of death is bound up with the believers' possession of bodies which are subject to old age and corruption (47.17–19) and with their ownership of physical and external members which make them liable to death (47.33–48.3). Thus, the arrival of old age and that 'setting in life' which is its end are inevitable (49.16–21). These facts must be frankly acknowledged by the Elect (49.16–21), although they are only properly understood when viewed in the light of the Saviour's destruction of death's power (49.26–30).

(b) Resurrection yet to be Realized

As with respect to his view on death, the author of our Letter

[128] Our summary here re-states the conclusions of our study of 'death' in the Letter undertaken *supra*, pp. 117–22.

[129] The view that death is the universal fate of men is widespread in the OT: Gen. 3.19; 15.15; 28.8; Josh. 23.14; I Kings 2.2; Job 5.26; Ps. 39.13; etc. Classical Greek thought, however, did not conceive of death as a natural event. On this, see Rudolf Bultmann, 'θάνατος', *TWNT*, III (1938), p. 9; and especially the Classical texts offered in the notes on pp. 7–10.

manifests a certain ambiguity in his conviction, on the one hand, that
the Elect are 'already raised' and, on the other, that they will not be
fully raised until death.[130] This ambiguity may be discerned from a
comparison of such passages as 49.9–30; 47.26–29; 44.6f. with 45.32–
46.2:

45.32   . . . and we are
         enclosed by
         him until our setting, that is to say,
35   our death in this life.
         We are drawn to heaven
         by him like the beams
         by the sun, not being restrained
         by anything. This is
40   the spiritual resurrection
46.1   which swallows up the psychic
2   alike with the other fleshly.

These lines make clear that the resurrection entails an ascension from
this earthly sphere following death. At death the Elect are 'drawn' to
heaven (cf. John 12.32). This is the resurrection which destroys, i.e.
'swallows up', the psychic and fleshly resurrections, the resurrected
state being purely 'spiritual' (45.40–46.1).

The idea that resurrection involves the separation at death of the
spiritual from the body is also intimated in 47.19–24, where the
expressions 'absence' (ἀπουσία) and 'to depart' (ἀπέρχομαι) are
used.[131] In the same passage the 'worse part' (πεθᴀⲩ = apparently,
the corruptible body) is said to have 'diminution', i.e. it is destined at
death to be abandoned to corruption. Thus, the believer anticipates
being disjoined from his dead, external 'members' (47.38), as from
his physical 'body' (47.35) at death. In preparation, he 'practises

[130] To gloss over this ambiguity is to fail to comprehend correctly the eschatology
of the Letter. Thus, we disagree with C. F. D. Moule who, following Puech and
Quispel, states:
     The 'de resurrectione', despite future tenses such as (46.7f.) 'He who is dead
     shall arise' (cf. 46.10), really treats the resurrection of believers as a 'fait
     accompli' . . . This is just like the view attacked in II Tim. 2.18 . . .
'St Paul and Dualism: The Pauline Conception of Resurrection', *NTS*, Vol. XII,
No. 2 (Jan. 1966), p. 112.

[131] On the eschatological significance of ἀπουσία, see our note to 47.19–22, *supra*,
p. 84. ἀπέρχομαι becomes a *terminus technicus* among the Early Fathers with the
meaning of 'departure at death'. Cf., for example, Const. *ap.* Eus. *v. C.* 2.36; and,
Chrysostom, *Hom.* 24.5 *in I Cor.*; *Hom.* 75.5 *in Mt.* These texts are cited in Lampe,
Lexicon, Fasc. 1, p. 184.

dying' that he might be freed from that inimical 'power' (στοιχεῖον) which has control over his physical body in this life (49.30–33). Having gained this freedom, the believer receives via his ascension his former state of pre-existence (49.34–36), an experience parelleling that of the Saviour (cf. 45.16–23; 46.14–17).

This conception of the resurrection reveals some interesting correspondences and contrasts to other Gnostic views. First, the author of our Letter shares in the depreciation of the physical body common to Orphic, Platonic, and Gnostic thought.[132] As we have seen, the resurrection involves the extrication of the inward and spiritual from the external and physical, an understanding of salvation necessarily presupposing a dualistic anthropology. At the same time, as will be seen in the following section, the author thinks in terms of a new resurrection *body*—an idea not exactly coinciding with Platonic or Gnostic views. Second, both our Letter and Gnostic systems generally conceive of an 'ascent' of the inner 'spirit' or 'spiritual nature' of the Elect after death (cf. Rheg. 47.7–8). But while Gnostic texts quite often indicate the need for fortification of the 'pneumatic' for his ascent with magical passwords and disguises, our Letter speaks of these not at all.[133] Third, while Gnosticism and 'Rheginos' anticipate that the ascent of the Elect will take him from earth to a separate, heavenly, realm, there is no elaboration on the nature of that realm in 'Rheginos'. That is, nothing is said in our Letter of the heavenly spheres through which the Elect must pass, of the guardians of these spheres, or of their names.[134] Fourth, our Letter does not demand as a prerequisite for resurrection that the Elect have a 'knowledge' ('gnosis') which is simultaneously 'knowledge' of the hidden, transcendent God and of the self's consubstantiality with that God.[135] The only 'knowledge' required seems to be that of recognizing and confessing the Saviour's preparation of the way of the resurrection!

[132] For the Orphic view, see Werner Jaeger, 'The Greek Ideas of Immortality', *Immortality and Resurrection. Death in the Western World: Two Conflicting Currents of Thought*, Krister Stendahl, Editor (New York, 1965), pp. 103–6. For the Platonic view, see Rohde, *Psyche*, pp. 470ff.; the Gnostic, Jonas, *Gnosis*, I, pp. 212ff.

[133] The 'heavenly ascent' of the Gnostic and his equipment with passwords, etc. are most fully described by Wilhelm Bousset, 'Die Himmelreise der Seele', *Archiv für Religionswissenschaft*, 4 (1901), pp. 136–69, 229–73.

[134] For descriptions of the heavenly world in Gnostic systems, see Jonas, *Gnosis*, I, pp. 181–90, 205–10; *The Gnostic Religion*, pp. 45, 250–65.

[135] That this 'self-gnosis' is basic to Gnostic theories of salvation is asserted by Grant, *Gnosticism and Early Christianity*, pp. 8–9; Quispel, *Gnosis als Weltreligion*, pp. 36–39.

In addition to these contrasts with other Gnostic views, our Letter's teaching on the resurrection also displays two fundamental differences from the Pauline view. First, for Paul the resurrection of both Christ and believers is part of a great history of the saving acts of God. The God who created the world, elected a people Israel, bound himself to them in covenantal promise, and fulfilled the promise in the Christ Event is the same God who will raise the dead and redeem his fallen Creation (Rom. 8.19–23). For the author of 'Rheginos', however, Christ's resurrection is severed from that history and its God. Theology, as we have indicated, is supplanted by Christology. And the world, which is not a purposive Creation but apparently a cosmic mistake, is not a sphere to be redeemed, but a sphere from which to escape. Second, the author of our Letter has 'individualized' the Apostle's resurrection teaching. Whereas Paul always places the resurrection of the believer within the resurrection of the whole of the faithful (notice, e.g., the 'we's' throughout I Cor. 15), the author of 'Rheginos' focusses on the resurrection-ascension of the individual at death.

(c) The Resurrection Body

The author of our Letter conceives of the resurrection neither as an escape of the bare 'spirit' (πνεῦμα) from the physical body, nor as the survival of the carnal flesh, i.e. the flesh identical to that utilized during earthly life. Rather, there is an ascension after death of the inward, invisible 'members' (μέλη), covered by a new, spiritual 'flesh' (σάρξ). The resurrected one retains the identifiable personal characteristics of his earthly 'flesh' despite its transformed nature. Therefore, in our author's view, discontinuity between the earthly and the resurrected body is provided by death and departure from the external, visible members and flesh; whereas, continuity is furnished by the inner, spiritual man and a spiritual flesh which retains personally identifiable characteristics. That this is our author's view we shall now attempt to show.

A key passage is 48.3–11 :[136]

. . . Then, what
is the resurrection? It is always the disclosure

---

[136] An interpretation of this passage and a study of its New Testament character are offered *supra*, pp. 18–19, 89–90. Cf. also the comments of A. Orbe, *Greg.*, 46 (1965), p. 173, on the inverted value placed upon both the Transfiguration and the Resurrection scenes by our author.

of those who have arisen. For if you
remember reading in the
Gospel that Elijah appeared and Moses
with him, do not think the
resurrection is an illusion.

It is important to note in this passage that the 'resurrection proof'
offered is the post-mortem appearance of two clearly recognizable
figures, Moses and Elijah.[137] That is, our author does not conceive of
the resurrection as an ascension of the bare 'spirit' following death,
its absorption in the Divine, and its consequent loss of all personal
identity. Rather, the resurrected Elect retain clearly recognizable
personal characteristics. A remarkable parallel to this idea appears
in the thought of Origen as reported by Methodius. Commenting on
how the 'soul' (our Letter does not use this term) must have a suitable body after the resurrection, Origen says (Methodius, *De res.*
i, 22.5):

> Just as if we had to be aquatic animals and live in the sea we should
> certainly need to have gills and other equipment of the fish, so we who
> are going to inherit the kingdom of heaven and be in places above
> must use spiritual bodies—not with the former appearance passing
> away, even if its change should be into something more glorious, as
> was the appearance of Jesus and Moses and Elijah in the transfigura-
> tion; it was not different from what it had been.[138]

If we press for more detail regarding this resurrection body,[139]
we are informed that the invisible, inward members of the Elect are
to be covered with a new 'flesh' in the resurrection (47.4-8):

> For if you did not exist
> in flesh, you received flesh when

[137] Such an appearance seems related to the author's declaration that the
resurrection always entails a 'making manifest' of the Elect in their risen state,
e.g. in 45.10–11 (?); 48.4–6; 48.34–35.

[138] The translation here follows the text established by Gottlieb Nathanael
Bonwetsch, *Methodius (Die griechischen christlichen Schriftsteller der Ersten Drei Jahr-
hunderte*, herausgegeben von der Kirchenväter-Commission der Königlichen-
Preussischen Akademie der Wissenschaft; Band 27; Leipzig, 1917), p. 246.5. The
same passage is quoted by Epiphanius, *Pan.* 64.14.8–9. Might there be allusion to
the retention of identifiable characteristics in 47.19–24 as well?

[139] Although our author never uses 'body' (σῶμα) to describe the resurrected,
he does think of the distinct personality in the spiritual state.

you entered this world. Why ((then))
will you not receive flesh when you
ascend into the Aeon?

Perhaps it is to the taking on of this 'spiritual flesh'[140] that the author
refers in his statement that the resurrection involves a 'transformation[141] of things, and a transition[142] into newness'. The reception of
this 'flesh' is implied in 48.38–49.1: 'For imperishability de[scends]
upon the perishable'. Thus, 47.4–8 does seem to make clear that a
flesh different from that used during life is received by the Elect at
his resurrection.

If the foregoing interpretation be correct, then this places Rheg.
45.39–46.2 in a new perspective:

> . . . This is
> the spiritual $(\pi\nu\epsilon\upsilon\mu\alpha\tau\iota\kappa\acute{\eta})$ resurrection $(\mathring{\alpha}\nu\acute{\alpha}\sigma\tau\alpha\sigma\iota\varsigma)$
> which swallows up the psychic $(\psi\upsilon\chi\iota\kappa\acute{\eta})$
> alike with the other fleshly $(\sigma\alpha\rho\kappa\iota\kappa\acute{\eta})$.

Of the three types of resurrection mentioned here, the 'psychic' and
the 'fleshly' are 'swallowed up' (ⲉⲥⲱⲙ̄ⲛ̄ⲕ), i.e. destroyed or denied.
The 'spiritual' is affirmed as being the true mode of resurrection.
Thus, the passage may reflect the author's implicit polemic against
those who affirm the immortality of only the naked 'soul', and
against those who contend exclusively for the resurrection of the
flesh.[143] But whether specific opponents be in mind or not in 45.39–
46.2, it is evident from our preceding study that the author could not
endorse either theory.

The foregoing leads us to an important conclusion, viz. that our

---

[140] We are in agreement with the first editors on the 'spiritual' nature of this
flesh, the implication being that nothing corporeal is involved in the resurrection.
See *De Resurrectione*, p. 34. By contrast, 'flesh' is here interpreted as being more
corporeal by Zandee, *NTT*, 16 (1962), pp. 370ff.; van Unnik, *JEH*, XV, No. 2
(1964), pp. 150f.; Daniélou, *VC*, XVIII, No. 3 (1964), p. 188; Goldsmith, *JR*,
45 (1965), p. 257.

[141] The Coptic expression ⲩϩⲉⲓⲉ ('transformation') is used to translate
$\mu\epsilon\tau\alpha\mu\rho\rho\phi\omicron\tilde{\upsilon}\sigma\theta\alpha\iota$ (Crum, 551b) in Matt. 17.2—a reference to Jesus' Transfiguration!
The same Coptic root renders $\mathring{\alpha}\lambda\lambda\acute{\alpha}\sigma\sigma\omega$ in I Cor. 15.51–52, a verb used to refer to the
change anticipated for the bodies of Christians at the final Resurrection.

[142] In later Patristic literature $\mu\epsilon\tau\alpha\beta\omicron\lambda\acute{\eta}$ is used with the meaning of 'change',
implying deification. Cf., e.g. Origen, *Con. Cels.* 3.37; Methodius, *Symp.* 4.2.

[143] Our interpretation here rests on earlier arguments and discussion given
supra, pp. 48f.

author's view of the *resurrection body* is a reasonably faithful interpretation of the Pauline view[144]—more faithful, in fact, than that of many of the heresiologists of early Christendom! That is,

> . . . Paul steered a remarkably consistent course between, on the one hand, a materialistic doctrine of physical resurrection and, on the other hand, a dualistic doctrine of the escape of the soul from the body.[145]

The author of our Letter apparently rejects both, too. In a rather Pauline fashion the Letter teaches that the resurrection body, while retaining some identifiable personal characteristics by which the earthly flesh was recognizable, is actually a new, spiritual body.[146] This contrasts sharply with those Fathers of the Church who, in their struggles with Docetic and Platonic theories of an immortal soul, affirmed in a very 'un-Pauline' fashion a crudely literal identity between the earthly, physical body and the flesh of the resurrected body.[147] Nevertheless, our author's negative evaluation of the 'world' and the corruptible body of 'flesh' does border upon a metaphysical and anthropological dualism which goes beyond Paul's views.[148] The Apostle thought of man as a somatic totality and of the resurrection as involving the transformation of the whole body.[149]

[144] We have purposely limited the comparison made here to the *nature* of the resurrection body. There are obvious differences between Paul's and our Letter's conceptions of the chronology of the resurrection, i.e. at what point after death a person is to be resurrected; but these will be discussed *infra*, pp. 152–3.

[145] The description is C. F. D. Moule's, as offered in *NTS*, Vol. 12, No. 2 (Jan. 1966), p. 107. We are well-acquainted with the long-standing controversy concerning the possible spheres of influence operative on the Apostle's resurrection teaching; but, having considered the evidence, we believe Moule's to be the most balanced generalization that can probably be made about Paul's conception. For a summary of the controversy, see E. E. Ellis, *Paul and His Recent Interpreters*, pp. 35–48.

[146] J. A. T. Robinson, *IDB*, IV, p. 52, summarizes the Apostle's understanding of the resurrection body: 'Paul's sole point is to stress that for all the identity of person there is a radical discontinuity of form (cf. I Cor. 15.36–38).'

[147] The disparity between the Pauline view of a spiritually transformed resurrection body and the Fathers' doctrine of the resurrection of the *flesh* has been ably demonstrated. See, e.g. Robert M. Grant, 'The Resurrection of the Body', *JR*, Vol. XXVIII (1948), pp. 124–30, 188–208; C. K. Barrett, 'Immortality and Resurrection', *The London Quarterly and Holborn Review*, Vol. CXC, Sixth Series, Vol. XXXIV (1965), pp. 96–102; cf. Harry A. Wolfson, 'Immortality and Resurrection in the Philosophy of the Church Fathers', *Immortality and Resurrection* (Stendahl, ed.), pp. 65ff.

[148] Further, we never find Paul using the term σάρξ—regardless of how spiritually interpreted—to identify the resurrection body, as we do in Rheg. 47.4–8.

[149] See, on this, M. E. Dahl, *The Resurrection of the Body* (Studies in Biblical Theology, No. 36; London, 1962), pp. 59–73, 94f.

(d) The Final Destiny

In one brief passage, 46.28–31, our author reveals his belief in the double predestination of mankind. On the one hand, some are elected to full participation in the 'wisdom (σύνεσις or σωφροσύνη: Crum, 715a) of the Truth' (46.30–31), a 'wisdom' which is apparently identified with the content of the Christian faith.[150] On the other hand, the non-Elect are described as 'falling into the folly (ἀφροσύνη or ἄνοια: Crum, 714b) of those who are without knowledge' (46.28–29), a 'folly' which is seemingly equated with disbelief in Christ's work.[151] Beyond what is stated in 46.28–31, however, nothing further is mentioned in our Letter concerning the final estate of the Elect, except for the implication that they shall be with Christ (45.36–39).

The ultimate goal of the saving work of the Saviour is alluded to in 44.30–33:

> . . . through the Son of
> Man the restoration (ἀποκατάστασις)
> to the Pleroma might occur . . .

This 'restoration'[152] seems to involve the return of the 'All', the whole body of the Elect, to its pre-existent state in the Pleroma. By this means, the 'deficiency' (ὑστέρημα) left in the Pleroma by the creation of the world and the coming into cosmic existence of the 'All' will apparently be overcome (49.4–5). But it is evident from the author's negative evaluation of the 'cosmos', e.g. in 47.5–6; 48.13–16, 22–28; etc., that the 'restoration' excludes any transformation of creation or redemption of the non-Elect. The II Future Tense of the main verb in 44.30–33 indicates that the 'restoration' is an event that has not yet occurred; rather, it seems to be the final goal towards which the whole process of salvation is moving.

---

[150] On the meaning of 'Truth' in our Letter, see *supra*, p. 131, n.85. Cf. also Paul's comments on 'wisdom' in I Cor. 1.24; 2.6.

[151] The contrast between 'wisdom' and 'folly', which is used here to describe the respective destinies of believers and non-believers, is part of the technical terminology of Wisdom Literature. Cf. Sir. 22.12; Wisd. of Sol. 3.12; 4.9. See, for additional texts and discussion, James A. Kelso, 'Fool, Folly', *Encyclopaedia of Religion and Ethics*, James Hastings, ed. (Vol. VI, Edinburgh and New York, 1914), pp. 68–69.

[152] 'Restoration' (ἀποκατάστασις), as the editors have shown, is a *terminus technicus* in Valentinian Gnosticism. See *De Resurrectione*, p. 23. Add to the parallels cited there some of the texts found in Rohde, *Psyche*, pp. x, 47, 519; Lampe, *Lexicon* Fasc. I, p. 195; Albrecht Oepke, 'ἀποκαθίστημι, ἀποκατάστασις', *TWNT*, I (1933), pp. 388–92.

D. THE TEMPORAL DIMENSIONS OF ESCHATOLOGY

Having surveyed the sphere, means, and goals of eschatology in our Letter, it will be important now to attempt a synthesis of that teaching through an examination of its temporal aspects. Unfortunately, the author of our Letter never makes use of any specifically temporal terms, such as καιρός or χρόνος, by means of which we might study his views on time.[153] Consequently, we must content ourselves with a study of allusions which shed only indirect light on this subject.

It seems that for this Gnostic teacher time has transpired between two poles. The first of these, the 'beginning' (ϣⲁⲣⲡ = ἀρχή in 44.33–34; 46.27), is conceived of as the pre-existent state of the Pleroma (46.35ff.), which in its perfection encompassed the Saviour (44.33–36), the 'All' of the Elect (46.38–47.1; cf. 47.26–27), and that which was potentially the 'cosmos' (46.35–38). The second pole, or end goal, to which, the author's thought extends is the 'restoration' (ἀποκατάστασις in 44.31–33), the final assemblage of all the resurrected Elect (49.4–5). Between this pre-existent 'beginning' and final 'restoration' is the period in which both 'cosmos' and the physical bodies of men are slowly perishing in corruption (45.16–17; 47.17–19). Thus the 'time'[154] of 'life' (βίος) in this 'cosmos' is viewed negatively as a period of illusion, flux, and change (48.22–27). From such time, as from the perishing world, the resurrected Elect shall depart, for his sojourn here has been only temporary (47.14–15). The implication of this is that time and the cosmic history of which it is a part represent spheres of imprisonment from which the Elect seeks to escape.[155] But, significantly, one decisive event has occurred within this history, viz. the descent, ministry, death, and resurrection of the Saviour (44.21–36; 45.14–21; 45.25–39; 46.14–20; 48.16–19). This event has provided a 'way of immortality' for the Elect, a way of escape from the sphere of cosmic existence. Thus, in apparent contrast to the general Gnostic view,[156] the Christ event is viewed as an

---

[153] It is true that the concept αἰών ocurs twice, viz. in 45.18 and 47.8; but in neither occurrence does it have any clear temporal meaning.

[154] The word 'time' is used here for convenience, although it does not occur in our Letter.

[155] Such, also, is generally the Gnostic view of time. On this, see Henri-Charles Puech, 'Gnosis and Time', *Man and Time: Papers from the Eranos Yearbook*, tr. Ralph Manheim (*Bollingen Series*, XXX.3; New York, 1957), p. 40; Jonas, *Gnosis*, I, p. 100.

[156] The uselessness and meaninglessness of historical events for the Gnostic is

event of historical significance! Only by entering the cosmos and suffering within it could the Saviour defeat death and provide the Elect with the means of escape from the temporal sphere of the world.

Despite this great framework within which the author's temporal consciousness moves, his real focus of attention is upon the present, i.e. upon what of significance for the believer's present has already taken place (43.34–37; 45.22–28; 46.20–24; 47.26–29; 49.15–16; 49.25–26). Thus, he explicitly emphasizes the *already* of both the believer's death and resurrection, while acknowledging less emphatically that *not yet* which characterizes those eschatological events still to occur.[157] An inner tension, therefore, manifests itself in the eschatological thought of the author: (1) the Elect man is *already* dead, but he has *not yet* physically died; (2) the Elect is *already* resurrected, but his resurrection is *not yet* fully consummated. But, as previously stated, the clear emphasis of our Letter is on the realized side of this tension.

The similarities of such a tension to the eschatologies of the Fourth Gospel[158] and the Apostle Paul[159] are striking. However, basic differences lie in the facts that whereas the author of 'Rheginos' identifies fulfilment of the 'not yet' with the physical death and resurrection-ascension of the believer, John's 'not yet' is characterized by the expectation of a 'last day' when the Son of Man shall raise the dead (cf. John 5.28–29; 6.39–40). Moreover, Paul's 'not yet' is distinguished by an 'eschatological reservation', i.e. the connection of the resurrection with the 'Parousia', thus giving it a futuristic character.[160] In 'Rheginos', however, the 'Parousia' is stripped away and vaguely replaced with a 'Restoration' (*ἀποκατάστασις*). Thus, the

---

discussed by Puech, 'Gnosis and Time', *Man and Time*, p. 63; Samuel Laeuchli, *The Language of Faith* (New York, 1962), pp. 81–82.

[157] This statement summarizes the main thrust of our argument in the preceding section on our Letter's 'Goals of Eschatology'.

[158] The eschatological 'paradox' in John has been made clear by C. K. Barrett, *The Gospel According to St John. An Introduction with Commentary and Notes* (London, 1965), pp. 56–58; C. H. Dodd, *The Interpretation of the Fourth Gospel*, pp. 144–50.

[159] On the 'already/not yet' tension in Pauline eschatology, see Bultmann, *Theology*, I, pp. 346ff.; J. A. T. Robinson, *IDB*, IV, p. 51; Ellis, *Paul and His Interpreters*, pp. 35–48; Béda Rigaux, *Saint Paul et ses Lettres: État de la Question* (*Studia Neotestamentica*, Subsidia II, ediderunt A. Descamps, E. Massaux, B. Rigaux; Paris, 1962), pp. 29–34.

[160] On the Pauline 'eschatological reservation', see James M. Robinson, 'Kerygma and History in the New Testament', *The Bible in Modern Scholarship: Papers Read at the 100th Meeting of the Society of Biblical Literature. December 28–30, 1964*, ed. by J. Philip Hyatt (New York and London, 1965/1967), pp. 122–7.

resurrection, which for Paul and the author of the Fourth Gospel was ultimately a matter of faith and future hope, has become for our author an almost automatic process for the Elect.

To sharpen even further our understanding of time in the Letter's eschatology, we may briefly compare it with some other recent portraits of Gnostic time and eschatology drawn by Henri-Charles Puech, Rudolf Bultmann, Hans Jonas, Jan Zandee, and Robert Haardt. First, Puech believes that in the Gnostic view time is 'shattered in pieces' since salvation must involve the negation of cosmic time as a reality.[161] By contrast, in our Letter there is a distinct consciousness of a 'beginning' and an end ('restoration'), as well as of the historically conditioned events of Christ's resurrection and the individual's death. Second, Bultmann and Jonas stress the 'atemporal' nature of Gnostic eschatology, i.e. all sense of time dissolves for the Gnostic in the face of the mystical appropriation of salvation through the reception of 'gnosis'.[162] Certainly this view, which relegates everything to the present experience of the Gnostic, is similar to our Letter's emphasis on the present but fails to do justice to the eschatological tension—unbalanced as it may be—in the Letter. Third, Zandee views Gnostic eschatology as cyclical. It is a process eschatology involving a return to their original state of all sparks of Light distributed among 'pneumatic' men.[163] In 'Rheginos', however, the resurrected Elect have spiritual bodies which they apparently did not possess in their pre-existence, and the 'world'—somehow included potentially in the pre-existent Pleroma (46.35–38)—is excluded in the 'Restoration'. Fourth, Haardt is convinced that the 'end time' in Gnostic speculation is decisive and controlling for all of Gnostic eschatology. Thus, Gnosticism's view of time could be characterized as linear.[164] The final 'restoration' in our Letter does seem significant, but it is certainly less emphasized than the present realization of eschatological goals. In actuality, time appears to be qualitatively distinguished in our Letter, there being a time of pre- and resurrection-existence as opposed to a temporary earthly so-

---

[161] See Puech, 'Gnosis and Time', *Man and Time*, pp. 40ff., 64f.
[162] For Rudolf Bultmann's views, see *Primitive Christianity*, pp. 161, 171f.; *Theology*, I, pp. 166, 183. The position of Jonas is expressed in his volumes, *Gnosis* I, p. 100; II, 1, pp. 138–43.
[163] Jan Zandee gives expression to this theory in *Numen*, Vol. XI, Fasc. 1 (January, 1964), pp. 19, 41, 49–51, 66–68; cf. also *X. Internationaler Kongress für Religionsgeschichte, 11–17 September, 1960* (1961), pp. 94–95.
[164] See Robert Haardt, *Vom Messias zum Christus*, p. 321.

journ. Major stress, however, is upon a realized/unrealized eschatological tension, with the realized aspect being most emphasized.

A diagram may best be used to portray the movement of time in
our author's eschatology. Rather than the circle, the linear line, the
fragmented line, or the spiral, the parabola seems to represent our
author's views most accurately:

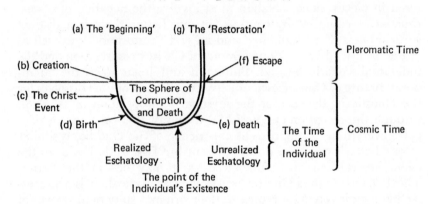

THE PLEROMA

EXPLANATION OF THE DIAGRAM

(a) 'The "Beginning".' The pre-existent state of perfection of the
   Pleroma. In this state were the 'All', the Saviour, emanations,
   and the potential 'cosmos'. From this point the time line dips
   downward, denoting a fall into an inferior state.

(b) 'Creation.' The coming into existence of the 'cosmos'. Note that
   creation corresponds with the beginning of cosmic time.

(c) 'The Christ Event.' The decisive descent into cosmic time of
   the Saviour and his defeat—within cosmic time—of death. This
   event decisively affects everything that follows: thus the double
   black line.

(d) 'Birth.' The beginning of the individual's 'life' within the cosmic
   sphere. The individual pre-existed in the 'All', but became an
   identifiable person in the flesh only within the cosmic sphere of
   death and corruption.

   We intersect the time line of the individual to indicate the
   point of present existence, i.e. the point from which our author

views things. Note that the intersection is made at a point nearer the individual's death than to his birth, thus representing the 'already/not yet' tension of the Letter's eschatology, but emphasizing the importance of the 'already'.

(e) 'Death.' The cessation of the individual's life and the beginning of his ascension.

(f) 'Escape.' The point of departure of the Elect from the cosmic plane of existence through his resurrection-ascension.

(g) 'The "Restoration".' The final goal toward which the time line of salvation moves. The parabola permits us to indicate that the 'Restoration' ends with the restored Pleroma and thus essentially on the same plane as the 'Beginning'. Nevertheless, the 'Restoration' differs from the 'Beginning' in that in the former the Elect have identifiable resurrection bodies which they did not have before; furthermore, the 'cosmos' is excluded, whereas it was included at the 'Beginning'.

V

THE AUTHORSHIP OF THE LETTER

THE PRECEDING INVESTIGATION of the eschatological teaching of our Letter has uncovered some matters important to the question of its authorship. It will be our purpose in this concluding chapter to set forth these matters and thereby submit to a critical re-examination the editors' hypothesis of authorship.

As indicated previously,[1] the first editors have argued that the Letter to Rheginos emanated from the Valentinian sphere of Gnosticism and that Valentinus himself was probably its author. To quote them:

> It has for (its) author a Valentinian: it may be a master of the 'Oriental' School of Valentinianism; it may be Valentinus himself. In choosing between these two possibilities, we have decided, on our part, with the reservations which are imperative, in favour of the second.[2]

Most others who have worked with the document agree on its Valentinian provenance, but not all concur in ascribing it to the hand of Valentinus.[3] Such dissent is not without foundation, and

---

[1] *Supra*, pp. viii, 13–16.

[2] Puech and Quispel, *De Resurrectione*, p. xxxiii. Actually, Quispel seems to have been the first to advance this thesis of authorship: see *VC*, VII (1953), p. 193. The following year, Puech added his support: see Puech and Quispel, *VC*, VIII (1954), pp. 50–51. Nevertheless, certain caution has appeared in Puech's affirmation of this view, e.g. in *The Jung Codex*, p. 19; in *Encyclopédie Française*, Tome XIX (1957), p. 19.42–8; and in *CRAIBL* (1964), p. 319. Gilles Quispel, however, supports the thesis with little qualification in *Orpheus*, X, No. 1 (1963), p. 12, and in 'The Writings of Valentinus Recently Discovered in Upper Egypt', *Acta Congressus Madvigiani*, Vol. I (1958), p. 230. Schenke, *OrL*, 60 (1965), cols. 472–3, has also sensed a difference between Puech and Quispel in the manner of their affirmation of this thesis.

[3] See, for example, the comments of Daniélou, *VC*, XVIII, No. 3 (1964), p. 188; Haenchen, in *ThR*, N.F. 30, Heft 1 (1964), p. 57 and in *Gnomon*, 36 (1964), pp. 361–2; Leipoldt, *TL*, 7, 90 (Juli 1965), col. 520; and, van Unnik, *JEH*, XV, No. 2 (Oct. 1964), p. 144. Schenke, *OrL*, 60 (1965), col. 473, even challenges—wrongly, we believe—the Valentinian nature of the Letter!

there appears room for another hypothesis. To present such, however, we must first deal with several facets of the authors' theory,
including their six arguments for Valentinus' authorship, and their
comparison of the D.R. with the E.V.[4] With these matters reviewed,
we may then confront afresh the teaching of the D.R. with what we
know of Valentinus' own thought.

Before proceeding, it is essential that we clearly delineate the
purposes of this chapter. We do not attempt here a thorough demonstration of the historical authorship of our Letter, as that would
require extensive study beyond the stated intentions of this investigation. Rather, on the basis of fresh insight derived from our study
of the D.R.'s teaching, we shall raise some probing questions about
the editors' hypothesis of its authorship and offer *as a suggestion* an
alternative hypothesis. Thus, our approach here is deliberately
critical. Where the editors have sought to show similarity, we shall
purposely stress difference. The reader himself must judge the success
or failure of this challenge to the view that Valentinus himself wrote
the D.R.

A. A CRITIQUE OF THE EDITORS' SIX ARGUMENTS

To strengthen their hypothesis that the founder of the Oriental
School of Valentinian Gnosticism composed the D.R., Puech and
Quispel have advanced six specific arguments. The nature of these
is such that their strength lies in their combination, i.e. considered as
a whole these arguments are relatively impressive; but, considered
separately, none of them are decisive. To show that this is so, we
treat them individually.

First Argument. Valentinus composed some doctrinal letters. This we
know from fragments of them preserved in Clement of Alexandria's
Stromata. Consequently, he could have written a letter like 'Rheginos'.[5]

As Ernst Haenchen has aptly remarked, the fact that Valentinus
was a letter-writer and the D.R. is a letter proves nothing;[6] it merely
suggests a possibility which, of course, cannot be excluded. Of in-

---

[4] The abbreviations D.R. (*'De Resurrectione'*) and E.V. (*'Evangelium Veritatis'*)
are used throughout this chapter to facilitate reference to these works.
[5] *De Resurrectione*, p. xxv.
[6] See *ThR*, N.F. 30, Heft 1 (1964), p. 57; *Gnomon*, 36 (1964), pp. 361–2.

terest, however, is the manner in which Clement introduces his quotations from Valentinus' letters:

. . . καὶ Οὐαλεντῖνος, ἔν τινι ἐπιστολῇ τοιαῦτα τινα ἐν νῷ λαβὼν αὐταῖς γράφεις ταῖς λέξεσι . . .

(*Strom.* II, c. VIII, 36.2–4)[7]

. . . Οὐαλεντῖνος . . . ἐν τῇ πρὸς 'Αγαθόποδα ἐπιστολῇ . . .

(*Strom.* III, c. VII, 59.3)

. . . καὶ Οὐαλεντῖνος πρός τινας ἐπιστέλλων αὐταῖς λέξεσι γράφει . . .

(*Strom.* II, c. XX, 114.3–6)

From the second of these citations it may be inferred that the letter about to be quoted contained a praescriptio in which Valentinus as the sender and Agathopous as the receiver were named. The same appears reasonably certain of the first and third letters, too. It seems curious, then, that the D.R., supposedly written by this same Valentinus, lacks such a praescriptio—especially since the letter was addressed to an individual.[8] The praescriptio, as we have suggested,[9] may have been removed from the original letter. However, it would be strange if the venerated name of Valentinus had been removed by other Gnostics who presumably preserved the letter.[10]

Second Argument. Valentinus was an educated 'Platonist' who reflected both hostility and attraction toward philosophy. The same background and ambivalent attitude are detected in the author of the D.R.[11]

This argument is partially apologetic since the authors (presumably in anticipation of being interrogated on the issue) have attempted to reconcile an attitude found in our Letter with what is otherwise completely unknown about Valentinus. That is, none of the records preserved by the heresiologists or Valentinian writers mention Valentinus' own rejection of philosophy; yet, in D.R. 46.7–13 such a rejection appears.[12] The editors explain away this

[7] The texts are quoted from Otto Stählin, Herausgeber, *Clemens Alexandrinus* (*GCS*, Band II–*Stromata*; Leipzig, 1906).

[8] The demonstration that the D.R. is a personal letter is presented *supra*, pp. 5–12.

[9] *Supra*, pp. 10f.

[10] The theory that our Letter is part of a library collected by Gnostic sectaries is mentioned *supra*, p. 12.

[11] *De Resurrectione*, pp. xxv–xxvi.

[12] This, at least, is the interpretation offered by Puech and Quispel, in *ibid.*, pp. xviii and xxvi.

discrepancy by attributing an ambivalent attitude to Valentinus. The argument is thus intrinsically circular.

The argument is further weakened by the fact that several of the Platonic conceptions identified in the D.R. as part of the philosophical background of the author seem on closer examination to rest upon some misinterpretations of the text. For example, a supposed contrast between κόσμος and αἰών in 45.16–18 is said to parallel the Platonic contrast between the 'image' and the 'living model'.[13] Such a comparison rests, however, on Puech's erroneous interpretation of 45.17–18; for in that passage Christ is said to *transform himself* into a divine αἰών, not that he *was transferred* to one.[14] In another passage, 46.35–47.1, the 'intelligible' world is said to be opposed to the 'sensible' world in a manner similar to Plato's thought.[15] We must reply, however, that the qualifying adjectives expressive of the contrast do not appear at all in the D.R. Further, whereas 46.35–47.1 indicates that the world's creation was a cosmic mistake, Platonic cosmology—especially as expressed in the *Timaeus*—understood the world to be the creation of the Good and to be sustained, even as an image, by that Good.[16] The opposition may owe something originally to Platonism, but in the D.R. it has become clearly gnosticized. Also, in D.R. 47.9–27 the editors state that the 'spirit' (πνεῦμα) is shown to be superior to the transitory, earthly 'body' (σῶμα).[17] But πνεῦμα is not mentioned in 47.9–27, the conception there being rather of inward, spiritual limbs—an idea probably developed out of the Pauline concept of the 'inner man'.[18] Finally, reference to the salvation of the 'All' in 47.26 is held to echo faithfully the Platonic view which identifies man completely, the integral man, with his 'mind' (νοῦς).[19] We, on the contrary, have argued that 'All' is a technical term used for the total group of the Elect.[20]

There are some Platonic features in our Letter, however, which the editors have omitted mentioning. Two of the clearest are the pre-

---

[13] *Ibid.*, p. xxv.
[14] See *supra*, pp. 67f.
[15] *De Resurrectione*, pp. xvii and xxv.
[16] See the comments of A. E. Taylor, 'Plato', *Encyclopedia Britannica* (Vol. 18; Chicago, London, Toronto, 1955), pp. 59–60. The *Phaedo* does present a different view, but, as Taylor shows (p. 57), it is wrong to speak of an absolute dualism even in that dialogue.
[17] *De Resurrectione*, p. xvii.
[18] See *supra*, pp. 83–87 and section 53.
[19] *De Resurrectione*, p. xvii.
[20] See *supra*, pp. 81, 107f.

existence of souls,[21] and the theme of 'practising for dying'.[22] Nevertheless, the 'Platonism' of our Letter is not pronounced. Its presence does no more than to add confirmation to what was already known, viz. that the influence of Platonism was widespread in the second century.[23]

Third Argument. Tertullian lauded Valentinus as being both 'ingenious and eloquent'. A re-translation of the Coptic text of the D.R. into its Greek prototype reveals a skilled and elegant stylist as its composer.[24]

Since the re-translation of our Letter made by Quispel[25] has not been published, this argument cannot be fully submitted to verification. Even so, several considerations make us hesitant to accept the editors' judgement concerning the quality of the underlying Greek text of 'Rheginos'.

In the first place, the problems encountered in trying to translate a Coptic text back into its original Greek are manifold and complex. For example, in deciding which of several possible Greek words may be rendered by a particular Coptic word, the best control available is afforded by the practice of translators of the Coptic Bible. In several instances, however, it is evident that Greek reconstructions offered by the editors are made without such a control;[26] even the explicit testimony of Walter Crum's standard *Coptic Dictionary* is neglected.[27] Moreover, the re-establishment of the Greek original of a Coptic Biblical text, even a text for which we possess a reasonably close Greek manuscript, is fraught with problems. As Walter Till comments:

> Moreover, it cannot be expected that the Coptic version will always accurately represent the tenses and moods of the Greek verbs or that these will always be translated in the same way. This is impossible because the very rich means of expression of the Coptic verb have developed in an entirely different way from the Greek. The forms of the Coptic conjunction have quite different values of meaning. Therefore,

[21] See *supra*, pp. 111f.
[22] See *supra*, pp. 98f, 132f.
[23] Compare the statements on Platonism in the second century offered by Eduard Zeller, *Outlines of the History of Greek Philosophy*, tr. L. R. Palmer (Thirteenth Edition, Revised by Wilhelm Nestle; New York, 1955), pp. 305–10.
[24] *De Resurrectione*, p. xxvi.
[25] We learn that such a re-translation exists in *ibid.*, p. xxxiv.
[26] Cf., for example, our notes to 44.7–8 (pp. 55f.); 45.16–23 (pp. 67ff.); 50.11 (pp. 102f.); also pp. 114–16.
[27] See, for example, our note to 49.7, *supra*, pp. 94f.

it is often impossible for the Coptic translator to find exact Coptic equivalents for the Greek moods and tenses. He must often choose amongst several possibilities of which none translates exactly the Greek form of the verb. That is why the Coptic version is always, to a certain degree, an interpretation by the translator. Moreover, the rules for the arrangement of the words in a Coptic sentence are different from those in Greek. These . . . few hints . . . are sufficient to show that it is often impossible even for one who knows Coptic to decide with certainty whether a difference between the Greek text and its Coptic translation is due to the peculiarity of the Coptic language or to a true variant of the Greek text.[28]

Coptic, therefore, could not easily capture the flexibility and rich nuances of Greek style. There is no clear distinction in it between the indicative and the subjunctive; the idiom lacks the past participle; and among Coptic translators there is a general tendency to be satisfied with the preterite.[29] In the light of these matters it is difficult not to be sceptical about the editors' claim to be able to find behind the 'often clumsy' rendering of the Coptic translator an elegantly-written Greek original of our Letter.[30]

In the second place, there is some room to question just how 'ingenious and eloquent' the writer of our Letter really is. For instance, we have detected a number of rather paratactic constructions in the Letter.[31] Also, the author's use of New Testament material by no means reflects the exegetical acumen of a Ptolemaeus, as may be shown by comparison with the latter's Letter to Flora.[32] He actually by-passes several opportunities to bring certain New Testament expressions more into conformity with his Gnostic views,[33] and thus gives the appearance of being in contradiction with what Valentinian Gnosticism generally taught. In addition, a lack of clear logic

[28] Till, *BJRL*, 40 (1957–8), p. 238.
[29] See Vööbus, *Early Versions*, p. 224.
[30] In *De Resurrectione*, p. xxvi, the editors state:
　　. . . several passages of the Treatise at first appear obscure and badly executed. But these defects, without a doubt, are to be credited to the Coptic translator who has often misunderstood and poorly rendered the original. It is only by re-translating the text into Greek that there may be recognized the mark of a good writer, or, at least, the procedures of one who pretends to be . . .
[31] See, e.g., our comments on the use of ⲁⲩⲱ ('and') in our notes to 43.29 (p. 52); 44.8–10 (p. 56.); 44.23 (p. 60); 46.8–13 (p. 77).
[32] Cf. C. Barth's comments on Ptolemaeus in *Die Interpretation* (1911), pp. 102–3.
[33] See *supra*, pp. 25f.

is apparent at certain points in the text.[34] Finally, the writer of our Letter (44.39–45.2) implicitly acknowledges his shortcomings in expressing himself clearly in his teaching[35]—a rather remarkable admission if the author was indeed the persuasive Valentinus himself!

Fourth Argument. Valentinus, as a Gnostic teacher, claimed to possess a secret tradition derived from the Apostle Paul through Theudas. The author of the D.R. also received such a tradition from Christ (49.37–50.1). Moreover, the author addresses the recipients of his Letter in the manner of a master of a school, i.e. as 'sons' and 'brethren'.[36]

The most serious flaw in this argument rests, as Haenchen has correctly indicated,[37] in the argument itself. That is, the author does not—like Valentinus—claim to have received what he has taught from Paul, but rather from Christ! And, apart from some allusions to Valentinian mythology, the Letter contains nothing esoteric. The author attempts as a Christian to interpret the New Testament view of the resurrection, and his teaching is generally straightforward and clear. In fact, 49.37–50.1 probably refers not to a secret tradition at all, but rather to the insight and interpretative skill which the author acknowledges as having been granted him by his Lord.

Further, the author makes no attempt to swear Rheginos to secrecy regarding the Letter's contents, and there is no explicit recommendation as to with whom the Letter might be shared. The editors' efforts to find such a recommendation in 49.37–50.1 must be rejected as tendentious.[38] Indeed, 50.11–13 makes explicit that 'many' may look at the Letter, there being no specification as to whom the 'many' may be. And, in 50.15–16 the author of the D.R. actually extends a greeting via his pupils to those outside their own circle![39]

Finally, while the author's manner of addressing Rheginos and his brethren as 'sons' does betoken a teacher-pupil relationship,[40]

---

[34] See *supra*, p. 50. Cf. also Schenke, *OrL*, 60 (1965), col. 472.

[35] See our note to 45.1–2, *supra*, p. 64; cf. also 48.19–20. To these comments we might add those of Leipoldt, *TL*, 90 (Juli 1965), col. 520; Haenchen, *ThR*, N.F. 30, Heft 1 (1964), p. 57. The latter quips that even a re-translation of the D.R. into Greek will 'not make any literary masterpiece out of it!'

[36] *De Resurrectione*, p. xxvi.

[37] *Gnomon*, 36 (1964), p. 361.

[38] See their 'Note Critique' to 50.8–10 in *De Resurrectione*, p. 47.

[39] Cf. our note to 50.16, *supra*, p. 103.

[40] See our comments supporting this, *supra*, pp. 100f.

such a manner by no means guarantees that the writer was the master of a school.[41]

Fifth Argument. Like Valentinus, the author of our Letter displays certain affinities of thought with the 'Asiatic Theology' represented by Ignatius of Antioch, Irenaeus of Lyons, and the Fourth Gospel. This is especially seen in the Christocentrism of both. In fact, nothing in the Christology of our Letter—including some new uses of the titles Son of God and Son of Man—prohibits attributing it to Valentinus.[42]

This argument contains several parts which must be dealt with separately. Initially, we would indicate that the 'Asiatic Theology', in which some parallels are sought to the Valentinianism of our Letter, actually differs radically from the teaching of the D.R. or Valentinus at two crucial points. First, Ignatius (*Smyrn.* 3.2), Irenaeus (*Adv. Haer.* V, *passim*), and the Fourth Gospel (cf. the Lazarus pericope in ch. 11; 5.25f.; 6.39–40, 44; 12.48) all stress that the resurrection will involve the 'flesh' ($\sigma \acute{\alpha} \rho \xi$) of the deceased. However, neither the D.R.[43] nor Valentinus[44] teach a resurrection of the physical 'flesh'. Indeed, the D.R. appears to support the view of a 'spiritual resurrection', and most early records indicate that Valentinus thought only of a rising of the 'spiritual element' in man. And, second, Ignatius (*Eph.* 7–9; *Magn.* 11; *Trall.* 9–11; *Smyrn.* 1–7; *Polyc.* 3); Irenaeus (*Adv. Haer.* I, *passim*; V, 14.2) and John (1.14) all display an anti-docetic emphasis on the flesh and blood body of Christ. But, whereas the D.R. also speaks of Christ 'taking on flesh' (44.14–15) and possessing human nature (44.23–26), Valentinus, according to the editors,[45] taught that Christ was completely 'spiritual', there being nothing carnal in him.

As part of their argument, the editors also try to show that two themes found in the D.R. are shared by Valentinus and Ignatius of Antioch:

(1) The theme of the Son as the agent of God's revelation:

---

[41] Yet this is precisely the editors' argument. See *De Resurrectione*, p. xxvi.

[42] *Ibid.*, pp. xxvi–xxix.

[43] See *supra*, pp. 214–17.

[44] See *De Resurrectione*, pp. xxvii–xxix, where the editors cite and discuss Valentinus' teaching.

[45] *Ibid.*, pp. xxiii–xxiv; xxviif. The editors here follow the views of the Oriental School of Valentinianism, that School which they believe has most faithfully preserved Valentinus' own teaching.

(Clem. Alex., *Strom.* II, 114.3)—εἷς δὲ ἐστιν ἀγαθός, οὗ παρρησία ἡ διὰ τοῦ υἱοῦ φανέρωσις, . . .

(Ign., *Rom.* 8.2)—Ἰησοῦς δὲ Χριστὸς ὑμῖν ταῦτα φανερώσει, ὅτι ἀληθῶς λέγω. τὸ ἀψευδὲς στόμα, ἐν ᾧ ὁ πατὴρ ἐλάλησεν ἀληθῶς.

(2) The theme that the Elect and Christ have co-operated in the destruction of death:

(Clem. Alex., *Strom.* IV, 89.1–2)[46]—ἀπ' ἀρχῆς ἀθανατοί ἐστε καὶ τέκνα ζωῆς ἐστε αἰωνίας καὶ τὸν θάνατον ἠθέλετε μερίσασθαι εἰς ἑαυτούς, ἵνα δαπανήσητε αὐτὸν καὶ ἀναλώσητε, καὶ ἀποθάνῃ ὁ θάνατος ἐν ὑμῖν καὶ δι' ὑμῶν.

(Ign., *Eph.* 19.3)—θεοῦ ἀνθρωπίνως φανερουμένου εἰς καινότητα ἀϊδίου ζωῆς· ἀρχὴν δὲ ἐλάμβανεν τὸ παρὰ θεῷ ἀπηρτισμένον. ἔνθεν τὰ πάντα συνεκινεῖτο διὰ τὸ μελετᾶσθαι θανάτου κατάλυσιν.[47]

The attempt to demonstrate Valentinus' dependence on 'Asiatic theology' from these parallels is weakened, however, by the fact that the themes of Christ as revealer and as destroyer of death can be explained by mutual use of the New Testament. Certainly, it is possible that the D.R. has drawn inspiration from the New Testament in its use of these two themes.[48] To have said these things, however, is not to deny that some historical connection does exist between Valentinianism and 'Asiatic theology', but the connection of such 'theology' with our Letter awaits convincing demonstration.

Another facet of this fifth argument is the editors' effort to compare what can be inferred from D.R. 44.17–21 with Valentinus' theory that Christ's conquest of death was actually the cosmic defeat of the Demiurge, the God of this world and Creator of the Law.[49] The problems involved in such a comparison are (1) that the Demiurge, whom the editors try to read into 44.17–21, is mentioned nowhere in our Letter; and, (2) that the 'Law of Nature' in 44.20 probably does not refer to the Jewish Law at all![50] This part of the

---

[46] In *ibid.*, p. xxvi, n.6, the editors actually cite Clem. Alex., *Strom.* IV, c. XIII, 89.4 in support of this comparison; but they obviously intend to allude to 89.1–2, which we cite here.

[47] These two passages are, in fact, not very similar. There is no mention of Christ's role in the quotation by Clement from Valentinus; and there is no mention of the participation of the Elect in the destruction of death in Ignatius' passage.

[48] See *supra*, pp. 54, 61f, 64–6, 78, 124–6, 142f.

[49] *De Resurrectione*, p. xxvii. A. Orbe, *Greg.*, 46 (1965), p. 173, appears to agree with the editors in finding an allusion to the Demiurge in 44.17–21.

[50] This issue is treated in detail, *supra*, pp. 117–20.

argument, therefore, must be viewed as so much *argumentum e silentio*.

Further, the editors' argument for a docetic Christology in the D.R. similar to that of Valentinus[51] falls to the ground in the face of the following: (1) The identification of Christ as a 'seed from above' (44.34–35) by no means indicates his completely spiritual nature. Rather, it emphasizes only his pre-existence, an affirmation quite congenial to New Testament Christology![52] (2) The 'humanity' of Christ as the Son of Man is clearly stressed, and this is distinguished from his 'divinity' as Son of God (44.21–26). (3) The author states that Christ 'existed in the flesh', raised himself 'from the dead', and 'suffered' (44.10; 45.25–26; 46.16–17, respectively). None of these statements are compatible with a docetic Christology. Yet, nowhere in the D.R. does the author seek to qualify these statements with such phrases as: Christ 'seemed to exist in the flesh', or he only 'appeared to possess humanity', or he bore a 'similitude of the body'.

Finally, the editors themselves concede that the title 'Son of God' used in the D.R. never appears elsewhere in writings attributed to Valentinus or in reports about his School. 'Son of Man', too, is not used to designate the human nature of the Saviour (cf. 44.21–26) in any other Valentinian texts known.[53] In the light of these admissions and the other matters we have raised, it is difficult to concur in the editors' judgment: 'That he (the author) could be Valentinus, nothing, after all, in the Christological themes which he works up, appears to present any obstacle thereto.'[54]

Sixth Argument. Valentinus seems to have held ambiguous views on the resurrection. He did not deny the resurrection and actually admitted that something of the corporeal could be involved. At the same time, he denied any identity of the resurrection body with the deceased earthly body. So also, the author of the D.R. affirms the resurrection only of the 'living members' within the physical body (47.33–48.3), but simultaneously speaks of 'receiving flesh' at the ascension of the Elect into the Aeon (47.6–13).[55]

---

[51] *De Resurrectione*, pp. xxvii–xxviii.

[52] Cf. *supra*, pp. 62, 111f, 124.

[53] *De Resurrectione*, p. xxviii. Haenchen, *ThR*, N.F., 30, Heft 1 (1964), p. 57, takes this fact as a counter-argument to the thesis that Valentinus himself wrote the Letter.

[54] *Ibid.*, p. xxix.

[55] *Ibid.*

This argument appears quite persuasive, and the Patristic citations assembled in support of it in the editors' 'Note Critique' to
47.2–8 do seem to show that the Valentinians entertained a view
very similar to that of our Letter.[56] Notably, Haenchen, who finds
some difficulty in accepting any of the preceding five arguments,
concedes that the editors have shown 'a close agreement' between
Valentinus and the author of our Letter in the matter of a 'spiritual
resurrection'.[57]

A problem presents itself, however, in the very parallels which the
editors offer to substantiate the views of Valentinus. In one instance,
the context of a parallel shows that it means something different from
what the editors imply. The parallel is from Tertullian's *De resurrectione mortuorum*, XIX.6:

> *Hoc denique ingenio etiam in conloquiis saepe nostros decipere consueuerunt, quasi
> et ipsi resurrectionem carnis admittant: 'Vae,' inquiunt, 'qui non in hac carne
> resurrexerint,' ne statim illos percutiant, si resurrectionem statim abnuerint.*

The context of this passage very clearly indicates that the heretics
discussed here (and they are not named) are talking about the resurrection which one may obtain *in the present* through gaining a knowledge of the 'truth' and being baptized. However, this passage does
not give their view of what happens to the Elect at his physical
death. Therefore, it is incorrect to refer to the passage as a proof that
Valentinus believed in the resurrection of some sort of body *at death*.

A more serious question must be raised, however, with respect to
the sources utilized by the editors in their Valentinian parallel
hunt, as well as with the methodology employed in making use of
these sources. A working presupposition of Puech and Quispel is that
while the Valentinian fragments in Clement's *Stromata* and certain
sections of the *Excerpta ex Theodoto* most faithfully preserve the Oriental and thus most original form of Valentinus' teaching, it is also per-
missible to derive material parallel to Valentinus' own thought from
Tertullian's *De Resurrectione Mortuorum*, Pseudo-Tertullian's *Adversus
omnes haereses*, Epiphanius' *Panarion*, and the E.V.[58] Is it not remarkable, however, that most scholars who have attempted to recover the

---

[56] *Ibid.*, p. 34.   [57] *Gnomon*, 36 (1964), p. 362.

[58] On the use of parallels from the *Excerpta*, see *De Resurrectione*, pp. xxiii–
xxiv. Pseudo-Tertullian (*Adv. om. haer.*, IV, 5) and Epiphanius (*Pan.*, XXXI, 7. 6)
are cited to show that Valentinus taught a spiritual resurrection in *De Resurrectione*,
p. xxix, n.3. The line of argument pursued on pp. xxivf. shows that the *Evangelium
Veritatis* is considered as giving important testimony to Valentinus' own teaching.

original teaching of Valentinus not only consider the task extremely complex, but also have made no significant use whatsoever of Tertullian, Pseudo-Tertullian, and Epiphanius?[59] The evaluation of Sagnard concerning the worth of two of these sources for the study of early Valentinianism is perhaps representative:

> One could add: Pseudo-Tertullian (*Adversus omnes haereses*), Philastrius (*De haeresibus*), Epiphanius (*Panarion*), three writings derived from the same source (which was, perhaps, a first *Syntagma* of Hippolytus, containing thirty-two heresies from Dositheus to Noetus); . . . but their late date scarcely permits their utilization.[60]

Moreover, the editors' use of parallels from these sources very often displays a circular mode of argumentation, e.g. if the view of the resurrection presented in the D.R. is parallel to that propagated by Tertullian's opponents in *De Resurrectione Mortuorum*, then these Valentinian opponents must surely preserve Valentinus' own teaching on the subject, as the D.R. itself proves!

As a result of these considerations, it appears that the crucial task remaining in the effort to determine whether Valentinus himself did write the D.R. is to compare what we have found to be its teaching with what has been previously isolated by scholarship as the original thought of Valentinus. But before this can be undertaken, we must give attention to one other major facet of the editors' argumentation.

B. THE *EVANGELIUM VERITATIS* AND THE *DE RESURRECTIONE*: A BRIEF COMPARISON

In order to strengthen their argument that Valentinus was the author

[59] Three of these major attempts to study Valentinus' own teaching have been those of Werner Foerster, *Von Valentin zu Herakleon: Untersuchungen über die Quellen und die Entwicklung der valentinianischen Gnosis (Beihefte zur Zeitschrift für die neutestamentliche Wissenschaft, 7;* herausgegeben von Hans Lietzmann; Giessen, 1928), esp. pp. 1–3; François M.-M. Sagnard, *La gnose valentinienne et le témoignage de Saint Irénée* (1947), esp. pp. 112–39; Gilles Quispel (!), 'The Original Doctrine of Valentine', *VC*, Vol. I (1947), pp. 43–45. It is also notable that Tertullian's *De Resurrectione Carnis* has not been used either.

[60] Sagnard, *La gnose valentinienne*, p. 120. Other scholars reflect some divergence of opinion concerning whether the *Adversus omnes haereses* of Pseudo-Tertullian does or does not represent an accurate summary of the lost *Syntagma* of Hippolytus. Contrast, on this, the views of Robert Grant, *Second Century Christianity: A Collection of Fragments (Translations of Christian Literature,* Series VI; London, 1957), p. 124; Johannes Quasten, *The Ante-Nicene Literature After Irenaeus (Patrology,* Vol. I; Westminster, Maryland, 1953), pp. 272, 319, 412–13.

of the D.R., as well as to establish a possible date for our Letter,[61] the editors have made a rather extensive comparison of it with another writing from the Jung Codex, viz. the *Evangelium Veritatis* or 'Gospel of Truth'.[62] For purposes of their argument,[63] the editors seem to accept the thesis propounded originally by Willem C. van Unnik, viz. that Valentinus himself wrote the E.V. shortly before or after his break with the Church of Rome, ca. AD 140–5.[64] However, the editors themselves are well aware of some obvious differences between the D.R. and the E.V., differences which must be taken into account if the thesis be accepted that Valentinus penned both writings. Consequently, such differences are attributed to Valentinus' literary versatility that could express itself in different styles and moods as the occasion demanded.[65] We, on the contrary, find such an explanation to be inadequate. Thus, after reviewing the editors' summary of dissimilarities and commenting upon each, we shall offer some other, more decisive differences.

The first contrast noted between the two writings is in the manner of their usage of the New Testament.[66] Being a shorter document than the E.V., the D.R. does use fewer references to the New Testament. But more important is the fact that whereas the author of the E.V. always 'echoes' the New Testament material he has worked in,[67]

[61] We have mentioned the use of the E.V. in the dating of the D.R. *supra*, pp. 16f.

[62] Most of the parallels offered are from the terminology rather than the teaching of the two writings. See *De Resurrectione*, pp. xxiv–xxv, and the 'Notes Critiques', *passim*.

[63] Certainly the line of argumentation in *ibid.*, pp. xxv, xxx–xxxiii, presupposes that Valentinus wrote the E.V. However, on p. xxxiii and also in the critical edition of the E.V. the editors are careful to state: 'The "Evangelium Veritatis" must have seen the light about AD 150 and may be the work of Valentinus or of one of his disciples.' See Michel Malinine, Henri-Charles Puech, and Gilles Quispel, *Evangelium Veritatis* (Zürich 1956), p. xv. Elsewhere, Puech and Quispel show the same caution: *VC*, VIII (1954), p. 39. But, in *ZRGG*, VI, Heft 4 (1954), we find Quispel arguing strongly for Valentinus as the author of the E.V., despite a few limply expressed reservations (pp. 293–6); Puech expresses his support of Valentinus as the author without qualification in *Encyclopedie Française*, Tome XIX, pp. 19.42–7f. Cf., finally, Quispel in *ACM*, I (1958), pp. 228 and 233, where all reservations about Valentinus as the author of the E.V. have disappeared.

[64] van Unnik's argument is presented in *The Jung Codex*, pp. 89–104; also in the Dutch original of this article, 'Het Kortgeleden Ontdekte "Evangelie der Waarheid" en Het Nieuwe Testament', *Mededelingen der Koninklijke Nederlandse Akademie van Wetenschappen, Afd. Letterkunde*, Nieuwe Reeks, Deel 17, No. 3 (1954), pp. 71–101. That Quispel is basically captive to this argument may be seen by reference to his comments in *ACM*, Vol. I (1958), pp. 227ff.

[65] See *De Resurrectione*, p. xxxiii.   [66] *Ibid.*, p. xxx.

[67] See van Unnik, *The Jung Codex*, p. 107.

the author of the D.R. uses clear citations-formulae to introduce quotations from the 'Gospel' and the 'Apostle' in addition to 'echoes'.[68] The other differences noted by the editors—viz. (1) that the E.V. is more influenced by John's Gospel, the D.R. by Paul; (2) that the E.V. uses Hebrews and Revelation, whereas the D.R. uses neither—can probably be explained on the basis of the subject matter of the two writings or the idiosyncrasies involved in citation.

The editors find a second major difference between the E.V. and the D.R. in the greater degree of heterodoxy reflected in the latter. That is, the E.V. (presumably written earlier) is said to contain a relatively simple, undeveloped form of Valentinian Gnosticism; whereas, the D.R. presupposes a more developed Valentinian system of a later date.[69] Such a judgment is weakened, however, by two facts: first, other studies have made it clear that the E.V., too, makes use of an already-developed system.[70] The infrequency of reference in the E.V. to distinctive features of the developed Valentinian myth may actually be due to the author's presupposition that his readers already thoroughly understand that to which he alludes only briefly. But, second, a comparison of the more heterodox features detected

[68] See *supra*, pp. 18–21. Haenchen, *Gnomon*, 36 (1964), p. 362, judges the manner of citation of the New Testament in the E.V. to be far superior to that in the D.R.

[69] *De Resurrectione*, p. xxxiii. This view of the editors presupposes van Unnik's 'developmental theory' of Valentinus' thought according to which it was not until after the arch-heretic's break with the Church of Rome ca. AD 140–5 that his system became flagrantly heterodox. Thus, the more orthodox nature of the E.V. may be explained by dating it just prior to or after this break. Cf. n.64 of this chapter above. Dr van Unnik's view may be somewhat weaker than hitherto supposed, however, in that the pivotal passage on which he builds his theory, viz. Tertullian's *Adversus Valentinianos*, 4, has been found on solid historical grounds to be a polemical fabrication of Tertullian's, rather than reliable historical information. See, for example, the negative judgments of Erwin Preuschen, 'Valentinus and his School', *The New Schaff-Herzog Encyclopedia of Religious Knowledge*, ed. by Samuel Macauley Jackson (Vol. XII; Grand Rapids, Michigan, 1957), p. 130; R. A. Lipsius, 'Valentinus', *A Dictionary of Christian Biography, Literature, Sects, and Doctrines during the First Eight Centuries*, ed. by William Smith and Henry Wace (Vol. IV; London, 1887), p. 1077; Ernest Findlay Scott, 'Valentinianism', *Encyclopaedia of Religion and Ethics*, ed. by James Hastings, with the assistance of John A. Selbie and Louis H. Gray (New York, 1922), Vol. XII, p. 572; Hans Leisegang, 'Valentinus, Valentinianer', *Paulys Realencyclopaedie der Classischen Altertumswissenschaft*, Neue Bearbeitung begonnen von Georg Wissowa; Mitwirkung Zahlreicher Fachgenossen, herausgegeben von Karl Mittelhaus und Konrat Zeigler (Zweite Reihe; Vierzehnter Halbband; Band VII A.Z.; Stuttgart und Waldsee, 1948), col. 2262.

[70] See, for example, Helmer Ringgren, 'The Gospel of Truth and Valentinian Gnosticism', *Studia Theologica*, Vol. 18, Fasc. 1 (1964), p. 53.

in the D.R. by the editors[71] shows that similar features in the E.V. actually reflect a more advanced development: (*a*) A clear docetism is found, for example, in D.R. 44.30–38. Compared to E.V. 31.4ff., however, the docetism of the D.R. is hidden and implicit at the most. (*b*) The symbols of 'light' and 'darkness' in D.R. 49.2–4 are taken to represent 'knowledge' and 'ignorance', as in more advanced Valentinian thought. Beside the fact that nothing else occurs in the D.R. which might be used to support this interpretation, the E.V. can be shown to use the same symbolism *and* to identify it specifically with 'knowledge' and 'ignorance' (cf. E.V. 25.17–19; 24.37–25.1; 18.16–19). (*c*) The editors argue that mention of the 'Law of Death' in D.R. 44.20 clearly implies the existence of the Demiurge as its author. However, the Demiurge is never mentioned in the D.R., although the figure of '$\pi\lambda\acute{a}\nu\eta$' ('Error') in the E.V. clearly plays the role of the Demiurge (E.V. 17.15–21, 30–33).[72] (*d*) D.R. 46.36–38 is said to imply that the 'world' was produced outside the Pleroma. However, whereas this is only an inference that may be drawn from one passage in the D.R., in the E.V. we have an elaborate account of how the heavenly aeons, frustrated in their search after the One from whom they had come into existence, are cast into dread, fear, and forgetfulness (17.4–6, 24). This condition gives rise to the birth of 'Error' (17.6–15), who in turn gives birth to Matter and forms from it the earthly world as an image of the heavenly world of the Aeons (17.15–21, 30–33). It is obvious which document has the most developed system here. (*e*) A final feature pointed out in the D.R. is the creation of the Son of Man before the world came into being. Certain statements in the E.V., on the other hand, show that this view was clearly entertained by the author of that homily as well: E.V. 26.5ff.: 'the Word appeared in visible form'; 37.4ff.: '. . . While they (the aeons) were still in the depth of his thought, the Word who was the first to emerge . . .'; cf. 32.17–22; 38.6ff.; 40.23ff.—all pointing to the Saviour's pre-existent origin. Beyond these comparisons, the editors themselves seem to have forgotten that they earlier pinpointed quite a number of technical Valentinian terms in the E.V., such as 'Aeon', the 'All', the 'Pleroma' as a designation of the upper world or a place in it, 'Deficiency' as a designation of

---

[71] These features are offered in *De Resurrectione*, p. xxxi.
[72] Cf. the interpretations of Hans-Martin Schenke, *Die Herkunft des sogenannten Evangelium Veritatis* (Göttingen: Vandenhoeck & Ruprecht, 1959), p. 17; Ringgren, *ST*, Vol. 18 (1964), p. 54.

the lower world, 'the place of Rest', 'Rest' as the final state of the redeemed in the upper world, 'Hylics', and 'those from the Midst or Middle'.[73] Thus, it is difficult to see how the editors could say that the system of the D.R. is more advanced than that of the E.V.

A third contrast found between the D.R. and the E.V. is in the style and tone of the writings. The E.V. is said to treat 'gnosis' as a warmly personal experience. The document itself has no real organic structure, the development of thought taking place by the association of words or ideas. The D.R., on the other hand, is apologetic and discursive.[74] The differences, as we have indicated, are attributed by the editors to the literary genre of the two writings. That is, the versatile Valentinus, they say, was quite capable of writing either a homily (the E.V.) or a didactic and apologetic letter (the D.R.); he would change his style accordingly. On this basis, both writings could still be thought of as emanating from the same author.[75] If, as the editors say, salvation is connected with the reception of 'gnosis' in both writings, however, it is difficult to see why we do not find more of the same expressions used to describe such an experience in the D.R. Also, the editors' description of Valentinus changing his style and mood to conform to literary patterns[76] makes the production of both writings far more mechanical than the content and implied 'Sitz im Leben' of either seems to allow. Could conformity to a letter form so obliterate the metaphysical concerns and mystical piety we find in the E.V.?

A fourth contrast not included by the editors may be drawn between the teaching of the E.V. and the D.R., a contrast which provides the most serious difficulties for the thesis which attributes both writings to the same author. A number of differences have already been pointed out in a monograph by Sasagu Arai.[77] We summarize his conclusions here and then add some of our own:

1. *Differences in cosmology.* The 'Pleroma' in the E.V. has cosmological, anthropological, and soteriological meanings; whereas, in the D.R. it has only cosmological (44.33; 46.36) and soteriological (49.4) significance. Moreover, 'Aeon' in the E.V. is considered both a cosmological and anthropological entity, but in the D.R. it is only

---

[73] See *Evangelium Veritatis*, pp. xiif.   [74] *De Resurrectione*, p. xxxii.

[75] *Ibid.*, p. xxxiii. Cf. Haenchen's challenge of this view, *ThR*, N.F. 30, Heft 1 (1964), p. 57.

[76] *De Resurrectione*, p. xxxiii.

[77] Sasagu Arai, *Die Christologie des Evangelium Veritatis: Eine religionsgeschichtliche Untersuchung* (Leiden, 1964), pp. 125–8.

cosmological (45.18).[78] Thus, the D.R. does not make use of the plural forms of 'Pleroma' and 'Aeon' as does the E.V. Finally, the relationship between cosmology and anthropology is not clearly indicated in the D.R. It is no accident that the 'Plané', who in the E.V. plays the great role of Demiurge, is not mentioned in the D.R.

2. *Differences in anthropology*. The anthropology of the D.R. is more physical than metaphysical—just the opposite of what we find in the E.V. E.g., the E.V. does not yet know the clear distinction of the three substances of man—the 'spiritual, psychical, and fleshly'—which the D.R. knows.[79] Likewise, nothing is said in the E.V. of man as an 'ἀκτίς' (ray, beam) of the Saviour.

3. *Differences in Christology*. The pre-existent Christ in the D.R. is called 'σπέρμα of the Truth' (44.35), not 'ὄνομα' of the Father, as in the E.V. The earthly Christ in the E.V. does not speak of 'the Law of Nature' (D.R. 44.19f.). In the E.V. there is no mention of Christ's possession of 'divine' and 'human' natures, nor of his corresponding designations as 'Son of God' and 'Son of Man' (D.R. 44.21–34). The E.V. says nothing about Christ 'transforming himself into an imperishable Aeon' (D.R. 45.17f.), whereas the D.R. has no parallel to the E.V.'s words about the 'Cross' of Christ. Finally, the word ἀνάστασις, which forms the theme of the D.R., never appears in the E.V. Indeed, the Coptic verb for ἀνάστασις is used once in the E.V. (30.11), but its meaning in that context cannot be clearly established.

In addition to these differences, Arai gives four points which he thinks must necessarily render problematic the identification of the author of the E.V. with the author of the D.R.[80]

1. E.V. 31.4f. ('He has come in a flesh of likeness') is actually more docetic and heterodox than D.R. 44.15 ('Christ was in the flesh'). Further, the 'two natures' Christology of D.R. 44.21ff., which Quispel and Puech hold to be really docetic in intent, is actually quite similar to the Christology of the Great Church (cf. Herm., *Sim.* 5.6.4–8).

2. The Editors of the D.R. explain the reference to the 'flesh' of Christ in 44.15 and 44.21ff. as alluding to the Valentinian doctrine of a '*carnem spiritalem*' (Tert., *Res. Carn.* ii, 3; xv, 1). Unfortunately,

---

[78] This statement should probably be modified in the light of D.R. 45.17–18 where Christ is said to have changed himself into an 'incorruptible Aeon' at his ascension. Elsewhere, however, the word never carries the anthropological sense it has in E.V. 18.35; 19.9f.; 21.14–18.

[79] Contrast our interpretation of the use of these three terms in the D.R., *supra*, pp. 74f., 148f.

[80] Arai, *Die Christologie des Evangelium Veritatis*, p. 128.

this teaching cannot be substantiated for the D.R., although it clearly appears in the E.V. (31.6ff.).

3. Puech and Quispel suppose that Rheg. 'presupposes a system more clearly formed' (than the E.V.). But if, as Quispel has stated elsewhere about the E.V. (*ZRGG*, VI, p. 296), the formation of the Valentinian system moves from the simple to the more complex, then Quispel is in self-contradiction when he says that the D.R. was written somewhat later than the E.V.[81]

4. Arai also finds it somewhat remarkable that if the same author wrote both documents, the D.R. would not refer once to the E.V. by name. The reference to a 'Gospel' in the D.R. makes this omission all the more curious, since presumably the 'Gospel of Truth' was revered among the Valentinians as a fifth Gospel.[82]

Some other differences in the teaching of the two documents which we may add to Arai's would include: (1) the central function of the Saviour in the E.V. is to bring 'gnosis' of the Father and thus of the true origin of pneumatic men and the aeons (cf. E.V. 18.12ff.; 19.18–32; 22.38–23.31; 24.38–42; 30.23ff.; 31.4ff.; and 40.23ff.). This 'Father', who is called 'God' only once (in E.V. 37.33), is described with a variety of adjectives[83] and is mentioned by name no less than ninety-one times in the E.V. Yet in the D.R. the name 'Father' does not appear once, and nowhere is anything said about the Son revealing the Father. As we have shown (above, pp. 111, 127, 131f.), the highest God is not even alluded to in the D.R. (2) In the D.R. πίστις ('faith') is as important as γνῶσις ('knowledge') in the appropriation by the Elect of their salvation (above, pp. 130f.). Int he E.V., on the contrary, 'faith' is mentioned only twice,[84] and it plays a clearly subordinate role to 'knowledge'. Unlike the D.R., 'faith' in the E.V. does not have Christ's resurrection as its object. (3) Certain significant expressions are omitted from the E.V. which appear in the D.R. Of the five terms the D.R. uses to describe the 'world' (above, pp. 108f.), στοιχεῖον, σύστασις, and ⲛⲓⲙⲁ do not appear at all in the E.V. The D.R. uses μέλη to describe the 'inner man' (above, p. 113), but the

---

[81] This conclusion only makes sense if Arai believes, as he seems to, that the system reflected in the E.V. is just as complex, if not more complex than that in the D.R.

[82] Of course, Arai presupposes here that the author of the E.V. would reverence it as Scripture as much as his pupils. However, as with Paul, such a writer need not have considered his own work canonical.

[83] These adjectives are collected by Ringgren, in *ST*, Vol. 18 (1964), p. 51.

[84] Both times the Coptic ⲛⲁϩⲧⲉ is used (E.V. 20.6; 23.32), but πίστις or πιστεύω never appears as in the D.R.

term is not found in the E.V. Χρηστός and κύριος, although used as Christological titles in the D.R., never appear in the E.V. On the other hand, the titles given the Saviour in the E.V. of 'Logos', 'Name', and 'Son' never appear in the D.R. (4) Although we have shown a distinction made between βίος and ζωή in the D.R. (above, pp. 114–16), the E.V. never uses the Greek loanword βίος. (5) 'Rest' (ἀνάπαυσις), which in the D.R. is associated with realized eschatology (above, pp. 142f.), seems to refer almost exclusively in the E.V. to the repose of final salvation (cf. E.V. 22.12; 24.18ff.; 41.29f.; 42.17ff.). (6) Nothing is said in the E.V. about the need for the Elect to 'practise' (γυμνάζω or ἀσκέω) for the attainment of salvation, although such ideas do appear in the D.R. (above, pp. 132f.). (7) Many of the key expressions used in the E.V. to describe the condition of the unsaved man do not appear in the D.R. These include 'forgetfulness' (E.V. 18.1ff.), 'sleep' (E.V. 29.33–30.9); 'drunkenness' (E.V. 22.17f.); and, 'error' (E.V. 22.22–25). (8) Although two classes of men are distinguished in the E.V., the 'Seed' and the 'Hylics',[85] we find no similar distinction in the D.R. (9) Similarly, although the E.V. clearly refers to the 'Place of the Midst' or 'Middle' (17, 34f.), the supposedly more developed teaching of the D.R. contains no such reference. (10) The D.R. teaches both the reception of spiritual 'flesh' and the retention of identifiable personal characteristics in the salvation of the individual at death (above, pp. 146ff.), whereas the E.V. implies a complete destruction of Matter, exempting only the πνεῦμα (E.V. 25.12–19). (11) In the E.V. the totality of the aeons which are fallen and are found enclosed in the bodies of earthly men is called the 'Soul' or the 'Seed' of the Father (E.V. 43.35–37; 43.14). Indeed, only those who possess such a fallen aeon within themselves can receive 'gnosis' (E.V. 21.3–6; 21.25–22.4). But although such a conception would have been very useful to the author of the D.R., he uses it not at all.

To summarize, we believe the foregoing has shown two things: first, that the D.R. and the E.V. were most likely *not* written by the same author; and, second, that the E.V. reflects a Gnostic system which actually appears more developed than that of the D.R., although such an impression may be due to a more elaborate expression of the Valentinian system in the former than in the latter.

[85] See, on this, Schenke's comments, *Die Herkunft des sogenannten Evangelium Veritatis*, p. 18.

C. THE TEACHING OF VALENTINUS AND THE
DE RESURRECTIONE: A COMPARISON

Our concerns in the two preceding sections of this chapter have been
(1) to demonstrate the intrinsic weaknesses of the six arguments presented by Henri-Charles Puech and Gilles Quispel to prove that
Valentinus himself penned the D.R.; (2) to show that because of
fundamental differences between the D.R. and the E.V. it is not
possible to argue that the same author, viz. Valentinus, wrote both.
Indeed, if the choice were forced upon us, we would be more strongly
inclined to favour Valentinus' authorship of the E.V. than of the
D.R.[86] The most decisive reason for rejecting the Master of Valentinianism as author of the D.R., however, lies in the fact that this
writing displays basic differences from and glaring omissions of major
elements in what has been called the original teaching of Valentinus.
And what better way to show this than to compare the teaching of
the D.R. with Gilles Quispel's own reconstruction of Valentinus'
original teaching?[87]

The highest God, in Valentinus' view, was essentially a dyad, con-
sisting of two parts conceived of as One (Iren., *Adv. Haer.* I, 11.1).[88]
This Deity was called 'Depth', the 'perfect Aeon', 'Father' (Iren., I,
1.1). Co-existent with 'Depth' was 'Silence' (elsewhere called
'Ennoia'), and from these two beings who were really One proceeded
all other aeons (Iren., I, 1.1 and 2).[89] In the D.R. we look in vain for
any mention of a highest God, by whatever name he may be called.
Nevertheless, in Valentinus' own teaching this was not only the ultimate Source of all beings, the Incomprehensible One whom the
Saviour came to reveal, but also the vision of him was considered the

[86] Thus, we would be in accord with Kendrick Grobel, *The Gospel of Truth*,
pp. 26–28; and with Willem C. van Unnik, *The Jung Codex*, pp. 89–104, on the
authorship of the E.V.

[87] See *VC*, Vol. I (1947), pp. 43–73. Sagnard himself states his general agreement with Quispel's presentation in *La gnose valentinienne*, p. 615 n.1. It should be
added that while Robert M. Grant (*Gnosticism and Early Christianity*, p. 135) states
that Quispel no longer believes that his published reconstruction of Valentinus'
original teaching is in fact representative of the original, this writer received just
the opposite evaluation from Quispel when the latter was questioned on this matter
at a meeting of the Society of Biblical Literature in New York City (December,
1964). Quispel affirmed that the most important texts for our study of Valentinus'
own thought are still to be found in his article of 1947.

[88] *VC*, Vol. I (1947), p. 45.

[89] *Ibid.*, pp. 49f.

final eschatological goal (*Exc. Theod.*, 63.1).[90] Yet the eschatology of 'Rheginos', despite its mention of a 'restoration' (44.30–33), never implies that knowledge of the incomprehensible Father is the goal of the resurrection.

From 'Depth' and 'Silence' there proceeded a gradual emanation of divine beings, the first being the 'syzygy' of 'Conscience' and 'Truth', and from them there came forth 'Reason' and 'Life', 'Man and Communion', and the remainder of the Thirty Aeons (Iren., *Adv. Haer.* I, 1.2; I, 2.1).[91] It is important to note that according to Valentinus 'Truth' was the consort of 'Conscience', the 'Spirit' was emitted by 'Truth' (Iren., *Adv. Haer.* I, 11.1), and 'Truth' was emanated from 'Grace'.[92] Moreover, 'Jesus' is said to be the emanation of 'Sophia' (Iren., *Adv. Haer.* I, 11.1); the 'Son' is really 'Conscience' who was emanated by 'Depth' and 'Silence' (Iren., *Adv. Haer.* I, 2.5; cf. *Exc. Theod.*, 31.2); 'Christ'—who is also called 'Saviour', 'Reason', 'All', and 'Paraclete'—was brought forth through the combined activity of the 'Spirit', the 'Father', and the Thirty Aeons (Iren., *Adv. Haer.* I, 2.6; I, 4.5; *Exc. Theod.*, 23 and 43).[93] Now it appears that the author of the D.R. was familiar with some system of Aeon speculation, as is evidenced by his use of the *terminus technicus* προβολή in 45.12 and mention of two, possibly three Aeons in 45.12–13.[94] However, the relationship of these Aeons to one another and to the Saviour (= 'the Solution')[95] is at no point similar to that found in the teaching of Valentinus. The Saviour (= 'Solution') is an emanation of 'Truth' and 'Spirit' in the D.R., but not of 'Sophia'; 'Depth' and 'Silence'; or the 'Father', 'Spirit', and the 'Thirty Aeons' combined. 'Truth' and 'Spirit' are paired together in the D.R., but in Valentinus' teaching 'Spirit' is emanated by 'Truth'. And, finally, whereas in the D.R. 'Grace' may be an emanation of 'Truth', for Valentinus 'Truth' was actually emanated by 'Grace'!

The origin of matter from which the world was created came, in

[90] *Ibid.*, p. 73.

[91] *Ibid.*, pp. 48–51. Quispel shows in his Commentary that Epiphanius and Hippolytus give slightly divergent versions of the Valentinian series of Aeons, but they both agree with Irenaeus on the total of thirty Aeons.

[92] Although this last-mentioned sequence of 'Truth' from 'Grace' seems to contradict what is said in Iren., *Adv. Haer.*, I, 1.2, the Editors declare that this was the teaching of the Valentinians. See their remark in the 'Note Critique' to 45.11–14, *De Resurrectione*, p. 26.

[93] Quispel in *VC*, Vol. I (1947), pp. 58–59.

[94] Cf. our note to 45.11–14, *supra*, pp. 66f., 107.

[95] On this identification, see *supra*, pp. 124f.

Valentinus' view, from the despair, sorrow, ignorance, and fear to which Sophia (the last of the Aeons) was subjected in her striving to know the Inconceivable Father (Iren., *Adv. Haer.* I, 4.5; I, 4.2; I, 5.4; cf. Tert., *Adv. Valent.* 15).[96] She, in turn, gave birth to an Aeon called the Demiurge who created the visible world (Iren., *Adv. Haer.* I, 5.1; *Exc. Theod.*, 47.1; Iren., *Adv. Haer.* I, 5.2; I, 5.3; I, 5.5; I, 5.6; Clem., *Strom.* II, 36.2–4; VI, 52.3–4).[97] It is obvious from the stanza of a Valentinian hymn which the author of the D.R. cites in 46.35–47.1 that he, too, knew of a cosmogonic theory involving the creation of the world through some disruption in the Pleroma. It could be that the clause 'small is that which broke loose' (46.36–37) is an indirect reference to Sophia, but neither her name nor her association with the creation of matter are referred to anywhere in the Letter. Also, the Demiurge makes no appearance. If the author knew of these Aeons, they were apparently too unimportant for him to name.

Three kinds of existence are said to have come into being through Sophia: 'matter', 'soul', and 'imagination' (Iren., *Adv. Haer.* I, 5.1; *Exc. Theod.*, 47.1).[98] The Demiurge took these and fashioned them into things heavenly and earthly (Iren., *Adv. Haer.* I, 5.2). He made the 'fleshly' part of man and breathed into him the 'psychic', but the 'spiritual' was implanted in man without the Demiurge's knowledge (Iren., *Adv. Haer.* I, 5.5; I, 5.6; cf. *Exc. Theod.*, 2; 50.2; 67).[99] Thus, there appears a tripartite division of man in Valentinus' thought. In the D.R., on the other hand, the author's anthropological views reflect a fundamentally dualistic conception of the physical, fleshly, outer man and the inner, invisible, spiritual man.[100] The editors' attempt to find the Valentinian tripartite division of man in D.R. 45.39–46.2 has been rejected on grammatical grounds[101] and out of consideration for the author's apologetic intent.[102]

Valentinus also taught that the Saviour, Christ, descended as a power upon Jesus, raising the latter aloft (*Exc. Theod.*, 58ff.).[103] In the same passage it is recorded that the Spirit had originally descended upon Jesus at his baptism, and it withdrew from Jesus at his death.[104] However, Clement's report lacks consistency here, for he goes on to cite Theodotus as saying, 'For when the body died and

[96] *VC*, Vol. I (1947), pp. 59–63.   [97] *Ibid.*, pp. 64–67.
[98] *Ibid.*, pp. 62–65.   [99] *Ibid.*, pp. 66–67.   [100] See *supra*, pp. 112–14.
[101] *Supra*, pp. 74–75.   [102] *Supra*, pp. 148f.
[103] Quispel, *VC*, Vol. I (1947), pp. 68–69.
[104] *Ibid.*, pp. 70–71.

death seized it, the Saviour sent forth the ray of power which had come upon him and destroyed death and raised up the mortal body which had put off passion.'[105] In the D.R., on the other hand, we never find any distinction between the Aeon Christ and the person Jesus. These are both the same being, the titles Jesus and Christ being used interchangeably of him.[106] Also, while the D.R. speaks of the self-transformation of Jesus and of his raising himself up, the teaching of Valentinus seems to indicate that the Father, through the instrumentality of the Aeon Christ, raised Jesus. Then, too, while Quispel emphasizes that the original Valentinus taught that Jesus was a spiritual human being,[107] we have shown that the D.R. does not appear to be very docetic, if at all.[108] In fact, several things have been left unaltered in the D.R. to which a Docetist could scarcely subscribe.[109]

One of the most well-attested features of Valentinus' eschatological thought was that pertaining to the Bridal Chamber. That is, every 'pneumatic' (Elect individual) is considered to have a personal angel. After death, the 'pneumatics' are said to ascend, still enclosed in their souls (their 'wedding garments'), to the Place of the Midst, the abode of Sophia. But when all the 'pneumatics' have thus ascended, they put off their souls and are united to their angelic counterparts. Thereby they pass into the heavenly Bridal Chamber, becoming by their marriage ($\sigma\acute{v}\zeta\upsilon\gamma\sigma\varsigma$) to their personal angels fully spiritual aeons ($\alpha\acute{\iota}\hat{\omega}\nu\epsilon\varsigma\ \nu\sigma\epsilon\rho\sigma\acute{\iota}$), and they attain a perfect vision of the Father (*Exc. Theod.*, 63.1; Iren., *Adv. Haer.* I, 6.1; Clem., *Strom.* II, 114.3–6).[110] When we examine the D.R. closely for traces of such a teaching, however, we find absolutely none! This is indeed remarkable, for Quispel himself has argued convincingly in two other places[111] that the conception of the $\sigma\acute{v}\zeta\upsilon\gamma\sigma\varsigma$ of 'pneumatics' with their angelic counterparts is one of the features most deeply embedded in the original teaching of Valentinus. Here, then, is a decisive difference between Valentinus and the teaching of the D.R.

[105] *Ibid.*
[106] *Supra*, pp. 123f.
[107] See *VC*, Vol. I (1947), p. 46.
[108] See *supra*, pp. 57, 112–13, 165.
[109] *Supra*, pp. 25f.
[110] Quispel, *VC*, Vol. I (1947), pp. 72–73. Cf. also Sagnard, *La gnose valentinienne*, pp. 193–5, 413–19.
[111] See Quispel's comments in *Gnosis als Weltreligion*, p. 84; and, his article, 'La conception de l'homme dans la gnose Valentinienne', in *Der Mensch: Eranos-Jahrbuch*, ed. by Olga Froebe-Kapteyn (Band XV; Zürich, 1948), pp. 255–70.

D. AN ALTERNATIVE HYPOTHESIS OF AUTHORSHIP

The preceding pages of this chapter have, we believe, brought into serious question the validity of the editors' hypothesis that Valentinus himself wrote the *De Resurrectione*. The difference, between what we know of Valentinus' own teaching and the D.R. have been shown to be far more numerous than the similarities, and the nature of these differences is so serious as to render the editors' hypothesis virtually untenable. Rather than end on this negative note, however, we should like to propose an alternative suggestion as to the authorship of the D.R. which to us better explains the facts.

The editors have shown decisively that our Letter bears traces of the influence of Valentinian Gnosticism. With this conclusion we are in full accord. Rather than finding the Letter an example of a rather undeveloped form of Valentinian Gnosticism, however, we believe it to be a rather late example. The allusions to such things as 'the Pleroma' and 'Emanations' seem to show familiarity with a fairly full development of the mythology of Valentinus. The fact that these allusions are infrequent does not necessarily indicate that the document must be early. Rather, a few allusions to something well-known are really all that are needed between a teacher and his pupil. But more than this, is it possible that Valentinianism not only became more and more degenerate, such as we find it in the *Pistis Sophia*, but also may have become more sober? That is, as one gets further away from the masters of the school in both time and geographical location, is it not possible that the Christian faith with which Valentinianism was interwoven could have become more dominant? This, in our opinion, is the type of Valentinianism reflected in the D.R.

It is clear that in our Letter the distinctively Gnostic features have somewhat receded into the background. The great emphasis on 'gnosis' as the means to salvation has been superseded by a stress on the importance of 'faith'. Whereas the content of this 'gnosis' in the systems of Valentinianism was knowledge of the unknown Father and of one's spiritual consubstantiality with that Father, for the author of the D.R. the principal content of 'gnosis' seems to be the acknowledgement of the reality of Christ's resurrection and his defeat of death. Moreover, the explicit docetism of earlier Valentinianism has been forgotten, and one can speak of Christ as having flesh, suffering, and rising from the dead without qualification of any kind. The tripartite division of man's nature, so central to Valentinian Gnosticism, has been refashioned under the influence of the Pauline conception of a spiritual resurrection body and his teaching of the 'inner man'. Moreover, the Valentinian affirmation that in receiving 'gnosis' one has really attained the resurrection has been transformed into a proleptic affirmation that the surety of the resurrection at death is so strong, one may speak of it as a present possession. In all of these ways, we think, we may see the Christian faith coming forth to dominate a loosely-held Valentinianism.

Furthermore, the way in which the author makes use of certain Valentinian features makes it appear that they are no longer well-understood, and that they are part of a tradition inherited and transmitted. For example, although he seems to know a Valentinian system of Aeon speculation, the exact relationship of the divine Aeons to one another has become unimportant and confused in his mind—perhaps not being too clearly remembered.[112] And, rather than referring by name to the 'dramatis personae' or events of the Valentinian myth of Creation, he alludes to them vaguely by the citation of a stanza of a Valentinian hymn probably long known (46.35–47.1). The relative unimportance of this mythology is evidenced by the awkward way in which the author has worked the stanza into his argument, where it stands like some erratic boulder.[113] Moreover, he confesses the difficulties inherent in some of the Valentinian imagery he utilizes to describe the Saviour's defeat of death in 44.39–45.4.[114] In so doing he reveals to us not one eloquent and zealous in explaining the nuances of the esoteric Valentinian myth, but one who may have lost some of his earlier enthusiasm for a system which he now finds difficult.

In sum, on the basis of internal evidence from the Letter we would maintain that the Letter to Rheginos was written in the last quarter of the second century by an anonymous but revered Valentinian-Christian teacher. Originally well-versed in the teaching of one of the Valentinian Schools, probably the Oriental, he has with time become more and more influenced by his fundamentally Christian faith and by the teaching of the New Testament, especially of Paul. The result has been a 're-Christianization' of his Valentinianism. Beyond this, our investigation will not permit us to go.

[112] See our comments on the Aeon speculation in the D.R., *supra*, pp. 175f.
[113] See our note to this passage, *supra*, pp. 81f.
[114] See our note to 45.1–2, *supra*, p. 64.

BIBLIOGRAPHY TO THE EPISTLE TO RHEGINOS

I. MONOGRAPHS AND PRIMARY SOURCES

BIANCHI, UGO (ed.), *The Origins of Gnosticism/Le origini dello gnosticismo* (*Studies in the History of Religion. Supplementum to Numen*, Vol. XII). Leiden: E. J. Brill, 1966. Esp. pp. 62, 68, 109, 125, 221–3, 517.

DORESSE, JEAN, *The Secret Books of the Egyptian Gnostics*. Translated by Philip Mairet. New York: The Viking Press, 1958; London: Hollis and Carter, 1960. Esp. pp. 118, 123, 141, 145, 238–9.

FRID, B., *De Resurrectione. Epistula ad Rheginum. Inledning och oversattning fran koptiskan.* (*Symbolae Biblicae Upsalienses, Supplementhaften till SEA*, 19.) Lund: Berlingska Boktryckeriet, 1967/Lund: C. W. K. Gleerup, 1967.

LABIB, PAHOR, *Coptic Gnostic Papyri in the Coptic Museum at Old Cairo*. Vol. I. Cairo, Egypt: Government Press, 1956. Plates 1 and 2 contain part of the text of 'Rheginos'.

MALININE, MICHEL, HENRI-CHARLES PUECH, GILLES QUISPEL, WALTER C. TILL, ROBERT McL. WILSON AND JAN ZANDEE, *De Resurrectione*. Zürich: Rascher Verlag, 1963.

QUISPEL, GILLES, HENRI-CHARLES PUECH, AND WILLEM C. VAN UNNIK, *The Jung Codex*. Translated by F. L. Cross. London: A. R. Mowbray and Company, 1955. Esp. pp. 19–20, 24, 45, 54–57.

II. ARTICLES

DORESSE, JEAN, 'Douze volumes dans une jarre', *Les Nouvelles Littéraires* (30 Juin 1949), cols. 1–5.

'A Gnostic Library from Upper Egypt', *Archaeology*, III (1950), pp. 69–73.

'Nouveaux documents gnostiques coptes découvertes en Haute-Égypte', *Comptes Rendus de l'Académie des Inscriptions et Belles Lettres* (1949), pp. 176–80.

'Sur les traces des papyrus gnostiques: Récherches à Chenoboskion', *Académie royale de Belgique: Bulletin de la Classe des Lettres et des Sciences Morales et Politiques*, 5e Série, Tome XXXVI (Août 1950), pp. 432–7.

'Une bibliotheque gnostique copte découverte en Haute-Égypte', *Académie royale de Belgique: Bulletin de la Classe des Lettres et des Sciences Morales et Politiques*, 5e Série, Tome XXXV (1949), pp. 435–49.

'Une bibliothèque gnostique copte', *La Nouvelle Clio*, No. 1 (1949), pp. 59–70.

DORESSE, JEAN AND TOGO MINA, 'Nouveaux textes gnostiques coptes découverts en Haute-Égypte: La bibliothèque de Chenoboskion', *Vigiliae Christianae*, Vol. III (1949), pp. 129–41.

FOERSTER, WERNER, 'Neuere Literatur über die gnostischen Papyri von Chenoboskion', *Theologische Literaturzeitung*, 79 (1954), cols. 377–84.

HAENCHEN, ERNST, 'Literatur zum Codex Jung', *Theologische Rundschau*, 30, Heft 1 (Juni 1964), pp. 39–82.

KRAUSE, MARTIN, 'Der Koptische Handschriftenfund bei Nag Hammadi. Umfang und Inhalt', *Mitteilungen des Deutschen Archäologischen Instituts, Abteilung Kairo*, Band 18 (1962), pp. 121–32.

MINA, TOGO, 'Le Papyrus Gnostique du Musée Copte', *Vigiliae Christianae*, II (1948), pp. 129–36.

PUECH, HENRI-CHARLES, 'Découverte d'une bibliothèque gnostique en Haute-Égypte', *Encyclopédie Française* (ed. Gaston Berger), Tome XIX (1957), pp. 19.42–4 to 19.42–13.

'Les nouveaux écrits gnostiques découverts en Haute-Égypte: Premier inventaire et essai d'identification', *Coptic Studies in Honor of Walter Ewing Crum* (ed. Michel Malinine; *Bulletin of the Byzantine Institute*, No. 2). Boston: The Byzantine Institute, Inc., 1950, pp. 91–153.

PUECH, HENRI-CHARLES AND JEAN DORESSE, 'Nouveaux écrits gnostiques découverts en Egypte', *Comptes Rendus de l'Académie des Inscriptions et Belles-Lettres*, Séance du 20 Fevr. (1948), pp. 87–95.

PUECH, HENRI-CHARLES AND GILLES QUISPEL, 'Les écrits gnostiques du Codex Jung', *Vigiliae Christianae*, Vol. VIII (1954), pp. 1–51.

'Le quatrième écrit gnostique du Codex Jung. Note Additionelle', *Vigiliae Christianae*, Vol. IX, No. 2 (April 1955), pp. 65–102.

QUISPEL, GILLES, 'Het oude Christendom in het licht van nieuwe Ontdekkingen', *Post Iucundam Iuventutem: Orgaan van het Utrechts Universiteitsfonds*, No. 36. Utrecht: Kromme Nieuwe Gracht 29, Juni 1962, pp. 1–11.

'Il Cristianesimo primitivo alla luce delle recenti scoperte', *Orpheus: Rivista di Umanità Classica e Cristiana*, X, No. 1 (1963), pp. 3–18.

'Neue Funde zur Valentinianischen Gnosis: Der Codex Jung', *Zeitschrift für Religions- und Geistesgeschichte*, ed. Hans Joachim Schoeps, Vol. VI, Heft 4 (1954), pp. 289–305.

'The Writings of Valentinus Recently Discovered in Upper Egypt', *Acta Congressus Madvigiani*, Vol. I (1958), pp. 225–34.

QUISPEL, GILLES, 'Note sur "*De Resurrectione*"', *Vigiliae Christianae*, vol. XX (1968), pp. 14–15.

VAN UNNIK, WILLEM C., 'The Newly Discovered Gnostic "Epistle to Rheginos" on the Resurrection: I and II', *The Journal of Ecclesiastical History*, Vol. XV, No. 2 (1964), pp. 141–52 (I), and 153–67 (II).

ZANDEE, JAN, 'De Opstanding in de brief aan Rheginos en in het Evangelie van Philippus', *Nederlands Theologisch Tijdschrift*, 16 (1962), pp. 361–77.

III. REVIEWS

ADAM, A., *Göttingische Gelehrte Anzeigen*, Vol. 215 (1963), pp. 56–39.

ANONYMOUS, *Bibliotheca Orientalis*, Jahrgang XXI, No. 3/4 (Mei-Juli 1964), p. 250.

BARNS, J. W. B., *The Journal of Theological Studies*, N.S., Vol. XV (1964), pp. 162–6.

DANIÉLOU, JEAN, *Vigiliae Christianae*, Vol. XVIII, No. 3 (1964), pp. 187–8.

GIVERSEN, SOREN, *The Journal of Ecclesiastical History*, XVI, No. 1 (April 1965), pp. 82–83.

GOLDSMITH, DALE, *The Journal of Religion*, Vol. 45 (1965), pp. 256–7.

GUILLEMONT, A., *Revue de l'Histoire des Religions*, 171 (1967), pp. 83–85.

HAARDT, ROBERT, *Wiener Zeitschrift für die Kunde des Morgenlandes*, 61 (1967), pp. 159–62.

HAENCHEN, ERNST, *Gnomon*, 36 (1964), pp. 359–63.
    Theologische Rundschau (Juni 1964), pp. 55–58.

LEBEAU, P., *Nouvelle Revue Théologique*, Vol. 87 (1965), p. 319.

LEIPOLDT, JOHANNES, *Théologische Literaturzeitung*, Nummer 7, 90 (Juli 1965), cols. 518–20.

ORBE, A., *Gregorianum*, 46 (1965), pp. 172–4.

PUECH, HENRI-CHARLES, *Académie des Inscriptions et Belles-Lettres. Comptes rendus des séances de l'année 1963* (1964), pp. 317–19.

SCHENKE, HANS-MARTIN, *Orientalische Literaturzeitung*, 60 (1965), pp. 471–7.

STIER, F., *Internationale Zeitschriftenschau für Bibelwissenschaft und Grenzgebiete*, X (1963–4), pp. 191–2.

WASZINK, J. H., *Vigiliae Christianae*, Vol. XVII (1963), pp. 55–62.

WILSON, R. McL., *New Testament Studies*, IX (1962/3), p. 401.

INDEX OF NAMES AND SUBJECTS

*Names marked with * are also referred to in the Index of References.*

INDEX OF MODERN AUTHORS

INDEX OF REFERENCES

DE RESURRECTIONE

OLD TESTAMENT

NEW TESTAMENT

APOCRYPHA AND PSEUDEPIGRAPHA

PAGAN WRITINGS

GNOSTIC LITERATURE